ORTHOPAEDIC ENGINEERING

Proceedings of the Orthopaedic Engineering
Conference held in Oxford, September, 1977

Edited by

J.DEREK HARRIS
Director,Oxford Orthopaedic Engineering Centre
Nuffield Orthopaedic Centre
Headington, Oxford
Great Britain

and

KEITH COPELAND
Biophysics Department
Faculty of Medical Sciences
University College London
London W.C.1.

OXFORD ORTHOPAEDIC ENGINEERING CENTRE
BIOLOGICAL ENGINEERING SOCIETY

ORTHOPAEDIC ENGINEERING

c   THE BIOLOGICAL ENGINEERING SOCIETY   1978

Orthopaedic Engineering

first published in 1978 by

THE BIOLOGICAL ENGINEERING SOCIETY

Honorary Secretary: Keith Copeland
Biophysics Department
Faculty of Medical Sciences
University College   London
Gower   Street   W.C.1E6BT

I.S.B.N.   0 904716 11 2

Printed in Great Britain by F.S.Moore Limited
Chancery Lane, London W.C.2

CONTENTS

Page

Acknowledgements   1

Foreword   2

Introduction   3

SPINAL RESEARCH

Chapter 1
   A review of spinal biomechanical research   5
   P.R. DAVIS

Chapter 2
   Is the shear stiffness of the intervertebral disc
   dependent on the intervertebral compressive force?   12
   B.M. CYRON, W.C. HUTTON

Chapter 3
   Surface strain measurements on the cadaveric
   lumbar spine   20
   W.G.J. HAMPSON, M. JAYSON, J.S. SHAH

Chapter 4
   Myoelectric back muscle activity, lumbar disc
   pressure and intra-abdominal pressure in
   standardized working-postures   21
   G.B.J. ANDERSSON, R. ÖRTENGREN, A. NACHEMSON

Chapter 5
   The methods used to observe work factors in a
   study of back pain in industry   30
   B.J. SWEETMAN

Chapter 6
   Investigations of the in vivo biomechanics of the
   lumbar spine   35
   J.W. FRYMOYER, E. BUTURLA, D.G. WILDER, M.H. POPE

Chapter 7
   Some physical effects of lumbar spinal support
   orthoses   39
   G. DEANE, N.D. GREW

Chapter 8
   The mechanical role of the vertebral processes
   investigated by neutron diffraction   47
   R.K. GRIFFITHS, G.E. BACON, P.J. BACON

Chapter 9
    Biostereometrics, shape replication and
    orthopaedics   51
    R.G. BURWELL

Chapter 10
    Investigation of changes in the posture of the
    spine. The effects of a heel raise and the
    working day   86
    R. ROGER, J.W. FRYMOYER, I.A.F. STOKES

Chapter 11
    Three-dimensional measurement of trunk shape
    with Moiré topography   92
    B. DRERUP

Chapter 12
    A computerised 3-D bodyshape description
    light-screen technique   101
    J.W. SMIT, L. SCHILGEN

Chapter 13
    The effect of spaceflight on regional body
    volume, studied by a biostereometric technique   108
    M.W. WHITTLE

Chapter 14
    Objective measurements from 90°-radiographs   113
    B. DRERUP, W. FROBIN

Chapter 15
    The display-stereocomparator. A new apparatus
    for the evaluation of stereoradiographs   117
    E. HIERHOLZER

Chapter 16
    A kinematic roentgen stereophotogrammetric method
    for studying movements between spinal segments   122
    S. WILLNER, T. OLSSON, G. SELVIK

Chapter 17
    Recent advances in morphanalysis and their
    implications in human orthopaedic measurement
    and replication   124
    G.P. RABEY

Chapter 18
    CODA: a new instrument for three dimensional
    recording of human movement and body contour   128
    D.L. MITCHELSON

Chapter 19
    Clinical shape measurement and replication   132
    S.J. COUSINS M.F. NEIL

Chapter 20
    Measurement of the lumbar spinal canal by
    diagnostic ultrasound   139
    R.W. PORTER, D. OTTEWELL, M. WICKS

Chapter 21
    Gait analysis   145
    J.P. PAUL

Chapter 22
    Measurement of knee torque/angle characteristics
    during the swing phase of gait   156
    G. JUDGE

Chapter 23
    Calculation of the loads transmitted by the
    joints of the body   163
    N. BERME

Chapter 24
    Objective assessment of locomotor function in
    the lower limb   169
    D.W. GRIEVE

Chapter 25
    The clinical assessment of gait using the
    polarised light goniometer   174
    D.L. MITCHELSON

Chapter 26
    The calculation of three-dimensional positions
    from optical data   180
    L.J. HUNTINGTON, B.R. TIETJENS

Chapter 27
    Kinematic assessment of arthritic knees   183
    A. MUKHERJEE

Chapter 28
    The measurement of foot contact patterns   189
    J.C. WALL, J. CHARTERIS, J.W. HOARE

Chapter 29
    Skeletal transients on heel strike in normal
    walking   195
    L.H. LIGHT, G. McLELLAN, L. KLENERMAN

Chapter 30
    A direct telemetric method for measuring hip load   198
    T.A. ENGLISH, M. KILVINGTON

Chapter 31
    Measurement and analysis of movement in the hip
    joint   202
    T.A. GORE, M. FLYNN, G.R. HIGGINSON, R.J. MINNS

Chapter 32
    The use of force plate analysis in the assessment
    of treatment for tendon injury in the racehorse   206
    A.E. GOODSHIP, L.E. LANYON, P.N. BROWN, C. PYE

ORTHOTICS DESIGN AND FABRICATION

Chapter 33
    Orthotics design and fabrication   211
    G.K. ROSE

Chapter 34
    The instrumentation of hip-knee-ankle stabilising
    orthoses   219
    G.G. REEVE

Chapter 35
    DHSS Biomechanical R and D Unit field trial of
    CARS-UBC valgus/varus knee brace   226
    S.J. COUSINS, D.L.V. LUSBY, J. CHODERA

Chapter 36
    The unstable elbow - the limitations of orthotic
    management   235
    J.H. MILLER, W.G. DYKES, J.V. TAYLOR

Chapter 37
    Lumbar scoliosis corrective orthosis   242
    R.G.S. PLATTS

Chapter 38
    Body support systems   246
    P.J.R. NICHOLS

Chapter 39
    Seating for assymetric hip deformity in non-ambulant
    multiply handicapped children   251
    D. SCRUTTON

Chapter 40
    One application of carbon fibre reinforced plastic
    for orthotics fabrication   254
    R.L. NELHAM

Chapter 41
    The use of carbon/glass fibre hybrid laminates for
    the constructoon of orthoses   260
    G.R. JOHNSON

Chapter 42
    Research and service applications of vacuum
    consolidation   265
    J.D. HARRIS

Chapter 43
    Vacuum consolidation techniques for limb
    replication - some practical experience   269
    G.R. JOHNSON, G.R.H. CROOKS

ACKNOWLEDGEMENTS

Chairmen of the Sessions

Professor P.R. Davis, M.B., B.S., Ph.D.(London), F.R.C.S.(Eng.), F.I.Biol.

Professor of Human Biology, University of Surrey, since 1967; previously Reader in Anatomy and Director of Biomechanics Laboratory, Royal Free School of Medicine. Research interests are human trunk anatomy and biomechanics, with special reference to industrial problems and avoidance of back pain.

Professor R.G. Burwell, B.Sc., M.D., F.R.C.S.

Professor Burwell holds the Chair of Human Morphology and Experimental Orthopaedics in Nottingham. He previously held the Chair of Orthopaedics in the University of London. He has a strong interest in orthopaedic research, currently into children's growth diseases, especially scoliosis and Perthe's disease. He is a Member of the British Editorial Board of the Journal of Bone and Joint Surgery.

Professor J.P. Paul, B.Sc., Ph.D., A.R.C.S.T., C.Eng., F.I.Mech.E., F.B.O.A.

Professor Paul graduated B.Sc. in Mechanical Engineering from the University of Glasgow and graduated Ph.D. following research into the functional loading of the human hip joint. He is a Fellow of the Institution of Mechanical Engineers and a Fellow of the British Orthopaedic Association and his present post is Professor and Chairman of the Bioengineering Unit, University of Strathclyde. His research interest is the mechanical loading of the human body structures and their replacements, prostheses and orthoses.

Mr. G.K. Rose, F.R.C.S.,(Eng.), M.B., Ch.B.(Hons.), L.R.C.P.

Mr. Rose is Consultant Orthopaedic Surgeon at the Robert Jones and Agnes Hunt and Shrewsbury Hospitals, and is Director of the Orthotic Research and Locomotor Assessment Unit at Oswestry. His professional interests are orthotic and surgical integration; design of orthoses for the severely handicapped; orthotic and gait assessment; and research into normal and abnormal feet.

The Oxford Orthopaedic Engineering Centre

The Oxford Orthopaedic Engineering Centre is a research unit set up jointly by the Nuffield Department of Orthopaedic Surgery and the Department of Engineering Science in Oxford University, with a grant from the Department of Health and Social Security. Situated in the Nuffield Orthopaedic Centre, research is centred on studies of mechanical aspects of orthopaedic disabilities and the treatments for these conditions.

The Biological Engineering Society

The Biological Engineering Society was founded in 1960 to further co-operation of workers in the fields spanning the Physical and Life Sciences. The B.E.S. is a multi-disciplinary learned society representing over thirty professions and encourages collaboration between all institutions having an interest in the subject, including industry. A number of the speakers and chairmen at this Conference are members of the Society.

FOREWORD

I am most happy to write the foreword to this
publication reporting the international meeting
arranged by the Oxford Orthopaedic Engineering
Centre and the Biological Engineering Society
in September, 1977. The subjects included much
new work, extending from gait analysis to orthotic
design and fabrication, to biostereometrics, and
shape replication in orthopaedics.

Speakers from the United States of America,
Canada, Sweden, Germany and India added
enormously to the success of this meeting, but it
is most reassuring to see the work coming from
numerous centres in the United Kingdom which are
now involved with orthopaedic engineering projects.
Bioengineering has gradually become an "in"
subject, with new university under-graduate
courses, numerous graduates, and Ph.D. and M.Sc.
theses; but with this publication it has become of
age. Real structural and functional problems in
humans are being measured and quantified, and from
there, improved management and care of patients
will hopefully result.

                    Robert B. Duthie

INTRODUCTION

The 1977 Orthopaedic Engineering Conference in Oxford was held to explore areas of bioengineering research applicable to orthopaedics, and it is encouraging to see that, both by papers and by attendance, a high degree of interdisciplinary interest was achieved.

Orthopaedic engineering is naturally directed towards measurement and observation. Facilities for improved accuracy and ease of measurement, after a comparatively late start apart from some dramatic and well-known exceptions, are now available for the researcher in quantity and variety. The abundance of techniques can lead to an uncritical acceptance of results, which, whilst apparently impressive, may yet not encompass the extreme complexity of the human situation under study.

Frequently the development of a technique becomes a major part of the intentions of the research worker, leaving others to establish its validity in any but a comparative straightforward assessment of normal subjects. The difficulties of obtaining an objective result in human test procedures using equipment attached to or near the subject are well known. Too short a test and normal rhythms are not achieved. Too long, and elderly or frail subjects become fatigued. Locomotion tests in a laboratory introduce restraints which may be of crucial importance to the understanding of the disability.

Systems of objective examination may be entirely practical for a small group of subjects. To what degree do these studies represent the total situation? Techniques designed for mass throughput of subject and information impress by the size and scale of the exercise, but the information captured must be relevant, and some way of representing the important variants must be found, and be acceptable to other workers of different disciplines.

The constitution of the Oxford conference was strongly influenced by the need to demonstrate the practical validity of the new engineering techniques for measurement and rehabilitation now available.

There is an urgent need for accurate clinical indicators of the progression of orthopaedic disabilities. Certainly in the field of gait analysis, which has been in existence for many years, the need to establish its value in the clinic is pressing, and perhaps in the other areas of study the honeymoon period for technology myst be regarded as over.

Clinical indicators must be simple in operation if they are to be used to assess the efficacy of alternative treatments. At present the gulf between laboratory and clinic is too large, leading to discouragement in the laboratory and scepticism in the clinic.

There also remains the challenge to apply the better understanding provided by engineering insights into orthopaedic problems to the design and construction of orthoses.

The Biological Engineering Society has been a prime mover in the development of multi-disciplinary study groups, so the Society's sponsoring of the Conference is seen as a guarantee for the future of orthopaedic engineering. It is hoped that the conference marks the beginning of a new productive phase in engineering applied to orthopaedics.

This is an opportunity to thank the four chairmen of the seesions, who each presented masterly review papers of their subjects. These can be read in full at the start of each of the four sections presented, and provide most valuable introductions to the subjects.

I am also particularly grateful for all the time and attention provided by Julia Thornton in the preparation, compilation and typing of this book.

Derek Harris

Oxford, 1978

SPINAL RESEARCH

A REVIEW OF SPINAL BIOMECHANICAL RESEARCH

P.R. DAVIS, M.B., B.S., Ph.D.(Lond.), F.R.C.S., L.R.C.P.(Lond.), F.I.Biol.

Department of Human Biology and Health, University of Surrey, Guildford

Modern bio-engineering approaches to the problems of the spine and trunk have very deep foundations. Backache has beset Man throughout recorded history, and although rarely fatal in outcome, it clearly has had great consequences for family life, particularly in ages when human energy was the main source of power for food production. Thus, it is not surprising that the Hippocratic School (ca. 430 B.C.) devoted a large part of a script to bones and joints of the human vertebral column.

However, as in so many other fields, progress in reported vertebral research was very slow over the next two thousand years, until the age of Leonardo (1452-1519), when artists dissected human material to assist with the accuracy of their representation. Regretfully, Leonardo da Vinci himself did not dissect the human spine, and in his drawings it is represented only in diagrammatic form. However, his general approach stimulated human research culminating in the production by Vesalius (1543) of his great work "De Humani Corporis Fabrica", which described the outward form of the vertebrae in very considerable detail, and laid the foundations for objective research on human material.

The first analysis of vertebral function, and the first use of serial measurements of external bone form at different levels in the body is attributable to Winslow (1732), and to Cheselden in his Osteographia (1733). Here we are told that the vertebral bodies and discs resist compression and that the articular processes direct the movements. We note that the ranges of movements correlate with disc thickness, and that discs narrow during the day and expand again at night. The physiological thoracic kyphoscoliosis is described, and is explained as accommodating the heart and increasing the size of the right chest to make it 'better founded' for right handedness. The lumbar lordosis is attributed to the need to bring the lumbar vertebral bodies beneath the centre of gravity of the trunk.

Barthez (1798) extended this analysis by showing that, in bipedal Man, the vertebral column above a given vertebra constitutes a lever whose fulcrum is formed by the vertebra in question, and whose force is resisted by the muscles and ligaments attached to its neural arch. The brothers Bell (1826) pointed out that muscle contraction in such a mechanism would increase the pressure within the discs, which would also be compressed by the direct weight of the limbs above them, and by the weight of the loads carried on the back or in the hands.

Studies of the internal form of vertebrae were initiated by Wyman in 1857. He noted that the corporeal trabeculae run vertically to form pillars resisting compression, and are braced by horizontal tie bars to limit angulation under load.

Weber (1823, 1827), was the first to record experiments designed to analyse spinal movements. He measured regional movements in the living and segmental movements in cadavers by use of marker pins, but lacked the advantage of photography to extend this to live studies.

Perhaps the true father of spinal bio-engineering is Humphry, who in 1858 collated these previous findings, added many more accurate and detailed observations of his own, and synthesized the whole into a general picture of spinal biomechanics. He used accurate serial measurements of bone to deduce changes of stress at various levels; he investigated the roles of the various articular processes, and he described the nuclei pulposi of the discs as 'forming a series of fluid balls around which the respective vertebrae revolve in their movements'. He deduced that rotation in the thorax would occur around an axis within the vertebral bodies; that in the lumbar region it could occur in some around a more posterior centre, and that the thoraco-lumbar transition was an area of fixity deriving from functional necessity.

Since Humphry's time, vertebral research has mushroomed, and, in summarising present knowledge, one can only include some of the outstanding contributions that have been made.

Looking first at the vertebral bodies, we now know that they form, with the discs, a complex, pliable and compression resistant strut permitting angular and rotational movements. Fick (1911), Schmorl (1919), Beadle (1931) Ubermuth (1929) and Bohmig (1931) showed that the small foraminae in the central area of the end plates transmit fine vessels which lie in the canals of the overlying cartilage, and allow fluid interchange between the nucleus puposus and the vascular fluid compartment, and that the central regions of discs and vertebral bodies are fully designed for compression resistance. The outer part of this mechanism consists of the peripheral cortex of the vertebral body and the annulus fibrosus of the disc, anchorage between them being obtained by the annular epiphysis in youth which becomes the bony ring of the adult end plate (Schmorl, 1928, Bick & Copel, 1950), all these structures forming a tensile sleeve around the central areas of compression.

Studies similar to those of Davidson & Woodhall (1959) and Mitchell et al (1961) have shown that the nucleus pulposus is dependent for its integrity upon its content of water-attracting polysaccharides, and studies such as those of Hirsch and Nachemson (1954), Brown et al (1957), Rolander (1966) and Galante (1967) have shown that there are changes in hydrostatic powers with age and with disease which lead to a decreased capacity of the nucleus for compressive energy absorption, with an increased liability to damage in the bones and in the annulus. Our modern environment imposes additional stresses from vertical vibrations, and Rosegger and Rossegger (1960) and Christ and Dupuis (1966) have shown that vertical vibrations in the 2-4Hz range at 0.5G magnitudes are common and may be damaging in Western societies.

External dimensions of human vertebrae are now well established. As long ago as 1883 Anderson produced first class data on the external measurements of the vertebral bodies, his data agreeing well with some published previously by Aeby (1879), and later ones obtained by Cyriax (1919) and Todd and Pyle (1928).   The slight ventral wedging of thoracic vertebrae, and the more marked dorsal wedging of the lower lumbar series, was recorded by Cunningham (1886), Martin (1928) and Vallois and Lazorthes (1942).

Since the vertebral column is a compression resistant strut, its cross sectional area at different levels can be taken as a crude guide to its regional strengths, and this measurement has been recorded by Davis (1957) in various races.

Linkage of the anterior components of the neural arches with their attached muscles and ligaments is by means of the pedicles. Gallois and Japiot (1925) demonstrated a complex internal architecture in which trabeculae from the lower end plates pass through the pedicles to expand into superior apophyses, and others from the upper end plates pass to the inferior apophyses. The relative and absolute size of the pedicles have been measured by Davis (1960), who noted that the necks of the ribs may play a part in parallel with that of the pedicles in transmitting forces in the thoracic region, and who also noted an inverse relationship between the cross sectional areas of the lowest lumbar vertebrae and the sizes of their pedicles, which he attributed to varying inclination of the lumbo-sacral transition (Davis, 1961).

The spaces between the pedicles which transmit the spinal nerves have naturally attracted attention, particularly from neuro-surgeons. They have been measured radiographically in adults by Elsberg and Dyke (1934), and in children by Landmesser & Heublein (1953) and Simril & Thurston (1955).

The neural arches contribute to the posterior wall of the spinal canal, and form the mechanical base for the apophyseal joints, the muscular and ligamentous attachments, and the costo-vertebral articulations.

While in general their form is well known, it is sometimes forgotten that the lower thoracic laminae of adults have spicules on their anterior surface which reinforce the junction of the lateral border of the ligamentum flavum with the capsule of the apophyseal joint, and they may indicate a need for reinforcement of an area subject to high stress in axial rotation (Le Double, 1912; Shore, 1931; Naffziger, Inman and Saunders, 1938; Olivier, 1954; Davis, 1957).

The apophyseal joints have been the subject of many studies, particularly in respect of the ways in which they dictate the forms of movement which can occur between pairs of vertebrae. Briefly, the studies of Humphry (1858), Morris (1879) and Capener (1944) have shown that the lumbar apophyses allow sagittal and lateral flexion, and can also permit some lumbar rotation around a posterior axis. In the thorax, Humphry (1858), Holder (1887) and Frazer (1933) demonstrated that the facets allow limited sagittal and lateral flexion, and that rotation can occur around an axis lying within the line of the vertebral bodies. Davis (1957) has shown that the rotational axis varies in position at different levels, lying within the bodies T4 - T9, but being in front of them at higher and lower levels.

At the levels of transition between regions, there are specialisms of the apophyseal joints which are worthy of note. At the thoraco-lumbar transition a certain specialisation is commonly found. Here Struthers (1875), Topinard (1877) and Le Double (1912) found that the level of functional transition varied between T9 and L_1, Topinard noting that it was sometimes marked by the formation of a mortice joint, a finding studied in further detail by Davis (1955). These studies make it clear that the thoraco-lumbar transition is relatively rigid, and that this reduces the liability of these vertebrae to shearing forces during axial rotation of the trunk as a whole. It does, however, increase their liability to crush fracture in excessive longitudinal compression. The lumbo-sacral transition has its own peculiarities, but as these will be described in another chapter of this book they are not considered here.

While the general form and outline of the muscles of the spine has been well known since the days of Humphry, it is only recently that Etemadi (1963) has elaborated quantitatively on these descriptions. He carefully weighed the muscle tissue in each of the 400 or more slips of muscle attached to the thoracic and lumbar vertebrae, and was thus able to indicate the weight of muscle available across each intervertebral joint. We thus have some guide to the relative power of the spinal musculature at different levels, and this shows an excellent correlation with the bone sizes of the vertebral bodies. Etemadi also found that the spinal muscles include some small slips of muscle with very long fine tendons which may well be concerned more with sensory activity than with motor power.

Bone strength is, of course, of major concern, and one of the earliest observations is that of Virgin (1951) using an engineers compression testing machine. He found that healthy lumbar discs and vertebral bodies could withstand compression of the order of 400Kg without bad effect, and his findings have since been confirmed by Hirsch and Nachemson (1954) Evans and Lissner (1955), Bartelink (1957) and many others. However, mechanical analyses of the trunk functions such as that by Bradford and Spurling (1945) indicated that compression of a far greater magnitude could be imposed by quite ordinary activities, which finding suggested that some other load bearing mechanism existed. Such a non-spinal mechanism had been proposed by Keith in 1923, and studies by Davis (1956, 1957, 1959), Bartelink (1957) Morris Lucas and Bresler (1961), and Davis and Troup (1964) have demonstrated that a rise in intragastric or intrarectal pressure accompanies activities which should theoretically overcompress the vertebral bodies. That these rises derive from abdominal parietal muscle contractions and not from intestinal activity has been demonstrated in studies by Rushmer (1946), Adno (1956), Sasaki (1969) and others. Mechanical analysis of the contributions such pressure might make to spinal stability is given by Morris Lucas and Bresler (1961), and by Troup (1968), and intra-abdominal pressure measurements are now widely used as an indirect measure of trunk stress during heavy physical activity, such as the analysis of spinal stress in the construction industry by Stubbs (1976).

At present there is a large gap between this fairly extensive knowledge of the normal and the little we know of the causes and effects of abnormality. The modern bio-engineer has to take account of these various factors in his appraisals. Back disorders are common afflictions of modern man, and some of their manifestations, such as scoliosis, can be severely crippling or lethal (Zorab, 1977). It is this gap that the bio-engineer is perhaps best placed to fill, and I hope that this new Oxford Centre will greatly speed the work that has to be done to this end.

REFERENCES

Adno, J. (1956). Some aspects of the mechanics of the abdomen. South African Med. J. 30, 535-539.

Aeby, C. (1879). Die Altersverschiedenheiten der menschlichen Wirbelsraule. Arch. Anat. Physiol, Lpz, 77-137.

Anderson, R. J. (1883). Observations on the diameters of human vertebrae in different regions. J. Anat. Lond., 17, 341-344.

Bartelink, D. L. (1957). The role of abdominal pressure in relieving the pressure on the lumbar intervertebral discs. J. Bone Jt. Surg., 39B, 718-725.

Barthez, P. J. (1798). Nouvelle mechanique des mouvements de l'homme et des animaux. Carcassone.

Beadle, O. A. (1931). The intervertebral discs. Spec. Rep. ser., M.R.C. London. No. 161.

Bell, J. & Bell, C. (1826). The anatomy and physiology of the human body. London

Bick, E. M. & Copel, J. W. (1950). Longitudinal growth of the human vertebrae, J. Bone Jt. Surg., 32A, 203-814.

Bohmig, R. (1930). Die Blutgefassversorgung der Wirbelbandscheiben. Arch. Klin. Chir., 158, 374-424.

Bradford, F. K., & Spurling R. G., (1945). The intervertebral disc. 2nd. ed., p 28, cc. Thomas,Springfield, 111.

Brown, T. Hansen, R. J . Yorra, A. J. (1957). Some mechanical tests on the lumbosacral spine with particular reference to the intervertebral discs; a preliminary report. J. Bone Jt. Surg., 39A 1135-1164.

Capener, N. (1944). Sciatica - anatomical and mechanical study of the lumbo-sacral region. Ann. Rheum. Dis., 4, 29-36.

Cheselden. W. (1733). Osteographia. London.

Christ, W., & Dupuis, H. (1966). Uber die Beanspruchung der Wirbelsaule unter dem Einfluss sinusformiger und stochastischer Schwingungen Int. Z. Angew. Physiol., 22, 258-278.

Cunningham, J. (1886). Memoir No. 2., Royal Irish Academy, pp 1-116.

Cyriax, E. F. (1919). On certain absolute & relative measurements of human vertebrae. J. Anat. Lond., 54, 305-308.

Davidson, E. A. & Woodhall B. (1954). Biomechanical alterations in herniated intervertebral discs. J. Biol. Chem., 234, 2951-2954.

Davis, P. R. (1955). The thoraco-lumbar mortice joint. J. Anat. London 89, 370-377.

Davis, P. R. (1955). Variations of the intra-abdominal pressure during weight lifting in various postures. J. Anat., 90., 601(P).

Davis, P. R. (1957). Studies on the functional anatomy of the human vertebral column, with special reference to the thoracic & lumbar region. Ph.D. Thesis, University of London.

DAVIS, P. R. (1959). The causation of hernia by weight-lifting. Lancet, 2., 155-57.

Davis, P. R. (1960). Observations of vertebrae in different races. Extrait des Actes due Vl^e Congress International des Sciences Anthropologiques et Ethnologiques. Paris 1960, 1, 443-450.

Davis, P. R. (1961). Human lower lumbar vertebrae, some mechanical and osteological considerations. J. Anat., London, 95, 337-344.

Davis, P. R. & Troup, J D.G. (1964). Pressures in the trunk cavities when pulling, pushing and lifting. Ergonomics, 7, 465-474.

Elsberg, C.A. & Dyke, C.G. (1934). The diagnosis of localizations of tumours of the spinal cord by means of measurements made on X-ray films of the vertebrae. Bull. neurol Inst., N.Y. 3, 359-394.

Etemadi A. A. (1963). Observations on the musculature and innervation of the human spine. Thesis, London.

Evans, F. G. & Lissner, H. R. (1955). Studies on the compressive strength of human lumbar discs and vertebrae. Anat. Rec., 121, 290.

Fick, R. (1911). Manuel d'anatomie et de mecanique des articulations chez l'homme. Paris.

Frazer, J. E. (1933). The anatomy of the human skeleton. 3rd ed. London.

Galante, J. D. (1967). Tensile properties of the human lumbar annulus fibrosus. Acta Orthopaed. Scand., Suppl., 100.

Gallois & Japiot. (1925). Architecture interieure des vertebres. Rev. Chir, Paris, 63, 688-708.

Hirsch, C. & Nachemson, A. (1954). New observations on the mechanical behaviour of lumbar discs. Acta. orthopaed. Scand., 23, 254-283.

Holder, L. (1887). Osteology. 7th ed., London.

Humphry, G. M. (1858). A treatise on the human skeleton (including the joints). London.

Keith, A. (1923). Mans posture: its evolution and disorders. Lecture 1V. The adaptations of the abdomen of its viscera to the orthograde posture. Brit. med. J., I, 587-590.

Landmesser, W. E., & Heublein, G. W. (1953). Measurement of the normal interpedicular space in the child. Conn. St. med. J., 17, 310-313.

Le Double, A. F. (1912). Traite des variations de la collonne vertebrale de l'homme. Paris.

Martin, R. (1928). Lehrbuch der Anthropologie. 2nd ed., Jena.

Mitchell, P.E.G. Hendry, N.G.C. & Billewicz, W. Z. (1961). The chemical background of intervertebral disc prolapse. J. Bone Jt. Sur., 43B, 141-151.

Morris, H. (1879). The Anatomy of the joints of man. London.

Morris, J. M. Lucase, D. B. & Bresler, B. (1961). Role of the trunk in the stability of the spine. J. Bone Jt. Surg. 43A, 327-351.

Naffziger, H. C. Inman, V. & Saunders, J. B. de C.M. (1938). Lesions of the intervertebral disc and ligamenta flava: clinical & anatomical studies. Surg. Gynec. obstet., 66, 288-299.

Olivier, G. (1954). Les tubercules lamellaires anterieures. Sem. Hop. Paris, (Archives d'Anat), 30, 1-2.

Rolander, S. D. (1966). Motion of the lumbar spine with special reference to the stabilising effect of posterior fusion: an experimental study on autopsy spcimens. Acta Orthopaed. Scand, Suppl. 90.

Rosegger, R., & Rosegger, S. (1960. Arbeitsmedisinische Erkentnisse beim Schlepperfahren. Arch. handtech., 2, 3-66.

Rushmer, R. F. (1946). Nature of intraperitoneal & intrarectal pressures. Amer. J. Physiol., 147, 242-249.

Sasaki, N. (1969). Effect of weight lifting by push and pull on intrathoracic pressure. J. Sc. Labour, 45., 410-421.

Schmorl, G. (1929). Uber Knorpelknotchen an der Hinterflache der Wirbelbandscheiben. Fortachr. Rontgenstr., 40, 629-634.

Shore, L. R. (1931). A report on the nature of certain bony spurs arising from the dorsal arches of the thoracic vertebrae. J. Anat., Lond., 65, 379-387.

Simril, W. A. & Thurston, D. (1955). The normal interpediculate space in the spines of infants and children. Radiology, 64, 340-347.

Struthers, J. (1875). On variations of the vertebrae and ribs in man. J. Anat., Lond., 9, 17-96.

Stubbs, D. A. (1975). Trunk stresses in construction workers. Ph.D. Thesis. University of Surrey.

Todd, T. W. & Pyle, S. I. (1928). A quantitative study of the vertebral column by direct and roentgenoscopic methods. Amer. J. phys.Anthrop., 12, 321-337.

Topinard, P. (1877). Des anomalies de nombre de la colonne vertebrale chez l'homme. Paris.

Troup, J.D.G. (1968). The function of the lumbar spine: a biomechanical and peripheral neurological study. Ph.D. Thesis. University of London.

Ubermuth, H. (1929). Uber die Altersveranderungen der menschlichen Zwischenwirbelshiebe und ihne Beziehung zu den chronischen Gelenkleiden der Wirbelsaule. Ber. sachs. Ges. (Akad) Wiss., 81, 111-124.

Vallois, H. V. & Lazorthes, G. (1942). Indices lombaires et indices lombaire total. Bull. Soc. Anthrop. Paris, 3, 116-131.

Vesalius (1543). De Humani Corporis Fabrica. Basel.

Virgin, W. J. (1951). Experimental investigations into the physical properties of the intervertebral disc. J. Bone Jt. Surg., 33-B, 607-611.

Weber, E.H. (1823). In Hildebrandt, F. (1823). Lehrbuch der Anatomie des Menschen. Leipzig.

Weber, E. H. (1827). Anatomisch-physiologische Untersuchung uber einige Einrichtungen in Mechanismus der menschlichen Wirbelsaule. Arch. Anat. Physiol., Lp., pp. 240-272.

Winslow, J. B. (1732). Exposition anatomique de las structure du corps humain. Paris.

Wyman, J. (1857) On the cancellate structure of some of the bones of the human body. Boston J. Nat. Hist., 6, 125-140. (quoted by Evans, 1957)

Zorab, P. A. (1977). Scoliosis, proceedings of the fifth symposium Academic Press. London.

IS THE SHEAR STIFFNESS OF THE INTERVERTEBRAL DISC DEPENDENT ON THE INTERVERTEBRAL COMPRESSIVE FORCE?

B.M. CYRON, B.Sc., Ph.D., and W.C. HUTTON, M.Sc., C.Eng., M.I.Mech.E.

The Polytechnic of Central London, New Cavendish Street, London W1M 8JS

INTRODUCTION

Flexion/extension movements of the lumbar spine are allowed through the anterior and posterior borders of the disc extending or shortening. The amount of movement at each intervertebral level is dependent on the elastic properties of the disc, the position of the instantaneous centre of rotation and the thickness of the disc. The latter is illustrated through an average total range of movement of 16° for the L5 - S1 joint as against 8° for the L1 - L2 joint; the lumbo-sacral disc is much thicker than the discs at higher lumbar levels (Tanz 1953).

The fibres of the annulus fibrosus of the intervertebral disc are set in concentric layers at about 30° to the vertebral end-plates, with each adjacent layer set in the opposite direction. This orientation of the fibres is a mechanical compromise offering minimum resistance to flexion/extension and lateral bending movements, and maximum resistsance to shear movements (Galante 1967). The disc is stiff enough to share equally with the neural arch in resisting anterior shear (Cyron 1977).

The intervertebral disc has also to resist compressive forces acting on the joint and these can be of an order of magnitude greater than the shear forces. While lifting a 500N weight the compressive force on the lumbo-sacral disc is about 9 kN, whereas while walking with a 500N pack on the back the force is about 1.5 kN. The comparable values for the shear force are about 750N and 500N respectively (Cyron 1977).

These high compressive forces can decrease the thickness of the disc and reduce the angle of the fibres in each concentric layer. This may alter the resistance of the disc to anterior shear. In addition, any change in resistance may be level dependent considering the variation in the disc thickness and wedging down the lumbar spine.

The following text reports on experiments carried out to investigate the shear stiffness of the lumbar intervertebral disc subjected to different ratios of shear force to compressive force.

MATERIALS AND METHODS

CADAVERIC MATERIAL

Lumbar spines from subjects aged between eighteen and forty four years were removed during routine necropsies. The material was collected from cadavers in whom there was no evidence of bone disease. The spines were dissected into joints consisting of two vertebrae and the intervening disc. During preparation of the specimens care was taken not to introduce any residual deformation within the disc. All the specimens were stored in sealed polythene bags at a temperature of -20 degrees Celsius until required for testing. Just before testing each joint was placed in a refrigerator for twenty-four hours to allow for slow defreezing. Of the eight intervertebral joints tested, two were L5 - S1, three were L4 - L5, one was L3 - L4 and two were L2 - L3 (Table 1).

EXPERIMENTAL METHOD

Each joint was stripped of the excess soft tissue, but the ligaments and muscles joining the vertebrae were not disturbed. Wood screws were fixed into the vertebrae to ensure a firm fixation in surgical cement (calestone). The joint was then mounted in cement (Figure 1) and wrapped in polythene to avoid dehydration. During mounting care was taken to ensure that the plane midway through the intervertebral disc, in its rest position, was parallel to the end-plates of the containers holding the upper and lower vertebrae. This method of mounting allowed a choice of pure compression (Figure 1), or a combination of compression and shear (Figure 2) to be applied to the joint.

Calestone is a stiff material which deforms very little under the forces applied during these tests. When hardening, it is also exothermic and a stream of cold air was directed on to the specimen during this stage, to avoid any damage from the heat generated.

In order to measure the properties of the disc alone the neural arch of the upper vertebrae was first cut with a chisel through the partes interarticulares. In our experimental method we had first to determine the compressive properties of the disc so that in subsequent tests, when we applied compression together with shear were able to calculate the relative displacement between the vertebrae due to anterior shear. The tests were carried out using the servo-controlled hydraulic testing machine. The upper cross-head of the machine incorporated a load cell while the base unit held a hydraulic actuator and a displacement transducer.

The following sequence of experiments was performed :

Experiment 1

The force/deformation characteristics of the intervertebral disc when subjected to a force perpendicular to the plane midway through the disc (pure compression) were determined (Figure 1). This was achieved by applying forces of known magnitude and direction to the joint through a roller. The roller was free to rotate but its axis was fixed. It was placed at the top of the upper container with its centre lying on the line between the point of application of the force and the centre of rotation of the joint. The position of the roller was located by trial and error; a small compressive force (up to 50 N) was applied at each position until it did not cause any tilting of the upper vertebrae. The outputs from the load cell and displacement transducer were fed on to the X-Y plotter which plotted the magnitude of the compressive force F_c and corresponding vertical displacement d.

Experiment 2

The force/deformation characteristics of the intervertebral disc when subjected to a force inclined to the plane midway through the disc (combined compression and shear) were then determined (Figure 2). By impinging on a plane inclined at an angle θ (in this case $\theta = 20^{\circ}$) the applied force F acted at an angle $(90 - \theta)$ to the plane midway through the intervertebral disc. The position of the roller was again adjusted so that the line of action of this force passed through the centre of rotation of the joint. The applied force F could be resolved into two components, F_S (equal to F $\sin \theta$) shearing the disc and F_C (equal to F $\cos \theta$) compressing the disc. As the magnitude of the applied force F was increased the upper vertebra moved forward while the roller travelled up the variable angle plate. The force F and resulting vertical displacement d_1 were measured directly. The corresponding shear force F_S was given by the expression $F_S = F_C \tan \theta$. The horizontal displacement h produced by F_S was calculated as follows. For a particular value of F_C, Experiment 1 gives the value of d and Experiment 2 the value of d_1. The horizontal distance through which the disc has been sheared can be evaluated since $h = (d_1 - d) \cot \theta$. A graph of F_S versus h gave the force/deformation characteristics of the disc. The slope of the main portion of this graph gives the shear stiffness K of the disc while the ratio of F_S/F_C was kep constant and equal to tan 20°. A typical result is shown in Figure 3 (graph (a)).

Experiment 3

The angle θ was changed to 10° and Experiment 2 was repeated. A second graph was plotted, the slope of which gave the stiffness K of the disc while the ratio of F_S/F_C was kept constant and equal to tan 10° (Figure 3 graph (b)). In a situation such as lifting the ratio of the shear component to the compressive component would vary since the magnitude of both components depends on different variables (Hutton et al. 1977). The values of 20° and 10° chosen for angle in these experiments only approximates to a partially flexed posture while carrying a 500N weight on the back. Earlier attempts to reduce θ (to simulate flexion) were abandoned due to the difficulty of accurately measuring the smaller values of d_1. When the experiments were completed the intervertebral disc was again subjected to pure compression. The force/ deformation characteristics obtained were nearly the same as those obtained in Experiment 1 suggesting that the compressive and shear forces applied during the experiments did not cause any great residual deformation within the disc. It should be noted that the disc was loaded slowly and allowed to recover before any subsequent test. After the tests the discs were examined for the degree of degeneration. Only results for normal discs and those in which the lack of a clear boundary between the annulus and nucleus was the only evidence of degeneration, were collected.

Figure 1

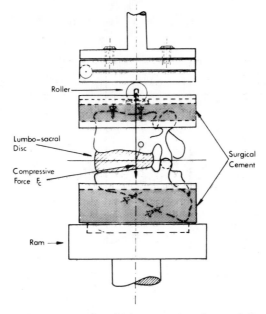

The arrangement of the apparatus for applying
pure compression to a lumbar intervertebral
joint

Figure 2

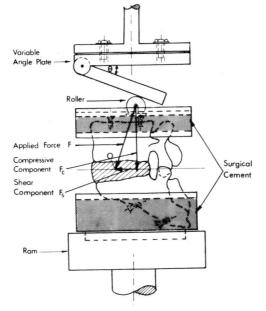

The arrangement of the apparatus for applying
a combination of compression and shear to a
lumbar intervertebral joint

Table 1: The details of the results obtained

Specimen Number	Age	Sex	Intervertebral Level	Shear Stiffness K for $\theta=20°$, kN/cm	Shear Stiffness K for $\theta=10°$, kN/cm
35	18	M	L2-L3	4.29	3.68
35	18	M	L4-L5	3.26	3.02
A2	35	M	L4-L5	3.70	6.42
38	38	M	L3-L4	4.32	3.39
38	38	M	L5-S1	4.54	3.05
53	44	M	L5-S1	2.64	1.67
A1	44	M	L2-L3	3.70	4.00
A1	44	M	L4-L5	3.58	3.90

Figure 3

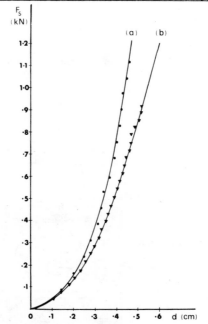

Typical result showing the force/deformation characteristics of a compressively loaded lumbar intervertebral joint subjected to shear. The main portion of graph (a) gives the shear stiffness of the disc while the ratio of Fs/Fc is equal to 0.36, whereas the graph (b) gives the shear stiffness while the ratio is equal to 0.18

RESULTS

The experimental results are summarised in Table 1 and the graphs in
Figure 3 illustrate a typical set of results obtained. The slope of
the main portion of each graph gives the corresponding stiffness of
the disc subjected to forward shear.

For angle θ equal to 10° the compressive force on the disc was about
twice that for θ equal to 20°, for the same value of applied shear
force. An increase in stiffness, after the angle was decreased, is
apparent in three out of the eight discs treated.

DISCUSSION

When the intervertebral disc is compressed the nucleus pulposus transmits
to the annulus fibrosus circumferential and radial stress. The
compressive force itself produces a longitudinal compressive stress,
and to compound the situation the invtervertebral disc can be under
shear stress. The truss model of the annulus fibrosus as described
by Galante (1967) is an analogy which may be too simple to predict
the behaviour of an intervertebral disc subjected to a complex
stress pattern. In addition the loaded disc will bulge and so
disturb any two dimensional model. The lack of consistency in our
results might possibly be explained by variations within individuals
and across the population, or the failure of the disc to behave in
a consistent manner due to changes in the position of the centre of
rotation while the disc is sheared.

In our experiment the position of the roller had to be adjusted at
the beginning of each experiment so that the applied force passed
through the centre of rotation. These three, possibly different
positions of the centre, may have allowed the disc to respond
differently to the forces applied in each test, so producing a new
result.

The experiments simulated an upright posture with the extensor
muscles inactive, while increasing load was placed on the shoulders.
This situation will seldom arise in life except in these cases where
the muscle attachments to the neural arch are absent or when the
neural arch is broken. As pointed out before, during spinal movements
the shear force and the compressive force acting on the disc are
somewhat independent variables, whereas in our experiments they were
related and increased proportionally.

Previous work has shown that the intervertebral disc is not subjected
to much shear in either the flexed or erect postures due to the
activity of the extensor muscles attached to the neural arch (Hutton
et al. 1977). This situation changes after a spondylolytic fracture

when the disc acts alone and spondylolisthesis may result. In our results the shear stiffness ranged from 1.6kN/cm to 6.4 kN/cm. This marked variation may explain why spondylolisthesis not always follows in those who develop spondylolysis.

Pure compressive tests on the intervertebral disc, after the neural arch had been fractured revealed an average stiffness for the disc of 29 kN/cm (Cyron and Hutton 1977). The overall average, as shown by these tests, for the stiffness of the disc in shear is 4 kN/cm. The nucleus pulposus of the intervertebral disc shares with the annulus fibrosus in resisting compressive forces, whereas shear forces are resisted by the annulus alone. Assuming that the annulus fibrosus is equally stiff in compression as in shear these results suggest that the nucleus pulposus plays the more important role in resisting compression.

If the fibres of the intervertebral disc are set at about 30° to the plane of the end-plates then a compressive force will produce slack in the fibres which must be taken up before the fibres can be subsequently stretched. This may have the effect that in vivo the disc will always be in a state of relative slack due to the very high compressive forces and it is only after spondylolysis that the fibres, now better orientated due to the compressive force, are asked to play a resistive role. In the intact joint the shear forces would be taken up initially by the neural arch alone until the slack in the fibres allowed the disc to aid in resisting shear. This may explain the increasing slope shown in the graphs of shear forces plotted against anterior displacement (Cyron 1977).

CONCLUSION

The object of these experiments was to determine whether the shear stiffness of the disc is dependent on the intervertebral compressive force. The considerable inconsistency in our results leaves the hypothesis still untested.

ACKNOWLEDGEMENTS

The authors wish to acknowledge the support of the National Fund for Research into Crippling Diseases and the help of Dr. H.J. Harris, Pathology Laboratory, Stoke Mandeville Hospital, Aylesbury, Bucks., who advised on some aspects of the work.

REFERENCES

CYRON, B.M. (1977)
    Mechanical factors in the etiology of spondylolysis.
    Ph.D. Thesis The Polytechnic of Central London.

CYRON, B.M., and HUTTON, W.C. (1977)
    Unpublished data.

GALANTE, J.O. (1967)
    Tensile properties of the human lumbar annulus fibrosus.
    Acta Orthopaedica Scandinavica, Supplementum 100.

HUTTON, W.C., STOTT, J.R.R., and CYRON, B.M. (1977)
    Is spondylolysis a fatigue fracture ?
    Spine (in press).

Tanz, S.S. (1953)
    Motion of the lumbar spine.
    American Journal of Roentgenology, 69, pp. 399 - 42.

SURFACE STRAIN MEASUREMENTS ON
THE CADAVERIC LUMBAR SPINE

W.G.J. HAMPSON, M. JAYSON, and J.S. SHAH

Southmead General Hospital, Bristol

The aims of this investigation are to examine in detail the sites, directions and magnitude of strains imposed on cadaveric lumbar vertebrae and discs under simplified loading conditions and to relate the findings to clinical conditions, particularly spondylolisthesis and disc degeneration.

In the first part of our investigation dried lumbar vertebrae coated with brittlecoat were loaded in a tensometer adapted for compression either singly, or in pairs separated by artificially prepared intervertebral discs. By examination of the crack patterns which developed in the brittlecoat layers, the sites and directions of the principal surface strain components were determined. Areas of stress concentration were found around the vertebral rims and near the pedicles, when direct axial load was applied. When the vertebrae were loaded in an inclined plane to simulate normal lumbar lordosis an additional very localised area of stress concentration occurred in the pars interarticularis.

In the second part of our investigation isolated sections of lumbar spines were freshly prepared from six young adults who died in road traffic accidents. Rosette strain gauges were attached at seventeen different sites on the fourth lumbar vertebra of each specimen, while simultaneous measurements of radial bulge and tangential strain were made on six sites on the surface of the L4-5 discs.

The results extend the findings of our brittlecoat test. They demonstrate that the highest compression strains occur at the base of the pedicles and on the pars interarticularis while loads to simulate extension further increase these strains. The highest tensile strains occur around the vertebral rims. Radial bulge circumferential strain measurements are maximum at the back of the disc. Furthermore, analysis of flexion/extension studies suggests that these movements are accompanied in life by the movement of the nucleus pulposus in the disc, a hypothesis since confirmed by cadaveric discography.

MYOELECTRIC BACK MUSCLE ACTIVITY, LUMBAR DISC PRESSURE AND INTRA-ABDOMINAL PRESSURE IN STANDARDIZED WORKING-POSTURES

G.B.J. ANDERSSON[1,2], R. ÖRTENGREN[2], and A. NACHEMSON[1]

1 Department of Orthopaedic Surgery, Sahlgren Hospital, Göteborg, Sweden
2 Department of Clinical Neurophysiology, Sahlgren Hospital, Göteborg, Sweden

INTRODUCTION

To reduce the incidence of low back pain in industry, ergonomic approaches to the workplace are used as well as instructions in manual materials handling. Difficulties, at present, to obtain direct measurements of back load during work have made it necessary to base these changes and instructions on experience and basic engineering concepts. In spite of these improvements the back injury rate is still very much the same as twenty-five years ago (Hult 1954a, b; Horal 1959; Andersson 1978). It would seem, therefore, that more accurate estimates of back load are needed to prove or disprove the theory of a relationship between low back pain and high back load, and to evaluate the importance of different measures introduced to reduce this load.

This chapter summarises a series of laboratory experiments undertaken to obtain knowledge about the magnitude of low back stress under standardized conditions of loading, to evaluate and compare different methods used to measure these stresses, and to achieve the necessary experience to conduct further studies on the factory floor.

MATERIAL

Three different groups of healthy volunteers participated in the investigations. Each of these groups has been described in detail in the paper in which the result was first reported (Andersson et al 1976a, b, 1977a, b).

The age range was from twenty-three to thirty-five years, heights between 169 and 188 cm and weights from 52 to 80 kg. Studies of the myoelectric activity were performed on groups of either ten or fifteen subjects. Simultaneous measurements of the myoelectric back muscle activity, the intra-discal pressure, and the intra-abdominal pressure were performed on four subjects.

METHODS

Equipment

The equipment used for recording of the myoelectric signals, the disc pressure and the intra-abdominal pressure has been previously described (Andersson et al 1976). It included a signal connection and monitoring unit and a fourteen-channel FM tape recorder. The monitoring unit made it possible to check the signal quality on any two channels simultaneously on an oscilloscope screen. All channels were checked consecutively before and during each recording period. The signals were recorded on magnetic tape for subsequent analysis.

The myoelectric signals were picked up by means of bipolar, recessed surface electrodes (inter-electrode distance 20 mm), which were glued to the skin using an alpha-cyanoacrylate adhesive, Cyanolit[R]. The electrode signals were fed to preamplifiers built into a small box which was strapped to the subject's chest. The signals were further amplified in main amplifiers and fed to the monitoring unit. For analysis, the tapes were played back and the amplitudes of the myoelectric signals were estimated by feeding the signals to linear-law detectors, thus producing full-wave rectified and averaged values (FRA-values).

The intra-discal pressure was measured by means of a subminiature pressure transducer built into the tip of a needle as previously described by Nachemson and Elfström (1970). The transducer signal was processed in a bridge amplifier and connected to the tape signal monitor and to a two-channel ink recorder.

The equipment for measuring the intra-abdominal (intra-gastric) pressure consisted of a pressure sensitive radio transducer and a receiver. The transducer was swallowed and the transducer signal picked up by means of a ferrite antenna and an FM-demodulator. The demodulated signal was connected to the tape signal monitor and to the ink recorder.

Recording Procedure

The guiding needle of the disc pressure transducer was inserted via a lateral approach into the centre of the third lumbar disc, the course being followed by TV-fluoroscopy.

Twelve (in the solely myoelectric studies) or ten electrodes were placed on each subject. They were located 3 cm lateral to the midline on both or one side of the trunk at the levels of T4 and T8, L1, L3 and L5. At the level of L3 a second electrode pair (or electrode) was placed 6 cm lateral to the midline.

The calibrated radio transducer for the intra-abdominal pressure was swallowed. With the ferrite antenna, the subject's abdomen was scanned for locations of highest strength of the radio signal. The antenna was then taped to the skin where it could be conveniently worn during the experiments.

Two series of experiments were performed. In the first, studies were made when the spine was loaded in fixed spinal postures. In the second, lifting was investigated both in static loading experiments (pulling) and in dynamic loading experiments.

In the first experimental series the subjects were placed in a reference frame, in which the positions of the feet, legs, pelvis, and spine could all be controlled. The pelvis was 'locked' with a transverse bar and wooden blocks - placed at the anterior superior iliac spines - in order to prevent lateral movement as well as rotation.

The second experimental series (lifting) fall into a static and a dynamic part. Static loading was accomplished by asking the subjects to pull on a handle with a force of 400 N using both hands symmetrically. The distance between the handle and the foot-support was 20, 40 and 60 cm in the myoelectric experiments, and 40, 50 and 60 cm in the experiments where the disc pressure and intra-abdominal pressure measurements were also included. At each height, one pull was performed with the back straight and the knees flexed (leg-lifting) and one pull with the back flexed and the knees straight (back-lifting).

The dynamic loading experiments were of several different types. With the subject standing, 100 N was lifted from 45 cm above the floor to the height of the freely hanging hands. Both hands were used symmetrically and two methods of lifting were studied, back-lifting and leg-lifting. One of the subjects repeated the lift while performing the Valsalva manoeuvre. In another experiment, a load of 50 N was lifted from a table, held with both arms straight and horizontal, and moved in close to the chest and out again. The 50 N load was then lifted from a 65 cm high table at different rates. Using both hands the lift was first performed in less than one second, then in about five seconds.

RESULTS

Loading in Fixed Spinal Postures

In upright relaxed standing without load the mean value (standard error of the mean) of the disc pressure was 0.331 MPa (0.034 MPa) and the corresponding values of the intra-abdominal pressure 0.20 kPa (0.20 kPa). The mean values of the myoelectric signal amplitudes recorded from the paraspinal muscles in that position were generally low, about 10 μV. The activity picked up from the trapezius muscles was considerably higher, about 50 μV.

All the measured variables responded systematically to changes in posture and load. When the subjects were loaded with 100 N in each hand and the angle of forward flexion was increased, there was an increase in intra-discal pressure and in intra-abdominal pressure (Figure 1). At the same time FRA-values of the paraspinal muscles increased at all levels of the back (Figure 2). The increase in the myoelectric activity was comparatively larger in the thoracic than in the lumbar region. Statistical analysis showed a significant linear relationship between the myoelectric signal amplitudes as well as the pressure values and the angle of flexion.

The intra-discal pressure and the intra-abdominal pressure both increased when the externally applied load was increased at a thirty degree angle of flexion. The relationships between pressures and load were statistically significantly linear (Figures 3a, b). Also, the FRA-values increased linearly at all electrode locations. The increase in myoelectric activity was greater at higher levels of the back.

The disc pressure and the intra-abdominal pressure both increased when the trunk was loaded in lateral flexion as well as in rotation. In these experiments consistent differences were found in the levels of myoelectric activity recorded on the left and the right side of the back. In the lumbar region, higher FRA-values were found on the side contralateral to the load; in the thoracic region the values were higher on the ipsilateral side. The disc pressure, the intra-discal pressure, and the FRA-values were throughout higher when the trunk was loaded in rotation than in lateral flexion.

Lifting (Static Loading)

The FRA-values of the myoelectric signals recorded when pulling with the back straight differed considerably from those found when pulling with the back flexed. When the handle was placed 20 or 40 cm above the floor, higher levels of activity were always found when the back was straight.

The differences were statistically significant at L1 and L3 levels. When the handle was at 60 cm, higher values were usually found when pulling with the back flexed but the differences were not statistically significant. There were only slight differences in the activity patterns obtained at the three lumbar levels. The FRA-values recorded at thoracic levels were significantly higher than those recorded at lumbar levels when the handle was placed 20 or 40 cm above the floor. With the handle at 60 cm, the activity was often higher in the lumbar region.

The disc pressure values were about the same when pulling was performed with the back flexed as with the back straight, the mean values being slightly higher when the distance between the handle and the floor was shorter. The intra-abdominal pressure differed significantly when pulling at 40 cm, the values being higher with the leg-lifting method. At 50 and 60 cm similar pressure values were obtained.

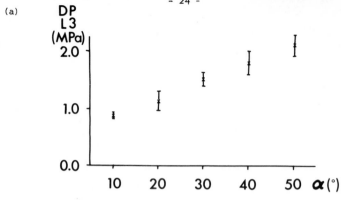

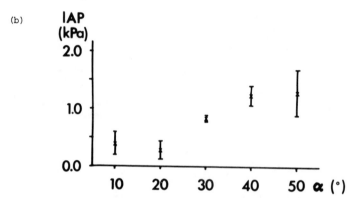

Figure 1   Lumbar disc pressure (a) and intra-abdominal pressure (b)
            recorded at different angles of forward flexion, with
            100 N in each hand

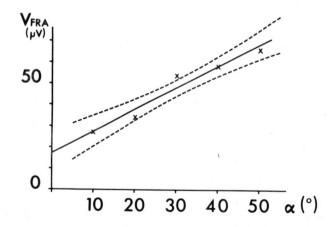

Figure 2   Mean values of myoelectric activity from the right side of
            the back at L3 level related to the angle of forward flexion.
            The relationship is statistically significantly linear
            (p < 5%). The dashed lines indicate 95% confidence limits
            for the mean values

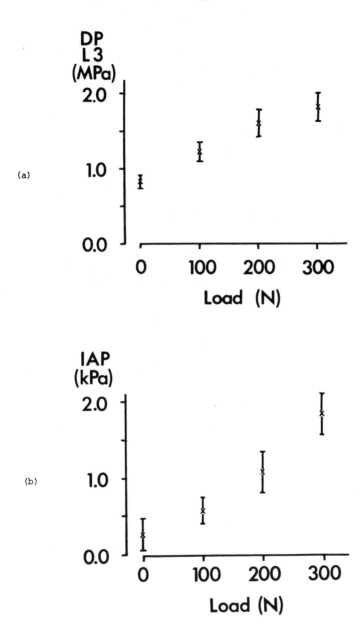

Figure 3   Lumbar disc pressure (a) and intra-abdominal
            pressure (b) at thirty degrees of forward
            flexion and different loads

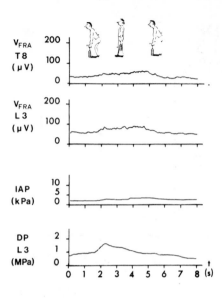

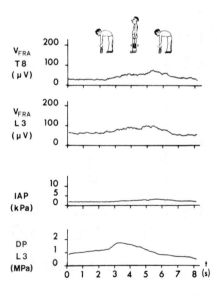

Figure 4   Temporal variations of myoelectric back muscle activity,
            intra-abdominal pressure and lumbar disc pressure when
            lifting 100N using the leg-lifting method (top picture)
            and the back-lifting method (bottom picture). The load
            on the back is similar in both methods.

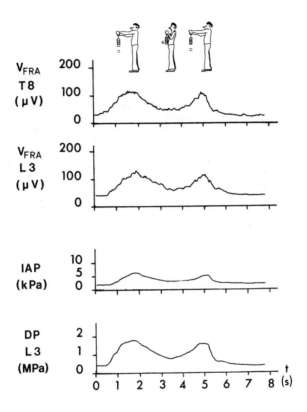

Figure 5.

Temporal variations in measured variables when a load of 50 N
was lifted with both arms, moved in close to the chest and out
again.

Dynamic Loading

During lifting of the 100 N load from 45 cm above the floor to an upright position, the FRA-values at all levels of the back and the disc pressure increased considerably, whereas the intra-abdominal pressure increased only slightly. Usually, peak values in myoelectric activity and disc pressure were reached slightly before the subject had reached the upright position. When the loads were put down again, peak values were reached slightly after the movement was initiated and then the values decreased gradually. Examples of temporal variations during lifting are shown in Figure 4. When leg-lifting was compared to back-lifting, no statistically significant differences were observed.

When the 50 N load was lifted with both arms straight and horizontal, high levels of myoelectric activity were recorded and the intra-abdominal pressure and the disc pressure was increased considerably (Figure 5). As the load was moved in close to the chest all values decreased and increased again when the load was moved away from the body. Both the intra-abdominal pressure values and the myoelectric activity values were higher in the extended position than when lifting was performed. Repeating the experiments **seated** similar values were obtained.

When the load of 50 N was lifted from a 65 cm high table using both hands, a change in the pace of the lift did not significantly influence the values recorded.

DISCUSSION

The myoelectric back muscle activities, intra-abdominal pressure and disc pressure all appear to relate to the turning moments acting on the spine: the measurement values increase when the trunk moment increases. In the static studies reported here, linear relationships were obtained between each of the parameters and the moment acting on the spine.

The studies on the different methods of lifting points in favour of the leg-lifting method. It is important to recognize, however, that the differences were small both in the static and dynamic experiments. The posture of the legs and the spine are probably of secondary importance. The main advantage of the leg-lifting method in our view is that it is possible to bring the object closer to the body. A reduction in the lever arm influenced the measured variables much more than the back posture during the lift. Thus, more emphasis should be placed on that aspect in the teaching of 'correct' lifting techniques, and efforts should be made to design the workspace and work methods accordingly. This requires also reductions in object sizes and attention to the distribution of load.

Regarding the use of the different methods of field studies, electromyographic and intra-abdominal pressure measurements are the only possibilities: disc pressure measurements must be carried out in laboratory settings. Studies performed at the Volvo assembly line using electromyography are encouraging (Örtengren et al 1974, 1975). Artifact-free signals of high quality can be obtained during unrestricted manual work, and the results can then be interpreted together with data on load and posture. The technical difficulties involved and the laborious data analysis - automatic   recording procedures and computerized analysis - precludes general use of this method at present, and necessitates further development.

CONCLUSIONS

The measurement methods all relate to the moments acting on the spine: the values increase when the trunk moment increases. In field studies electromyography and intra-abdominal pressure measurements are the only possibilities. From these parameters, together with data on posture and load, the disc pressure can be inferred. Further studies are needed to analyse differences between various techniques of lifting. The size of the object and the distance from the body in which the object is lifted is of greater importance than the technique of lifting.

ACKNOWLEDGEMENTS

Financial support was provided by the Swedish Work Environment Fund and AB Volvo.

REFERENCES

ANDERSSON G. (1978) Low back pain in industry: Epidemiological aspects. Scandinavian Journal of Rehabilitation Medicine. In print.

ANDERSSON G.B.J., HERBERTS P., and ÖRTENGREN R. (1976) Myoelectric back muscle activity in standardized lifting postures. In Biomechanics, editor Komi P.V., vol. 5-A, pp. 520-529, publisher University Park Press, Baltimore, USA.

ANDERSSON G.B.J., ÖRTENGREN R., and NACHEMSON A. (1976) Quantitative studies of back loads in lifting. Spine, 1, pp. 178-185.

ANDERSSON G.B.J., ÖRTENGREN R., and HERBERTS P. (1977) Quantitative electromyographic studies of back muscle activity related to posture and loading. Orthopedic Clinics of North America, 8(1), pp. 85-96.

ANDERSSON G.B.J., ÖRTENGREN R., and NACHEMSON A. (1978) Intradiscal pressure, intra-abdominal pressure and myoelectric back muscle activity related to posture and loading. Clinical Orthopaedics and Related Research. In print.

HORAL J. (1969) The clinical appearance of low back pain disorders in the city of Gothenburg, Sweden. Comparisons of incapacitated probands with matched controls. Acta Orthopaedica Scandinavica Supplementum 118.

HULT L. (1954a) The Munkfors investigation. Acta Orthopaedica Scandinavica Supplementum 16.

HULT L. (1954b) Cervical dorsal and lumbar spinal syndromes. Acta Orthopaedica Scandinavica Supplementum 17.

NACHEMSON A., and ELFSTRÖM G. (1970) Intravital dynamic pressure measurements in lumbar discs. Scandinavian Journal of Rehabilitation Medicine Supplementum 1.

ÖRTENGREN R. (1974) On multichannel acquisition of biomedical data, with special reference to the recording and analysis of myoelectric signals. Technical report 46, Chalmers University of Technology, Göteborg, Sweden. Thesis.

ÖRTENGREN R., ANDERSSON G.B.J., BROMAN H., MAGNUSSON R., and PETERSEN I. (1975) Vocational electromyography: Studies of localized muscle fatigue at the assembly line. Ergonomics, 18, pp. 157-174.

THE METHODS USED TO OBSERVE WORK FACTORS
IN A STUDY OF BACK PAIN IN INDUSTRY

B.J. SWEETMAN, M.R.C.P.(U.K.)

Guy's Hospital, London SE1 9RT

INTRODUCTION

Back pain is a major cause of absenteeism in Industry and this paper describes the several methods used to observe the way in which men worked, looking for aspects that might predispose to back pain. All the work study procedures were carried out with the co-operation of postmen from the letter and parcel sections of a London Postal Sorting Office. Each of the ten methods of assessment will be described.

1. Abstracting from duty schedules.

Each task which a postman undertakes during a particular shift is described on a numbered Duty Schedule upon which is recorded also the time and place. This information was converted to a numeric form suitable for analysis. The various tasks have been grouped by the Post Office into broad categories: for example office work, sorting work and its associated mail work. The hours spent per week undertaking each type of work were recorded.

2. Classical Ergonomics.

This term is used to relate anthropometric factors to measurements of the work space, although nowadays the term Ergonomics implies a wider spectrum of study. It is fortunate that Post Office work surfaces, fittings and equipment are standardised and their dimensions were noted. Elbow height and arm-reach relationships were recorded for a short, medium and tall subject. In addition, the various tasks were described on a check list, together with details of the objects handled, sitting and standing arrangements, work rates and variability in types of work.

3. The Score Sheet technique.

A score sheet was employed upon which could be indicated:

(i)	Item handled
(ii)	Neck posture
(iii)	Low back posture
(iv)	Stance

The posture grid (Fig. 1) is an adaptation of a clinical shorthand notation of movement with three gross ranges of posture indentified for each of flexion, rotation and lateral flexion and with one grade for extension. Observations were made each minute for 15 minutes. Cluster analysis identified main categories of work and in particular the analysis suggested that sitting and standing letter sorting were as markedly different from one another as were other distinctly labelled jobs and this led us to return and find out what proportion of time the men spent sitting and standing when letter sorting.

4. BAHLPS.

This method was developed (Anderson 1964) as part of the Industrial Survey Units' investigation of rheumatism in industry and described the upper limits of effort involved in a given task rather than describing what is actually done. The observer grades the job according to the usual limit of effort by Back, Arms, Hands and Legs and well as features of Posture and climatic features of Site of work. Increasing effort is graded from one to eight and the sub-sections allow extra information for each section to be appended.

FIG. 1

The Score Sheet Technique

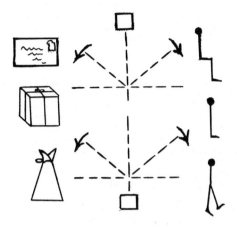

FIG. 2

BENESH NOTATION

	hands & feet	bent elbows & knees
Level with body	—	┿
In front of body	I	┼
Behind the body	•	✕

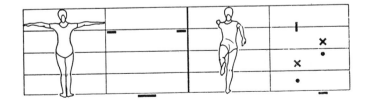

5. Choreology using the Benesh movement notation.

Notation in real time on a five bar stave (Fig.2) indicates posture and movement of the body. Practitioners trained at the Institute of Choreology observed men doing quarter hour samples of their work. The notation was coded numerically and each posture and movement transcribed. Choreology has been deployed in the ergonomic field observing variation in sitting posture (Kember 1976) and its use in the medical field has been described (Benesh and McGuiness 1974).

6. The Photographic Essay.

One photographer followed and one flanked the worker and took pictures at minute intervals using the flashlight to synchronise the process. This procedure was mainly useful as a descriptive reference record, information from which would be used to corroborate observation of the other techniques. Alignment of the photographers at right angles was not always possible when the job involved moving about the office and thus the records are not suitable for accurate measurements of limb geometry.

7. Actimeters. (Modified self-winding 'Automatic' watches.)
                (Sweetman et al 1977).

The principle underlying self-winding watches is that limb movement tightens the watch spring. This action can be modified to register limb movements.

The actimeters are made by modifying commercially available self-winding watches with date display, by removing the escapement mechanism, namely, the balance wheel and the pallet fork. Activity translates to movement of hour and minute hands as well as date display. Ideally the display of the actimeter should be all digital and have an automatic reset to zero. The system was unobtrusive and relatively cheap and simple to use. The devices were reliable with only one actimeter failing in 465 man hours of observation. Experience has suggested that the cheaper mass produced watches are the more suitable for conversion.

8. Intra-abdominal Pressure Recordings.

It has been shown (Davis 1977) that there is a close relationship between stress applied to the back and intra-abdominal pressures recorded using a miniature transmitting pressure transducer pill swallowed by the subject under investigation. Two volunteers participated in the study and each demonstrated a number of jobs for fifteen minute periods. The pressure spikes were recorded and annotated for the activities inducing them.

9. Oxygen Consumption.

A number of volunteers participated in quarter hour observations of their jobs. The system (Goldsmith 1973) involves the wearing of a face mask and expired air is sampled at volumes triggered by a flowmeter. The mixed samples were analysed for oxygen content and the oxygen consumption was then calculated correcting for inspired air temperature and vapour pressure. The procedure is now carried out automatically on a portable system carried on the belt called 'Oxylog'. It is difficult for the subject to talk when wearing the mask but none of the jobs we observed was hindered by this.

Electrocardiographs (ECG's) were recorded simultaneously on a portable minature tape recorder and the total respiratory flowmeter readings were also available.

10. E.M.G. Activity and Accelerometry.

A miniature analogue tape recorder was used to record these parameters (Sweetman et al 1976). Pairs of surface electromyographic (EMG) electrodes were placed over the muscles on either side of the lower back. A miniature accelerometer electronically damped was placed on the upper back such that it would behave as an inclinometer and record sagittal movements of the back. A second undamped accelerometer was placed on the belt to record vibration transmitted to the low back region.

The system was worn and observations for full shifts were made. It was worn also at the same time as using the other systems of observation.

SUMMARY

A variety of methods of observations have been described using systems developed specifically for the project as well as systems developed by other workers in the field. These methods range from simple documentary data extraction to comprehensive physiological recordings.

The observations were conducted at the normal place or work, and provided a great deal of information for the study of work factors in a study of back pain in industry.

ACKNOWLEDGMENTS

We should like to thank the Occupational Health Service and the Management of the Post Office and the Unions for their co-operation in making this study possible, and the staff of the London Postal Region for participation. We are indebted to Professor Davis, Professor Goldsmith and Julia McGuiness for the use of their various systems of observation. The ongoing work of Dr G. McMaster and Sue Ellam in the processing of the 'Medilog' recordings is gratefully acknowledged.

This work was part of a study of back pain in industry and was financed by a grant from the Arthritis and Rheumatism Council.

REFERENCES

ANDERSON, J.A.D.   (1964)
    Rheumatism in Industry. M.D. Thesis (Edinburgh).

BENESH, R and McGUINESS, J.   (June 1974)
    Benesh Movement Notation and Medicine.
    Physiotherapy Journal vol. 60 No.6 pp. 176-178

DAVIS, P.R., STUBBS, D.A., RIDD, J.E. (July 1977)
    Radio Pills, their use in monitoring back stress.
    Journal of Medical Engineering and Technology vol.1 pp. 209-212.

GOLDSMITH, R.;   TAN, G. Lin E.;   WALKER, C. and WRIGHT, B.M.   (1975)
    The validation of a miniature indicating and sampling electronic
    respirometer (MISER).
    Journal of Physiology   vol. 256   pp. 102-103.

KEMBER, P.A.   (Sept. 1976)
    The Benesh movement notation used to study sitting behaviour.
    Applied Ergonomics   pp. 133-136.

SWEETMAN, B.J.;   MOORE, C.S.;   JAYASINGHE, W.J. and ANDERSON, J.A.D.(1976)
    Monitoring work factors relating to back pain.
    Postgraduate Medical Journal   Vol. 52 (Supplement)   pp. 151-155.

SWEETMAN, B.J.;   EDWARDS, G.S. and ANDERSON, J.A.D.   (1977)
    A measurement of limb activity in a back pain study in industry.
    Postgraduate Medical Journal   (Supplement)   (In press).

INVESTIGATIONS OF THE IN VIVO BIOMECHANICS OF THE LUMBAR SPINE

J.W. FRYMOYER, M.S., M.D., E. BUTURLA, Ph.D., D.G. WILDER, B.S.M.E., and M.H. POPE, Ph.D.

University of Vermont College of Medicine, Department of Orthopaedic Surgery, Burlington, Vermont, U.S.A.

INTRODUCTION

The biomechanics of the lumbar spine have been clarified in part by three approaches: 1) Laboratory tests of mechanical properties of cadaveric specimens of the spine; 2) Analysis of spine function in living humans; 3) Mathematical modeling. At the University of Vermont Spine Research Laboratory, we have been interested in studying lumbar spinal mechanics in normal living subjects. Our objective has been to develop laboratory techniques which could be applied in comparative studies of subjects with and without lumbar pathologies. In our early studies, we used a biplanar radiographic system which permitted measurements of segmental vertebral motion in prone human subjects. The coupled characteristics of spinal motion, instant centre behaviour of vertebral motion segments, muscle strength in resisting torsion, and hysteretic behaviour of the spine were analysed. This report will detail a new apparatus designed to evaluate more completely muscle strength and spinal kinematics in living humans in a variety of standing postures.

METHODS AND MATERIALS

The apparatus (Fig. 1) consists of a frame fixed to an x-ray table which can be tilted from the horizontal to the vertical position. The subject is secured in a pelvic holder by straps. Load cells set at 120° are attached to the pelvic holder to measure reaction forces. The torsional reactive forces can also be measured by three additional load cells. The subject may actually impart motion isotonically, or resist motion imparted by a thoracic holder attached by a specially designed parachute harness. This thoracic ring is activated by cables to an inner ring to impart axial rotation or can be moved in other planes; for example, flexion-extension or lateral bend. Load cells attached at 120° intervals to the thoracic ring also can be used to measure reactive forces.

Measurement of imparted motion can be obtained by either a stereoradiographic x-ray system, or by analysis of surface topography by the Moiré fringe inferometry technique. The radiographic method depends upon locating x-ray sources by means of a calibration device. The position of each vertebra in space is defined from bony landmarks, usually inferior bases of the right and left pedicles, and the right superior articular facet. The centroid of the triangle created by these bony landmarks is used as a reference plane for segmental vertebral motion.

The Moiré fringe generates a topographic map which can then be digitised for each body position. Transverse and vertical profiles can be used to compare the subject's positions and displacements.

SUBJECTS

Eleven male subjects, ages twenty to thirty-seven, with no evidence of low back disease were studied. The subjects performed the following tests: 1) Lateral bend isometrically against an infinite resistance; 2) Lateral bend against a 4.5 kg resistance to a known displacement; 3) Isometric forward flexion; 4) Isotonic forward flexion; 5) Isometric axial rotation; 6) Axial rotation against 8 Nm; 7) Passive axial rotation applied via the thoracic ring, and; 8) Active resistance of axial rotation imparted by the thoracic ring in a constant rate.

RESULTS

Table I lists the mean reaction forces and torques measured from the load cells fixed to the pelvic ring. In this table, the conventions are as follows: F = Force in Newtons, θ = torque in Newton-metres, +X = superior (cephalad) direction, -X = inferior (caudad) direction, +Y = right bend, -Y = left bend, +Z = posterior, -Z = anterior, i.e. flexion.

DISCUSSION

The relevance of these data are two-fold: First, it gives semiquantitative, controlled estimates of muscle force in both isometric and isotonic motion performed in the usual directions of spinal mobility. Since the subjects were healthy, athletic males, these generated forces can be viewed as rather maximal for humans. Secondly, these preliminary data suggest a postural mechanism may exist to optimise resistance to forces and torques imparted to the spine, either isometrically or isotonically.

These data are viewed as preliminary. Methodologic problems remain in achieving a reliable interface between the subject and the thoracic and pelvic holders. These data contain an element of friction and soft tissue elasticities and displacements.

The displacements in these studies have been measured largely by surface topography, with limited radiographic exposure for position confirmation. Although preliminary analyses suggest a reproducible relationship between topographic and radiographic displacement measurements, this has yet to be precisely quantified. Thus, the displacement should be viewed as an approximation.

Our long range plans are to develop these methodologies, and to analyse the variations between subjects with and without lumbar spine disease. By electromyographic analysis, the muscle groups responsible for displacements may give valuable insights into the normal behaviour of the lumbar spine, as well as serve as important data for mathematical modeling.

Reference:Pope, Malcolm H., Ph.D., Wilder, David, G., B.S.M.E., Matteri, Richard E., M.D., and Frymoyer, John W., M.D.: Experimental Measurements of Vertebral Motion Under Load. Orthopaedic Clinics of North America, Vol. 8, No. 1, pages 155-167, January 1977.

Acknowledgement: A portion of this research has been supported by AFOSR grant #74-2738, The Foxboro Company, Foxboro, Massachusetts, U.S.A., and a Macy Foundation Sabbatical Scholar Award to Dr. Frymoyer.

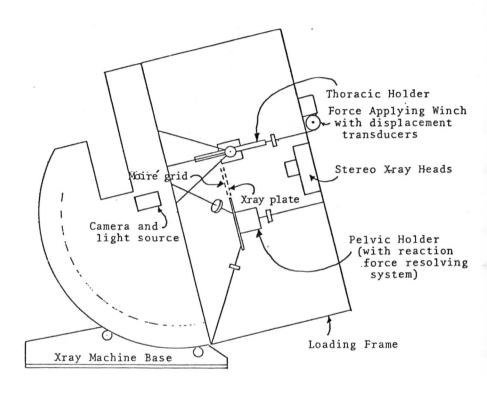

Figure 1   Schematic diagram of the spinal apparatus

TABLE I: LIMITED DEFLECTION TESTS (ISOTONIC), 11 SUBJECTS.
(Mean reaction forces in Newtons and torques in
Newton-Meters)

Right Lateral Bend	Forward Flexion	Right Axial Rotation
$F_y = 53.95$	$F_z = 56.14$	$F_z = 22.64$
$F_z = 6.61$	$F_x = 3.07$	$F_y = 12.91$
$\theta_z = 49.46$	$\theta_y = 7.76$	$\theta_x = 5.87$
		$\theta_y = 7.17$

LIMITED DEFLECTION TESTS (ISOMETRIC), 11 SUBJECTS.
(Mean reaction forces in Newtons and torques in
Newton-Meters)

Right Lateral Bend	Forward Flexion	Right Axial Rotation
$F_y = -80.10$	$F_z = -187.84$	$F_z = 34.47$
$F_z = 4.64$	$F_x = 145.15$	$F_y = 43.94$
$\theta_z = 74.46$	$\theta_y = 0143.76$	$\theta_x = 20.33$
$O_x = 336.43$		$\theta_y = -27.96$

SOME PHYSICAL EFFECTS OF LUMBAR SPINAL
SUPPORT ORTHOSES

G. DEANE, M.B., M.Sc., F.R.C.S., and N.D. GREW, B.Sc., M.Sc.

Oxford Orthopaedic Engineering Centre, Oxford

Introduction

There are over 250,000 lumbar spinal support orthoses prescribed
each year in England and Wales in the treatment of low back pain.
It is apparent that the basis upon which a particular orthosis is
prescribed is often largely empirical because there is insufficient
knowledge available as to the physical effects these orthoses produce.
This study sets out to determine some of these physical effects in
terms of five typical orthoses described as follows:

(i)	Long Fabric Support	(PH)
(ii)	Short Fabric Support	(S)
(iii)	Elasticated Support	(T)
(iv)	Plastic Jacket	(PJ)
(v)	Leather Covered Steel Brace	(G)

The range of orthoses available falls into two main categories, the
fabric or conforming support more commonly prescribed, and the rigid
spinal brace.

The Measurement Technique

The physical effects of the orthoses were assessed by investigating
the parameters of skin surface temperature, intra-abdominal pressure,
and spinal movement.

It has been shown that wearing a warming belt is often at least as
effective as wearing a fully re-inforced orthosis for the relief of
low back pain (St. J. Dixon et al, 1972). In order to assess the effects of each
orthosis upon the temperature of the back, two thermistors are
placed, one on the skin of the lumbar spine under where an orthosis
is worn, and the second on the thoracic skin outside the area of
influence of an orthosis. Thus, comparative spinal skin temperatures
can be recorded.

The role of the intra-abdominal pressure in the support of the spine
remains a subject of debate. It is generally accepted that an intra-
abdominal pressure rise acts to relieve spinal loading, but the
exact mechanism is not clear. The most obvious form of support is
purely that the cavity can act as a pressurised "balloon" attached
to the spine and giving a direct and mechanical distending force
proportional to the pressure produced and the horizontal area over
which it acts. In this study the intra-abdominal pressure is
measured in the colon by means of a rectally-introduced pressure
transducer of diameter 4mm inserted to a distance of at least 15cm
to ensure that the sensitive tip is within the abdominal cavity.

The temperatures from the two thermistors and the intra-abdominal pressure are continuously recorded on a miniature, four-channel cassette recorder capable of several hours of monitoring per cassette. The fourth channel is used to identify each activity a subject performs in the timed series which make up each test, lasting about twenty minutes. Because of its small size the recorder leaves the subject free to perform these everyday activities as listed below:

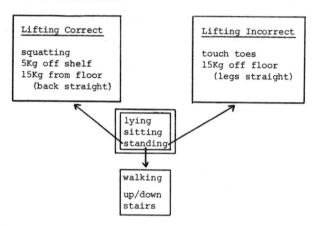

In order to assess the effects of each lumbar spinal support orthosis upon spinal movement, it was necessary to prevent pelvic and hip movements at the time of measurement. To this end a frame has been constructed (Agrippa) which is fully adjustable and enables each subject to be held at pelvic level and with the hips splinted as illustrated (fig. 1). The range of movement available to the lumbar spine is measured by means of the Vector Stereograph (used as a position measuring device in this study) following the T12 spinous process as the subject undergoes a full range of movement. The series of movements are comprised of forward and lateral flexion and extension from a neutral, upright posture, and moving first clockwise, then anti-clockwise, at the limit of possible movement. The resulting locus of movement when viewed from above is oval in shape.

The Tests

At this time the tests involved ten subjects. Of these, seven were normal with no history of low back pain, while three were chronic sufferers from low back pain whose long-term treatment involved the wearing of lumbar spinal support orthoses.

Each subject undergoes one full test while wearing no orthosis, and then up to five further tests in a variety of orthoses. In the case of a low back pain sufferer one of these latter tests is always

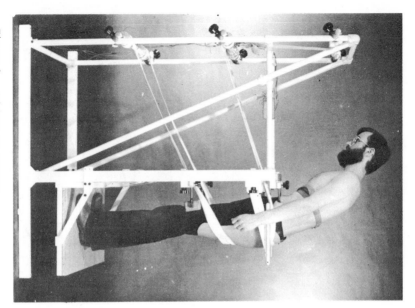

Figure 1   Subject in Agrippa

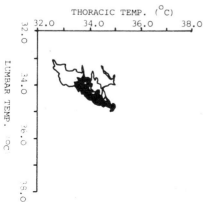
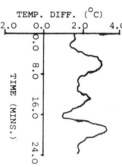
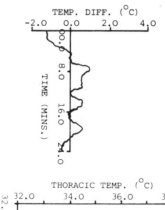
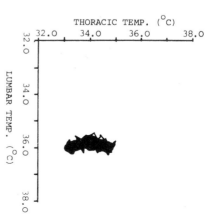

Figure 2   Temperature results

Typical Movement Pattern

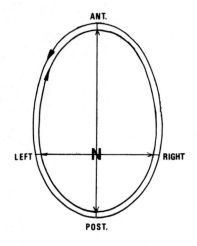

No Orthosis

Average Enclosed Area: 98.81 sq.cm.

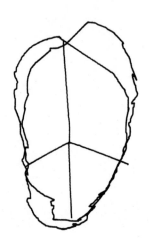

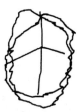

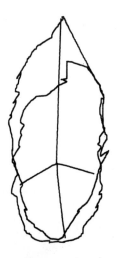

Plastic Jacket

Average Enclosed Area: 27.10 sq.cm.
Area Ratio to no Belt: 0.27

High Fabric Support

Average Enclosed Area: 81.94 sq.cm.
Area Ratio to no Belt: 0.83

Figure 3   Spinal movement patterns

whilst wearing his prescribed orthosis. In total forty-six tests
have been undergone by the ten subjects, but a maximum of only nine
of these tests have been whilst wearing any one type of orthosis.
Because of the numbers involved, no statistical analysis has yet
been applied and the following discussion of the results is of a
preliminary nature.

Results

(a) Temperature

Illustrated (fig. 2) are the results as plotted by computer from two
tests from the same subject wearing two different orthoses. The
graphs on the left are the lumbar minus thoracic skin temperatures
plotted against time for each twenty-minute test. These show that
the orthosis producing the upper graphs maintained the lumbar spine
at a higher temperature throughout all activities. This can also
be seen in the right-hand pair of graphs showing the two temperatures
plotted against each other. This presentation enables the relative
variations in the two temperatures to be examined, and it can be
seen that whilst in the lower graph the temperatures vary very much
in sympathy, the effect of the orthoses producing the upper graphs is
to insulate the lumbar spine from the external temperature changes
seen reflected in the thoracic skin temperature. An example of the
construction of the latter orthosis shows it to have two layers of
leather and further insulating fabric over the lumbar spinal region.
By contrast, the other orthosis was of a thin fabric construction.
These findings are typical of the results as they present so far.

(b) Movement

The movement of the top of the lumbar spine above a fixed pelvis is
plotted as viewed from above. In each case the area enclosed by the
pattern is calculated and, where appropriate, the ratio of this area
to that calculated from the pattern produced by the same subject
wearing no orthosis. The patterns illustrated (fig. 3) are all from
the one subject wearing no orthosis, a high fabric support, and a
plastic jacket.

The changes in area are very much as would be expected from
consideration of the construction of the supports. One possessing
rigidity in the spinal region but otherwise conforming in nature, the
other possessing a rigid structure. However, by the measurements
made it is possible to reach an objective figure for the degree of
total restriction. Other features of the patterns may well also call
for more detailed examination. It would appear, for instance, that
the degree of extension permitted by both orthoses is of a comparable
size - the main difference in restriction being upon the forward
flexion of the subject.

(c) Intra-Abdominal Pressure

For the longer-term activities in each test the presentation chosen
is that of histograms showing the percentage of the event time spent

SUBJECT 9 TEST 1 (NB)

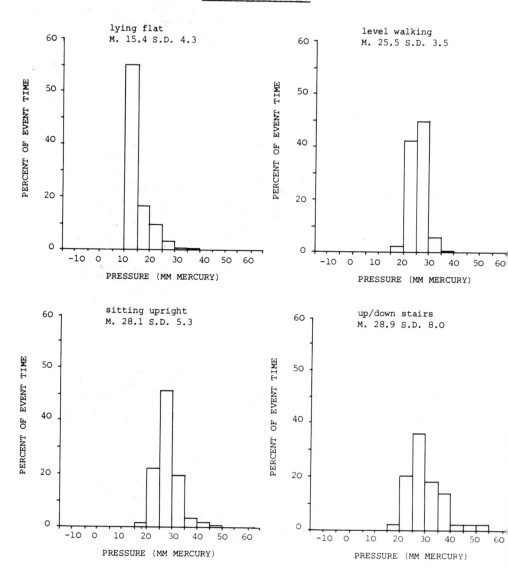

Figure 4   Intra-abdominal Pressure Histograms

between 5mm pressure bands as illustrated (fig. 4). From these
generalised formats, patterns and trends become apparent. In each
case the mean and standard deviations are calculated. The highest
peak in each distribution is called the mode (the pressure to which
the subject returns most frequently) which can be regarded as
representing the resting pressure during that activity. It is the
modal values which are used in the following comparative observations.

One feature of the patterns illustrated is that the distributions
from the upright activities are all centred about higher pressures
than that for lying flat. This is a consistent feature arising from
the position in the abdominal cavity where the measurements are made.
Because the rectum is in the lower part of the cavity the mass of
viscera above bears down upon it during upright activities, causing
effectively a hydrostatic offset in pressure. The average increase
over all the tests is 14mm mercury (8" of water) which is of the
order anticipated. Measurements made simultaneously in the upper
abdominal cavity confirm that this offset does not have any other
effect upon the pressures recorded.

The effect upon the intra-abdominal pressure of wearing a lumbar
spinal support orthosis is to raise the pressure.

Comparing the modal values of a typical upright activity (walking)
when wearing each orthosis with wearing no orthosis for each
subject, and then averaging the increases seen for each orthosis,
produces the following average pressure rises:

G	S	PJ	T	PH	
7	5.5	6	7	6	mm mercury

Figures adapted by Morris, Lucas and Bresler (1961) are used below to
calculate the significance of these figures in terms of spinal
unloading:

Maximum average pressure increase $= 7mm$ $= 948N/M^2$
Area of abdominal cavity $= 500cm^2$ $= 0.05M^2$

TOTAL VERTICAL FORCE $= 0.05 \times 948 = 47N$

For a man of mass 70Kg (700N weight), assuming 50% of the load is
carried by the spine, the load relief to the spine is 13%. Thus,
it would appear that the wearing of a lumbar spinal support orthosis
provides a significant degree of load relief to the spine.

The shorter events are plotted graphically as pressure against time,
but as yet it has proved difficult to assess these. With further
numbers of tests patterns will emerge. There are certain features
which are already obvious. For instance, when a subject stands up
after lying flat, resting, the maximum pressure seen whilst wearing
no belt is 20mm, and whilst wearing a plastic jacket, 60mm. On
examination it is apparent that the reason for the discrepancy is
that the plastic jacket imposes such a high degree of restriction
(as shown previously in the movement studies) that the subject has
to exert much more effort in order to perform the activity.

Undergoing the same activities a subject suffering from low back pain produces much higher pressures than a normal subject. For example, during the activity of lifting a 5Kg mass from a high shelf to a low shelf and back, typical pressures are 10mm for a normal, but for a low back pain sufferer, 25mm. However, throughout the tests the maximum pressures seen for the two groups has been similar (110mm and 100mm respectively).

Another discrepancy between normal subjects and those suffering from low back pain is that when bending to touch toes the latter produces an increase in intra-abdominal pressure while normal subjects nearly all produce a drop in pressure. The drop in pressure could be explained by the fact that in stooping the torso becomes horizontal, thus removing any hydrostatic offset. It would appear that whatever the mechanism, the response of intra-abdominal pressure to posture and load in the subject suffering from low back pain often differs from the response of a normal subject. This leads to the question "is intra-abdominal pressure directly related to spinal loading and in what way?" Study is underway which aims to answer this question.

Conclusion

The study of the physical effects of lumbar spinal support orthoses has already produced positive findings. These encourage us to believe that continuing this study along the lines indicated will produce results which will enable definite conclusions to be drawn. It is becoming clear that if these conclusions are to have relevance in improving the treatment of low back pain using spinal supports, it is important to begin to pursue the links between the physical effects and the specific relief of the various forms of low back pain.

References

ST. J. DIXON A., OWEN SMITH B.D., and HARRISON R.A. (1972)
    Cold sensitive, non-specific low back pain
    Clinical Trials Journal, 9, no. 4, pp. 16-21

MORRIS J.M., LUCAS D.B., and BRESLER B. (1961)
    The role of the trunk in stability of the spine
    Biomechanics Laboratory, University of California

THE MECHANICAL ROLE OF THE VERTEBRAL PROCESSES INVESTIGATED BY NEUTRON DIFFRACTION

R.K. GRIFFITHS, M.B., Ch.B., B.Sc.[1], G.E. BACON, M.A., Sc.D.[2], and
P.J. BACON, B.Sc.[3]

1 Department of Anatomy, University of Birmingham
2 Department of Physics, University of Sheffield
3 Edward Grey Institute, University of Oxford

INTRODUCTION

We have recently described a method of using neutron diffraction to measure the integrated orientation of apatite crystals in bulk samples of bone (Bacon, Bacon & Griffiths, 1977 a,b). Using this technique we have studied the crystalline construction of some spinous processes in human vertebrae. Analysis of the muscles attached to these processes suggests that they function as struts, rather like the spreaders on a yacht mast. The angulation of the strut varies along the length of the spine. Quantitative analysis of the muscle attached to the spinous processes (Griffiths, 1966) shows that there is a similar variation along the length of the spine. This seems to support the general hypothesis that the angulation of the vertebral processes is a function of the resultant pull of the attached muscles; probably they lie in the line of this resultant pull.

However, analysis of muscle weight does not offer a complete description of muscle activity. The internal engineering of the muscle, expressed as different fibre types may give different properties to muscles of the same weight. The information available from neutron diffraction provides an independant test of this hypothesis and offers the possibility of establishing a relationship between stress and structure in bone in a site which is readily accessable to operative intervention in experimental animals. This may provide a useful model in which the contribution of genetic and environmental influences on bone structure may be assessed.

MATERIALS AND METHOD.

Vertebrae from mature human cadaveric material were cleaned, degreased and heated in a continuous air stream to about 550 degrees centigrade. This effectively destroys the collagen which would otherwise lead to considerable incoherent scattering of neutrons. This process has not been found to alter the orientation of the apatite crystals. The diffraction pattern produced is characteristic of hydroxapatite and no other crystal patterns can be distinguished from the background. The whole thickness of the spinous process over a length of about 8 mm. was exposed to the beam of neutrons with a wavelength of 2.4 A on the neutron diffractometer D1B at the Institut Laue Langevin, Grenoble, France.

RESULTS

The intensities of neutron diffraction peaks were measured as the specimen was sequentially rotated in the beam through an angle of ninety degrees. Fig. 1 shows the characteristic pattern produced at one of these angles, compared with that of a powder for specimens of T1 and T7. The other half of this figure shows the height of the 0002 peak as the specimens are rotated. Fig. 2 shows the effect of rotation on the 0002 peak in four sites on the first lumbar vertebral one spine.

DISCUSSION

The organisation of the musculoskeletal system is such that muscles
are normally arranged to maximise velocity ratio at the expense of
mechanical advantage. This increases the possibility of mobility but
also means that the forces generated by muscles on bones are larger than
the actual loads carried by the lever systems as a whole.

It has been remarked for over a hundred years (e.g. Meyer, 1867) that
there appears to be a relationship between spongy bone structure and the
forces acting on the bone.   It is also clear that spongy bone is
found in the parts of bones where the muscular forces are concentrated.
The weight of serial sections of dry femurs shows that there is more material
at the ends of the bone, in the spongy areas, than there is in the compact
areas of the shaft (Raffle, 1977). This seems to correlate with the notion
that the muscular forces have a major effect on bone structure.

In the spine we are familiar with the presumed weight bearing role of the
vertebral bodies and discs but the vertebral processes seem to exist
entirely to provide muscle attachments. If this is the case then their role
must be to transmit the forces generated by the muscles to the main axis of
the skeleton. In this case we could expect that the structure of the
process will be adjusted in some way to the loading supplied.

The proposition is that each of these processes is carrying out an identical
task in functional terms. We might expect therefore that the internal
structure would be very similar. Our results (Fig. 1) show that this appears
to be the case. The average angulation of the spine of the first thoracic
human vertebra to the horizontal is 23.5 degrees (S.E. 2.9) while that of
the seventh is 52.1 (S.E. 1.8). In each of these spinous processes the
hydroxyapatite crystals have their 'c' axes largely orientated in the long
axis of the process despite the fact that their angulation to the spine as
a whole varies considerably.

The situation in the lumbar spine is more complicated because the spinous
processes are much wider and it becomes difficult to imagine the process as
a whole as a single strut. We have a sheet of material lying in the
saggittal plane. Fig. 2 shows how the crystalline orientation of the
sheet varies in the different parts of it. However, the crystals are lying
so that their long axes point along the line of a thrust from the surface of
the process towards the spinal axis; the direction of this line being
modified by the necessity of transmitting the thrust via the neural arch.

In every case in this investigation, and in our other observations
(Griffiths and Bacon, 1977 a,b and unpublished data) we have found a high
correlation   between a theoretical analysis of the expected stress in bone
and the direction of preferred orientation of the 'c' axes of the
hydroxyapatite crystals. This holds out the possibility that measurement of
the crystalline orientation by neutron diffraction may be an effective 'bio-assay'
method of plotting stress distribution within bone.

We can not say, however, how this relationship comes about. It may be that the
crystals are, as has been suggested (Justus and Luft, 1970), the transducers
which detect stress, and that the preferred orientation that we detect is the
result of continuous adaptation to the stress field operating on the bone.
On the other hand it may be that the crystalline structure is part of the
inherited species plan laid down to resist the stresses 'anticipated' by
Natural Selection.

We seem to have in the spinous process the potential for a model in which
this 'Nature/Nurture' question can be studied in relation to the control of

bone structure.

A weight bearing strut such as the spinous process appears to be most efficient if it lies along the line of the resultant muscle thrust. The external angulation of the processes varies in a way that follows the muscle structure and the internal structure of the process is well organised to resist linear compression. The two methods of traditional morphometrics and neutron diffraction analysis allow us to examine the external and internal structure of these bones. It remains to alter the functional environment experimentally, by disconnecting some of the muscles from the spinous processes in order to see the rates of change of the internal and external structure as they adapt to the changed stress field. These experiments are currently in progress.

SUMMARY

Neutron diffraction affords a method of measurement of the orientation of crystallites in bone which seems to provide an effective 'bio assay' of stress in the bone. The vertebral spinous processes may provide a useful experimental model in which the effect of changes in stress can be assessed.

ACKNOWLEDGEMENTS

We acknowledge the support of the Science Research Council in providing access to the service of the Institute Laue Langevin, Grenoble, France and the assistance of Monsieur J.L. Buevoz of that Institute with the experimental measurements and the design and construction of the rotating sample holder.

REFERENCES

Bacon, G.E., Bacon P.J., Griffiths, R.K.(1977a). The study of bone by
        neutron diffraction. Journal of Applied Crystalograph April, 1977
        10 124-126.

Griffiths, R.K. Bacon, G.E., Bacon, P.J.(1977b). The study of bone
        structure by neutron diffraction.Journal of Anatomy (1977, September,
        124 253.

Griffiths, R.K.(1966) The comparative anatomy of the spinal extensor muscles
        in primates. Thesis, University of Birmingham.

Justus, R. and Luft, J.H.(1970) A Mechano chemical hypothesis for bone
        remodelling induced by mechanical stress Calcified Tissue Research,
        1970 5 222-235.

Meyer, H.(1867) Die architektur der spongiosa Archives, anatomy and physiology
        1867.

Raffle, A.(1977) The effects of hypergravity of the rat thigh. Thesis
        University of Birmingham.

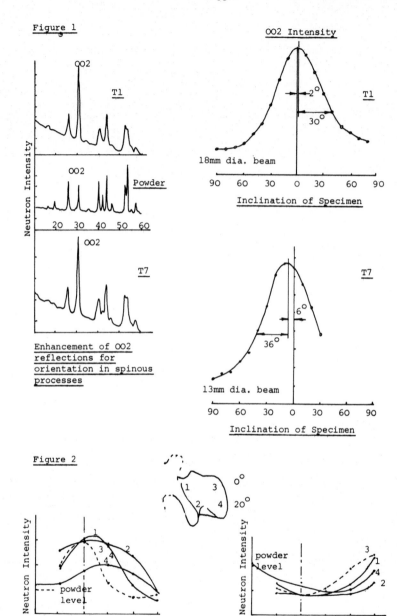

Figure 1

002 Intensity

T1

002 · T1

18mm dia. beam

2°
30°

Inclination of Specimen

Neutron Intensity

002
T1

002 Powder
20 30 40 50 60

002 T7

T7

6°
36°

13mm dia. beam

Inclination of Specimen

Enhancement of 002 reflections for orientation in spinous processes

Figure 2

Neutron Intensity

powder level

1
3
4
2

002

Neutron Intensity

powder level

3
1
4
2

310

Inclination of Specimen

1 3
2 4

0°
20°

L1 Spinous Process

Variation of Apatite Orientation with Position

THREE-DIMENSIONAL MEASUREMENT
AND REPLICATION
OF BODY SHAPE

BIOSTEREOMETRICS, SHAPE REPLICATION AND ORTHOPAEDICS

R.G. BURWELL, B.Sc., M.D., F.R.C.S.

University Hospital and Medical School, Clifton Boulevard, Nottingham

The science of measurement, or metrology, is widely used in orthopaedic surgery. Any summary of the subject must review techniques which were developed for very different purposes but which have been subsequently found to be relevant to the measurement of human shape, and to throw light on this surgical specialty.

I.   ASSESSMENT SYSTEMS IN ORTHOPAEDICS

Orthopaedic surgeons in their daily work involving the diagnosis and treatment of patients with disorders of the spine and limbs are constantly using three-dimensional systems of assessment. For this purpose, word description, images and mathematics are utilised.

Description in words is the principal method of stating and recording orthopaedic data, with the frequent use of images in the form of diagrams and photographs; and to a lesser extent models, drawings and paintings. The mathematics used is both arithmetic and Euclidean geometry.

The accurate description in space and time of the body regions as Cartesian coordinates is rarely, if ever, utilised. However, the use of such coordinates in the basic research of orthopaedics is beginning to grow, if it cannot yet be described as burgeoning.

II. DIMENSIONAL PROBLEMS OF ORTHOPAEDICS

The three-dimensional problems of orthopaedics relate to:-

1. Descriptive problems of injury, disease, growth and surgery.

2. Surface problems of treatment.

3. Internal problems of treatment.

4. Problems of basic research.

Descriptive problems of injury, disease, growth and surgery.

Problems are created by the need to express deformities of the spine and limb joints in three-dimensional terms. Movements of the spine and limb joints have also to be recorded. In this connection, the Benesh Movement Notation of Chore-ology has, as yet, been little applied to orthopaedics (Comparetti et al 1968,

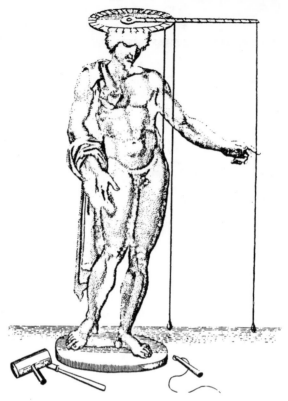

Figure 1   Alberti's 'definer', a modified surveyor's disc which he used
            to locate points on the body surface in three-dimensional
            coordinates. (Reproduced by kind permission of Dr. R.E. Herron
            and the Editor of Orthopaedic Review)

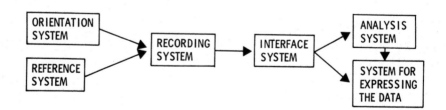

Figure 2   A flow diagram to show the relation of the systems used in
            biostereometrics.

Benesh and McGuinness 1974). Amputation stumps present problems of three-dimensional geometry to the prosthetist. The way a patient stands, walks, sits and lies (on a couch or bed) may also need to be recorded. Growth is measured in the management of deformities which develop in childhood; but this is usually a linear measurement, such as the standing height or the length of a limb.

Surface problems of treatment. The three-dimensional problems involved in the provision of clothing and footwear are managed by the use of arithmetical measurement. In connection with clothing for the normal population, new anthropometric data for men, women and children in the United Kingdom are now being acquired (Stone and Rae 1977). In connection with the provision of surgical footwear, moulding techniques using a plastic (Plastazote) are now available (Tuck 1972).

The application of a plaster-of-Paris cast rarely involves measurement unless the plaster needs to be wedged to correct a deformity. Fabric supports rely mainly for their preparation on measurements of the patient by a tape. Block leather pelvic supports, for the preparation of spinal braces and for the treatment of hip conditions are made by moulding the leather to a plaster-of-Paris cast; this is prepared from a mould of the patient's body. Plastic supports can now be moulded directly onto the patient's body surface (e.g. Plastazote, Tuck 1967, 1973). The three-dimensional problems created by the recumbent patient are usually overcome by nursing techniques; but different types of mattresses, plaster-of-Paris, vacuum consolidation, air-support and sand-bed nursing have their place (Scales et al. 1974, Kenedi et al. 1976). Other surface problems of treatment are posed in the design of orthoses (braces) and prostheses.

Internal problems of treatment. The internal fixation of fractures and osteotomies of spinal and limb joints by surgical treatment involves position-ing the skeletal parts in space. The prosthetic replacement of half or whole joints has posed problems of three-dimensional measurement, not only in manu-facturing the implant, but also in its insertion into the patient. Likewise, the more rare replacement of diseased bone segments involving a joint surface has created additional three-dimensional problems in implant design and insertion as well as needing to allow for movement of the artificial joint (Burrows et al. 1975).

Problems of basic research. Much of the recent application of spatial and spatio-temporal techniques of measurement to orthopaedics must be regarded as basic, in so far as it has not yet become part of established practice.

The surface of the human body has been measured with particular reference to the spine and limbs: the posture of the spine in relation to the effect of high heels and of leg inequality has been examined (Free 1974); and the deformity of structural scoliosis (a lateral curvature of the spine associ-ated with a rib hump on one side of the patient's back) has been measured (Hugg et al 1971, Morris and Harris 1976). In connection with amputees, the three-dimensional shape of limbs has been measured (Abdel-Aziz and Herron 1974) and a numerical control milling machine has been used to reproduce models of limbs (Duncan et al 1974, Kratky 1975a, Forsyth et al 1976, Foort et al 1977).

Body movements have been extensively studied particularly in relation to the major joints of the lower limbs, the hip and the knee. The methods have been reviewed by Jarrett et al (1976); they include ciné photography, electro-mechanical goniometers, opto-electronic goniometers and TV/computer goniometry. A new electro-mechanical goniometer for the knee joint has recently been reported (Townsend et al 1977).

In spinal radiology, three-dimensional techniques have been reported (Suh 1974, Jonason and Hindmarsh 1975, Kratky 1975b, Brown et al 1976, Olin et al 1976). At the knee joint, a three-dimensional radiological technique is being developed to record patellar movements (Lippert et al 1975).

In connection with internal problems of treatment, fractures of the tibia (Lippert and Hirsch 1974, Lippert et al 1974) and the internal fixation of the spine for scoliosis (Armstrong et al 1974, Jonason and Hindmarsh 1975) have each been evaluated using three-dimensional techniques.

In cadaveric specimens of the hip joint, a three-dimensional technique has been used to determine the shape of the femoral head and the acetabulum (Duncan et al 1970).

The growth of children, and their three-dimensional changes in body form is being evaluated (Herron 1975). The growth of limb bones in rabbits has been studied using a three-dimensional radiological method (Aronson et al 1977ab).

In the automobile industry, master models (mannequins, or 'golden shell' models) have been prepared from three-dimensional measurements of the human body to be used in road safety research (Radovich and Herron 1974, Herron 1975).

In aerospace medicine, Apollo 16 and all Skylab astronauts have been measured before and after their flights to reveal changes in body volume, body density and body volume distribution (Herron 1975, Whittle et al 1976).

Now let us turn to biostereometrics and shape replication and briefly review the methods which might be of help in solving orthopaedic problems. No reference will be made to research on three-dimensional force analyses of the spine or limb joints; but consideration will be given to the movement of limb joints.

III. DEFINITIONS

Biostereometrics is the spatial and spatio-temporal analysis of form and function based on principles of analytical geometry (Herron 1974).

The science of biostereometrics deals then not only with three-dimensional measurement of biological subjects in space, but also any variation of the measurements with time such as movement and growth. The potential of stereo-metric measurement of the human body was demonstrated over five hundred years ago in Florence by Alberti (Figure 1) (Herron 1975). Orthopaedics was founded over two hundred years ago by Andry (1743).

Shape replication is the reproduction of the shape and size of the body, or its components, for purposes of support, record, augmentation or research. As already outlined, much of shape replication of the spine and limbs for purposes of support has been executed without recourse to geometrical analysis.

IV. SYSTEMS FOR SPATIAL AND SPATIO-TEMPORAL MEASUREMENT

In basic terms spatial and spatio-temporal measurement of the human body involve the utilisation of the following systems (Rabey 1968, Herron 1972) (Figure 2):-

1. Orientation systems.

2. Reference systems.

3. Recording systems.

4. Interface systems.

5. Analysis systems.

6. Systems for expressing the data.

1. Orientation systems. The position of the body, or part of the body, in relation to the recording systems being used must be reproducible. This is relevant to cross-sectional studies of different subjects; and to longitudinal studies of the same subject at different time intervals.

2. Reference systems. The need for a reference (or datum) system is to enable a given part (or parts) of the patient's body to be recorded accurately in space.

In order to create such a reference system, markers can be placed on the body surface or rarely in the bones of the body; and, if the recording system needs it, reference points can be placed in the immediate environment of the patient. From the reference system(s) Cartesian coordinates (x, y and z) are then calculated.

3. Recording systems. A number of recording systems are available. Essentially they include the use of mechanical techniques, light, X-rays, ultrasound, electrical signals and television camera scanning.

Knowledge of the total body volume is of little interest in orthopaedics. However, blood volume is important in relation to injuries and surgical operations.

4. Interface systems. One example of an interface system is the transference of the data in the recording system into digital form for computer analysis. The data may be stored on media such as punch cards. For recording systems which involve a rapid collection of coordinate data, additional 'on-line' interfaces have been developed (Meier 1976, Jarrett et al 1976).

The remarkable progress of close-range photogrammetry in the last decade is due to the development of analytical methods. Most of the analytical methods have been applied in an 'off-line' mode. The use of the 'on-line' mode of data accumulation is making progress in the field so much more rapid (Kratky 1976).

5. Analysis systems. In the plotting of contour lines from stereoscopic photographs, a stereo-comparator and a stereoplotter are required. Computers are used to analyse the data using appropriate programmes.

6. Systems for expressing the data. After analysis, the coordinates can be used to express the results as:-

    a) Contours, profiles, perimeters, surface area, volume and movements.

    b) Models, using a numerical control milling machine.

    c) Three-dimensional television display.

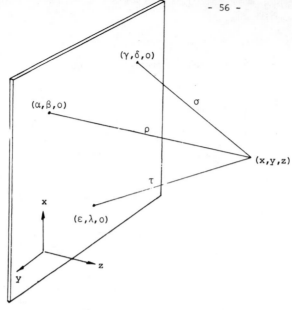

<u>Figure 3</u>   Geometry of the vector stereograph. (Reproduced by kind permission of Mr. J.D. Harris and the Editor of the Lancet).

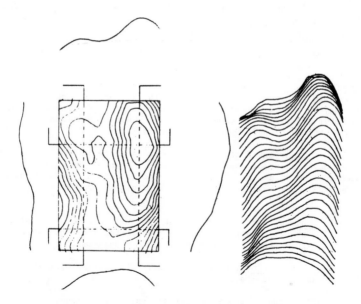

<u>Figure 4</u>   Expression of data obtained by the vector stereograph. Scoliotic deformity showing 10 mm contour map with four sections, and perspective view from 45° posteriorly and inferiorly. (Reproduced by kind permission of Mr. J.D. Harris and the Editor of the Lancet).

V. RECORDING SYSTEMS

1. Rod matrix. The simplest, but perhaps the most tedious, approach to the three-dimensional measurement of body shape is to use a matrix of rods. Lovesey (1974a) discussed the application of this method to measurement of the human face. A matrix consisting of 20 x 15 rods (= 300 rods) held in a metal plate is rigidly positioned in front of the subject's face and the rods are pushed through until they contact the facial tissue. Each rod is graduated, enabling a matrix of facial spot heights to be made by reading the rod positions in the plate. Disadvantages of this method are its tedium, the possibility of deforming facial tissue and the care needed in positioning the rods about the eyes.

The principle of the rod matrix has been applied to the spine to record principally x and y coordinates in patients with ankylosing spondylitis and scoliosis (see Thulbourne and Gillespie 1976). One such instrument is the Formulator Body Contour Tracer (Internuclear, 18 Bath Road, Swindon, Wiltshire, England).

2. The contour-graph. This instrument has been developed to measure the shape and volume of an amputation stump and the prosthetic socket of above-knee amputees (Abdel-Aziz and Herron 1974, Texas Institute for Rehabilitation and Research, Annual Report 1976). The cross-section of the stump is recorded by a 'feeler' which maintains gentle contact with the skin surface as it is rotated through 360 degrees. For simultaneous multiple level recordings, additional 'feelers' are attached. A graphical recording or a numerical expression of the findings can be obtained. In the most recent work, the biomechanics of the stump under a variety of load conditions is being evaluated using a finite element stress analysis. In this type of analysis, widely used in engineering, the structure is divided into a number of elements, and the material properties of each element are defined separately.

3. Triangulation - the vector stereograph. It is a principle of geometry that if three vectors meeting at a point are known, it is possible to define that point in space (a vector being a quantity with magnitude and direction). The method of triangulation is used for surveying and for navigation. In biology it has been used to measure parts of the skeleton such as the skull (Bunn and Turner 1960).

Morris and Harris (1976) have used the triangulation principle to record the size and shape of the posterior surface of the trunk in patients with scoliosis (Figure 3). The vector focal-point is run manually over the surface of the patient's back and the vectors are recorded by strings and feed bobbins which are placed in the frame of the apparatus. The length and direction of each of the three strings are recorded and the information is stored on magnetic tape. After computation, the data can be used to produce contour maps, projections of the back in perspective and sections of the body (Figure 4). The apparatus is termed 'the vector stereograph'.

In Chapter 7, Deane and Grew report the application of the vector stereograph to study the effect of spinal orthoses on the movement of the lumbar spine.

4. Stereoscopic photography with measurement (stereophotogrammetry). Like triangulation, stereophotogrammetry was developed for cartography and was later applied to medical problems (Hallert 1960, Beard and Burke 1967, Burke 1972, Beard and Dale 1976).

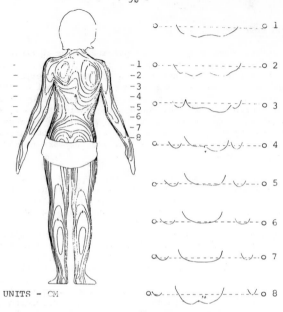

UNITS - CM

Figure 5   Stereophotogrammetry. Contour map and profiles of a patient with
             scoliosis in the standard pose. (Reproduced by kind permission
             of Mr. Hugg and the American Society of Photogrammetry).

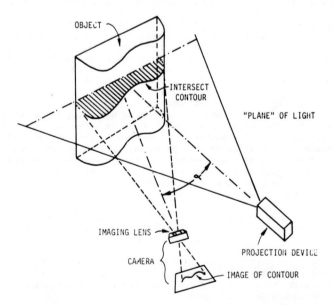

Figure 6   The principle of light sectioning technique (Reproduced by kind
             permission of Dr. H.C. Joel and the American Society of Photo-
             grammetry).

The method of close-range photogrammetry is based on the principle of looking at a subject simultaneously from two points of view as in stereoscopic vision. In place of the eyes, cameras are used to take overlapping photographs (or stereopairs). When the images comprising a stereopair are suitably orientated in a stereocomparator, or stereoplotter, the observer sees an image in three dimensions. The three-dimensional images can be plotted to produce a contour map and profiles using a stereoplotting instrument (Figure 5). In addition, using a stereocomparator (see Appendix) or stereoplotter, the position of chosen points on the body surface can be measured in terms of x, y and z coordinates which are amenable to subsequent computer analysis.

The method has been applied to patients with idiopathic scoliosis to provide contour and profile data (Hugg et al 1971). In the limbs, three pairs of photographs have been used to provide the data needed for the automated production of prostheses (Kratky 1975a).

In Chapter 13, Whittle reports the application of a stereophotogrammetric technique to study the effect of spaceflight on the regional body volumes of astronauts.

5. The light slit technique. The light slit (or Lichtschnitt) technique was one of the earliest photographic approaches for recording three-dimensional surface contours (Joel 1974). In the technique a thin sheet of light is projected on the surface of the subject and a photograph is taken of the image with the camera at an angle to the beam of light. The contours of the body surface may be reconstructed from the photograph knowing the angle between the plane of the incident light and the axis of the camera (Figure 6).

Multiple contour sections are obtained by scanning the subject sequentially by a series of light sheets obtained by moving the light source and the camera as a unit. The method is discussed by Joel (1974).

6. The projected grid technique. This method uses a pattern of equal width coloured straight lines projected onto the subject's body surface (Figures 7 and 8). It was developed by Cobb (1972) and used by Lovesey (1973, 1974ab) to provide a quick, simple and cheap means of recording individual face shapes for use in connection with improving the comfort and efficiency of aircrew oxygen masks. It has recently been used for contouring and measuring a child's face (Ainsworth and Joseph 1977).

By superimposing the image of a square graticule on each photograph it is possible to record the exact magnification and provide convenient measuring points. The method is accurate to within 1 mm. The use of a coloured straight line grid, instead of a black and white one, helps to avoid confusion when following contours in regions where they are close together, such as at the side of the nose and around the mouth.

7. The light screen technique. In Chapter 12, Smit and Schilgen describe their computerised three-dimensional description of body shape using a light screen technique. In their method, Cartesian x, y and z coordinates are projected sequentially onto the body surface: firstly, as a group of x light lines which are photographed; secondly, as a group of y light lines which are photographed as a separate image; and thirdly, as a group of z light lines which are also photographed.

Each of the three photographs is converted into a television screen image. The three photographs are analysed separately by a scanning programme which reads the numerical coordinate-value of each light line. An intersection programme combines the fields, which now bear x, y and z coordinate values.

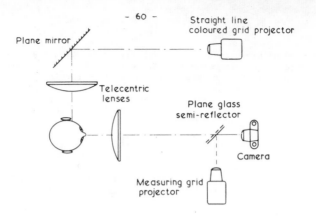

Plane mirror

Straight line
coloured grid projector

Telecentric
lenses

Plane glass
semi-reflector

Camera

Measuring grid
projector

Figure 7   The projected grid method.   Plan view of the telecentric system.
(Reproduced by kind permission of Dr. E.J. Lovesey and the
Editor of Applied Ergonomics).

Figure 8   Monochrome reproduction of coloured contours produced by the
projected grid on a girl's face (Reproduced by kind permission
of Dr. E.J. Lovesey and the Editor of Applied Ergonomics).

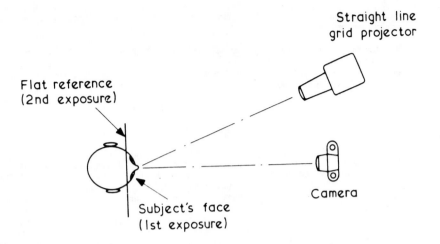

Figure 9   The additive Moiré method. (Reproduced by kind permission of
Dr. E.J. Lovesey and the Editor of Applied Ergonomics).

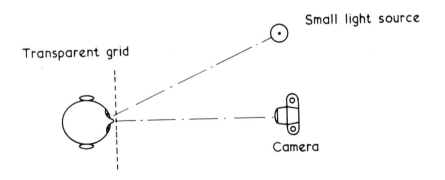

Figure 10   Takasaki's subtractive Moiré method. (Reproduced by kind permission of Dr. E.J. Lovesey and the Editor of Applied Ergonomics).

The results are expressed by a cross-section programme either on a television screen or on paper.

8. <u>Moiré fringe contouring (or topography)</u>. The contours of the surface of the human body can also be revealed by an optical interference technique known as Moiré fringe contouring (or Moiré topography). There are two principal methods (Lovesey 1974a).

(a) The additive Moiré method.

(b) The subtractive Moiré method.

(a) <u>The additive Moiré method</u>. In this technique the image of a straight line grid is projected onto the body surface at an angle normal to the subject and the subject photographed along the normal line (Figure 9). The subject is removed and replaced by a flat reference surface; the image of the grid projected onto the reference surface is again photographed onto the same photographic plate. Moiré fringes are formed between the distorted body-shape lines and the straight lines on the reference surface. Although fringes appear, they are of low contrast. Moreover, they only appear where the brightness of the body surface matches that of the reference surface. Hence the method is of limited use.

(b) <u>The subtractive Moiré method</u>. In this method a quasi-point source of light casts the shadow of the coarse grating onto the body surface (Figure 10). The fringes are formed between the distorted shadow, as seen from the camera position and the grating itself which is illuminated by light reflected from the body (Figure 11) (Takasaki 1970, 1973, 1974).

Using this method, the fringes are of high contrast and appear even over the entire body surface. The contour interval (dh) has a value given by dh = d/tan θ, where d represents the period of grating, and θ the angle between the light source and the normal line to the body surface from the camera (Balasubramanian 1976).

A disadvantage of the method, like that of the additive Moiré method, is that of divergence errors (Lovesey 1974a).

The Moire method of shadow contouring has been used on the lower limbs of normal subjects and on amputation stumps (Duncan et al 1974, Forsyth et al 1975, Foort et al 1977). Placing the limb along an axis around which the Moiré contouring apparatus could be rotated, made it possible to obtain contour patterns from three (or more) positions. Using a grating (or grid) which gave a 4.75 mm contour height interval, the contours were then digitized from each of the three photographs. The information was then used with a numerical milling machine to reproduce (as a model) the shape and size of the limb or of the amputation stump. The Moiré method has also been applied to cadaveric specimens of the acetabulum (using a silicone rubber cast) and the femoral head (Duncan et al 1970).

The subtractive Moiré method has been improved by Miles and Speight (1975). In their method, lines are projected onto the body surface and the subject photographed (Figure 12). Using the image on the photographic plate, an equispaced line grating is superimposed to create contour lines. The levels at which the contours are observed may be adjusted by lateral movement of the grating. In this way any point on the body surface may be made to coincide with a contour line and its coordinates determined.

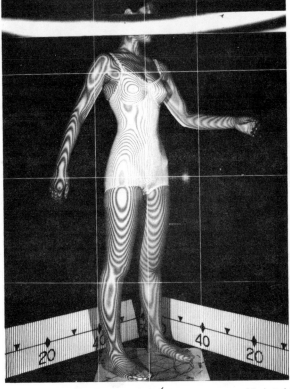

<u>Figure 11</u>   The contour Moiré topogram on a living body.   (Reproduced by kind
permission of Dr. Takasaki and the American Society of Photogrammetry).

<u>Figure 12</u>   The method of Miles and Speight (Reproduced by kind permission
of Dr. C.A. Miles and the Editor of the Journal of Physics).

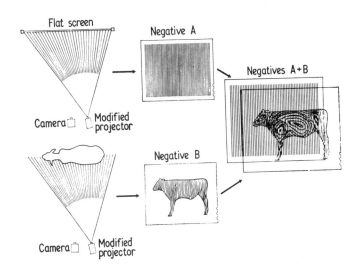

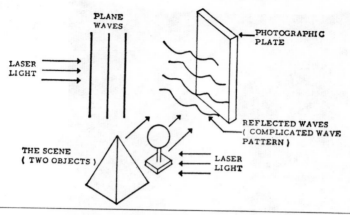

<u>Figure 13</u>   In making a hologram the scene is illuminated with laser light, and the reflected light is recorded, along with a reference wave from the same laser, on a photographic plate. The plate is then developed and fixed. (Reproduced by kind permission of Dr. W.E. Kock and the publisher, Heinemann, London).

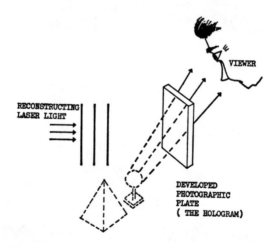

<u>Figure 14</u>   When the developed plate of Figure 13 is illuminated with the same reference laser beam, a viewer sees the original scene "reconstructed", standing out in space, with extreme realism, behind the hologram "window". (Reproduced by kind permission of Dr. W.E. Kock and the publisher, Heinemann, London).

In Chapter 10, Roger, Frymoyer and Stokes report the use of the method of Miles and Speight to study the changes in the posture of the spine during the working day and also the effects of a heel raise. Drerup reports the application of Moiré fringing to study the deformity of scoliosis before and after treatment. In addition, Cousins describes the use of Moiré contour data obtained from amputation stumps to prepare prostheses using a numerical control milling machine.

9. <u>Laser holography</u>. Laser holography is a means of encoding an image of a three dimensional scene onto a two dimensional photographic plate. Hologram is the term given to the recorded plate and the image can be observed when recreated by illuminating the plate with either laser or other suitably coherent light. The three dimensional effect is lost if one attempts to produce an ordinary photograph of the holographically formed image.

Holography, was conceived by Gabor (1948), but its full capability had to await the development of lasers in 1960. The word laser is an acronym formed from the words <u>L</u>ight <u>A</u>mplification by the <u>S</u>timulated <u>E</u>mission of <u>R</u>adiation (Kock 1972). Lasers are required because they provide light in a single frequency form in which the waves are 'phase-locked'; it is known as coherent light. The hologram is made by generating an interference pattern between a reference beam and light reflected from an object or subject. Both the reference beam and the object illumination are derived from the same laser beam and optically arranged to fall on a photographic plate together. The phase coherence of the two beams results in the interference pattern which makes the hologram.

Since a hologram is an optical interference pattern the object (or subject) and the optical system must be dimensionally stable to a precision measured in terms of a fraction of a wavelength during the period of exposure (about 0.1 of a micron). Notwithstanding this problem it has been possible to obtain holograms of people using the pulsed ruby laser since exposure times with this light source are reduced to about 25^{-9} second. (Ministry of Technology, 1969, Ansley 1970, Butters 1977, Phillips 1977; laser supplied by J.K. Lasers Ltd., Somers Road, Rugby, Warwickshire, England).

Lovesey (1974a) discussed some disadvantages when using laser holography to record the shape of the human face. Firstly it was claimed that an energy of 1 to 3 joules was required to expose the photographic plate and secondly measurement accuracy was found to be no better than 2 mm even when using a dummy head. However, recent advances in laser holography enable lower pulsed energies to be used and clearer images to be obtained. The size of the hologram can be chosen for convenience, it being easy to view from a large plate but all the information can be obtained from a very small area. Technically 1 mm^2 of holographic plate can easily store an image contained in 1 mm^3 (Butters 1977). Comments on the future of holography in biology and medicine have been made by Mikhail (1974) and Greguss (1975).

10. <u>Holographic radiography</u>. Shuttleworth et al (1969) described the technique of 'Holographic Multiplexing' for possible use in radiology. Essentially this involves:-

(a) Radiographs in sequence taken in an arc about a patient using a transaxial tomography unit (or a rotational radiotherapy simulator) (Figure 15).

(b) Preparing a holographic image using the laser beam divided such that one portion is projected through each radiograph and the other portion illuminates the photographic plate directly to form a reference beam as Figure 16. The successional radiographs are

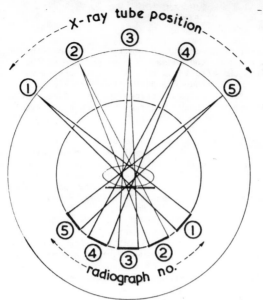

Figure 15   Holographic multiplexing.   Radiographs in sequence are taken
in an arc about a patient at the centre of rotation. (Reproduced
by kind permission of Dr. E. Shuttleworth and the Editor of the
British Journal of Radiology).

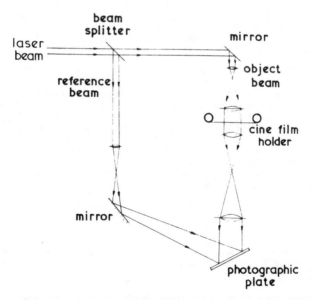

Figure 16   The optical system used to produce the multiplexed hologram.
The mirror and the photographic plate are linked to ensure the
reference beam is incident on the plate at a constant angle.
(Reproduced by kind permission of Dr. E. Shuttleworth and the
Editor of the British Journal of Radiology).

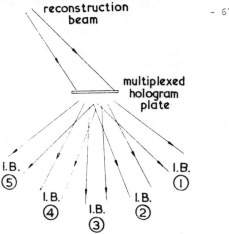

reconstruction
beam

multiplexed
hologram
plate

I.B.
⑤

I.B.
④

I.B.
③

I.B.
②

I.B.
①

I.B. = image beam

Figure 17 Illumination of the multiplexed hologram by a reconstruction
beam at the correct angle produces a series of image beams
identical with the radiographic views shown in Figure 15.
(Reproduced by kind permission of Dr. E. Shuttleworth and the
Editor of the British Journal of Radiology).

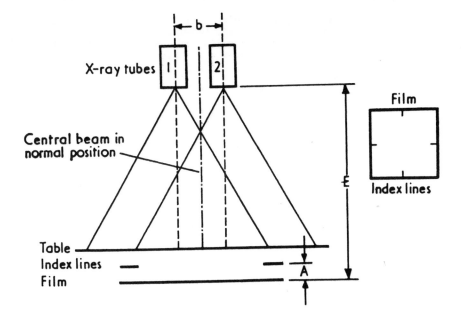

Figure 18 Stereopair X-ray photogrammetry. The two exposures are represented by X-ray tubes 1 and 2. The X-ray source is moved along
axis 'b' between each exposure. The patient remains in an
identical position between each exposure and the second film is
held in exactly the same position. (Reproduced by kind permission
of Dr. R.K. Jacoby and the Editor of Annals of the Rheumatic
Diseases).

exposed in positions related to their radiological location such that the holographic reconstruction shows a three-dimensional effect compounded from the two-dimensional radiographs.

(c) Illuminating the 'multiplexed hologram' so created with a laser beam and observing the three-dimensional image. By varying the angle of view, it was hoped to see the entire range of three-dimensional views from antero-posterior round to lateral (Figure 17); but in practice this has not so far been possible (Shuttleworth 1977).

The method is still being evaluated by Shuttleworth and his colleagues who now use a quartz iodine bulb instead of a laser beam to illuminate the multiplexed hologram (Shuttleworth 1977); and an alternative technique using parallel planes is being evaluated by Keane and Wright (1977).

11. X-ray stereophotogrammetry. In the three-dimensional measurement of X-rays, essentially three methods are available (see Hallert 1970).

(a) Using stereopairs of radiographs.

(b) Using two orthogonal radiographs.

(c) Using a single radiograph.

(a) Using stereopairs of radiographs. This method has been applied to the lumbar spine by Jacoby et al (1976). Their method involves two stages:-

(i) Paired radiographs of the spine are procured with constant position of the patient, film-focus distance and X-ray casette. Between exposures, the X-ray tube is shifted a known distance along an appropriate axis (Figure 18).

(ii) Using a stereoscopic plotter (Meier 1971) the paired radiographs are viewed to give a three-dimensional image. Selected points are chosen and x, y and z coordinates calculated as already described (vide supra, V, Recording Systems, 4. Stereoscopic photography with measurement).

This method has been developed to study the spine in patients with scoliosis (Kratky 1975, Jonason and Hindmarsh 1975) (Figures 19, 20).

In Chapter 15, Hierholzer reports a new apparatus for use with stereo-radiographs. In his method, a computer simulation is substituted for the stereoscopic images of the body. The display can be made to fit the structure as seen on the stereoradiographs with respect to position, size and shape. This is equivalent to measuring their geometry.

(b) Using two orthogonal radiographs. In this method the radiographs, say of the thoracic or lumbar spine are produced quasi-simultaneously in two planes at right angles, namely in antero-posterior (AP) and lateral views. Each of these radiographs is produced by an X-ray beam at right angles to the film.

In such orthogonal stereophotogrammetry, it is essential to ensure the following:-

(i) The region of the body to be X-rayed is the same in the AP and lateral radiographs.

Vertebra measured points.

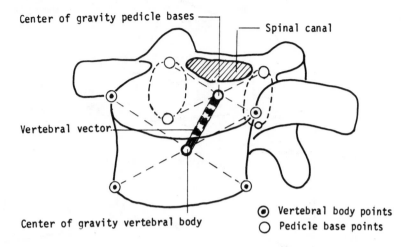

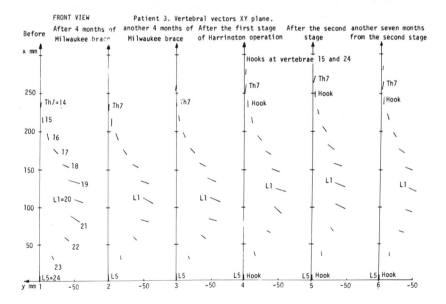

Figure 19   The measured points of a vertebra and the vertebral vector.
(Reproduced by kind permission of Dr. J. Hindmarsh and the
American Society of Photogrammetry).

Figure 20   The vertebral vectors in the x-y plane of a patient before and
after (1) brace treatment and (2) operative surgical treatment.
(Reproduced by kind permission of Dr. J. Hindmarsh and the
American Society of Photogrammetry).

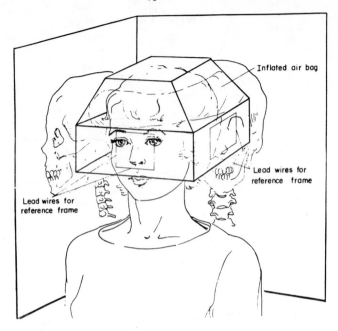

<u>Figure 21</u>   Orthogonal X-ray stereophotogrammetry. The helmet for computer-
             aided X-ray analysis of the cervical spine. (Reproduced by kind
             permission of Dr. C.H. Suh and the Editor of the Journal of
             Biomechanics).

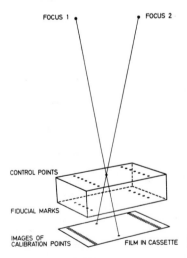

The radiation beams from the two
tubes. FFD 120 cm, distance between the foci
about 70 cm. Between film and table an airgap
of 20 cm.

<u>Figure 22</u>   Single film X-ray stereophotogrammetry (Selvik). The radiation
             beams from the two tubes are directed simultaneously across the
             calibration cage containing the subject onto the film.
             (Reproduced by kind permission of Dr. S. Willner and the Editor
             of Acta Radiologica Diagnosis).

(ii) A minimum of three reference sites can be identified on the AP and lateral radiographs; for example the tip of the spinous process and the inferior portion of the pedicles of a given vertebrae. The same reference points in adjacent vertebrae need to be identified if movement of one vertebrae upon another is to be calculated.

(iii) An additional reference (fiducial) system needs to be projected onto the X-ray films so that the x, y and z coordinates can be measured.

(iv) For the repeated study of the same patient, a framework (or cage) is used to reposition the patient exactly in space. For the cervical spine a helmet is used.

Orthogonal stereophotogrammetry has been applied to the normal cervical spine (Figure 21, Suh 1974) and the normal thoraco-lumbar spine (Brown et al, 1976).

In Chapter 6, Frymoyer, Buturla, Wilder and Pope report the application of orthogonal X-ray stereophotogrammetry to study the normal thoraco-lumbar spine combined with Moiré topology and electromyography. Drerup and Frobin also describe the application of the method to the spine.

(c) Using a single radiograph. Selvik (1974) has developed a stereophoto-grammetric method for radiography using the X-ray beams from two tubes directed simultaneously through the subject onto one X-ray film.

In the spine it has been applied to experimental scoliosis in pigs (Olin et al 1976). The method involves (Figure 22):-

(i) Inserting three radio-opaque tantalum spheres in three reference points in each vertebra - at the base of the spinous process and in the lateral part of each lamina (or articular process).

(ii) Placing the subject in a cage which carries at each end radio-opaque (fiducial) markers, the images of which are projected onto the X-ray film (Figure 22).

(iii) The images of both reference systems on the radiographs are measured in an 'Autograph' (A8, Wild, Heerbrugg) where the drawing table was modified to transmit the image via a closed television circuit to focus the points to be measured on a measuring mark on the television screen.

(iv) The x and y coordinates within the X-ray film were determined for the reference points in the vertebrae and the calibration cage. Cartesian (x, y and z) coordinates were then calculated by computer for each of the markers in bone.

(v) The movement of one vertebra in relation to another can then be described.

In Chapter 16, Willner, Olssen and Selvik report the application of this method to patients with scoliosis before and after the surgical operation for spinal fusion. The method has also been applied to determine the daily longi-tudinal growth in the rabbit's tibia (Aronson et al 1977ab).

Computed tomography. The technique of computed tomography (that is the head and body scanner) has been used for the measurement of x and y coordinates; it has not yet been utilised to create x, y and z coordinates, although this is technically possible (Ridyard 1977).

12. Morphanalysis. In Chapter 17, Rabey summarises the theory, practice, applications and implications of the method called morphanalysis. The approach is based upon the Fixed Relations Theory, which provides a solution to the central orientation problem of human imaging. The recording apparatus produces photographs and radiographs which relate to each other with three-dimensional validity, in the same patient and in other patients. The method has been applied extensively in the craniofacial field and is now extending into orthopaedics. One of the most interesting aspects of the method is its potential for standard- isation and improved communication (Rabey 1968, 1971, 1977abc).

13. Ultrasound. Attempts have been made to use ultrasonic holography to reproduce the size and shape of body regions; but the method has been found to be of very limited application (Greguss 1975).

The combination of ultrasonography and radiological transverse tomography has been evaluated as a means of obtaining cross-sectional anatomy for use in radio- therapy (Hughes and Sternick 1974).

A pulse modulated ultrasonic camera has been used by Short et al (1974) to measure the surface area, volume and cross-sectional area of human subjects. The patient stands upright with the arms above the head and the legs apart. The camera rotates about the subject in a rotating frame and takes about six minutes to complete a whole body scan using a vertical series of horizontal rings. The output devices include a lineprinter, digital plotter and visual display unit. This arrangement was used to demonstrate change in the body shape of obese patients on diet. The method appeared to be at least as accurate as that using conventional techniques of winding non-stretch paper tape around the subject, or conducting a series of anatomical measurements. It also makes it possible to relate other measurements to body coordinates (Anderson 1977).

Ultrasound can now be used to create three-dimensional images of body organs (5000 Multiplanar Scanning System, Sonicaid Ltd., Bognor Regis, Sussex, England). The method is currently being investigated largely in relation to obstetrics but also to liver, renal and general abdominal scanning. It would appear to have little application to orthopaedics as the acoustic impedance of bone and cartilage obviates the use of ultrasound (Young 1977).

In Chapter 20, Porter, Wicks and Ottewell report the use of ultrasound to measure the size of the lumbar spinal canal in normal subjects and in patients with low back pain.

Now let us summarise the methods which have been developed for spatio-temporal measurement with particular reference to movement.

14. Electromechanical techniques. Goniometers which produce an electrical signal corresponding to the angle between body segments have been used (Kettle- kamp et al 1970). Townsend et al (1977) have used an electromechanical instru- ment for total motion knee goniometry.

15. Opto-electronic techniques.

(a) Polarised light goniometry. This method utilises polarised light (that is where the oscillations constituting the beam of light are confined to one plane) to illuminate the room in which the patient is positioned for recording. Polarised light transducers are then placed on the lateral aspect of the patient's thigh and calf of the leg being studied; or of both lower limbs if this is required. The method has been developed by Grieve (1969), Reed and Reynolds (1969) and Mitchelson (1973) (Figure 23).

The light emitted from a DC light source is polarised by transmission through a disc of linear polarising filter which rotates in excess of 125 revolutions/ second. This produces polarised light whose plane of polarisation is rotating. The light is received by the transducers. Each transducer consists of a pair of matched photocells in front of each of which is mounted a piece of polarising filter. The system (manufactured by Crane Electronics Ltd., Twycross, Atherstone, Warwickshire, England and as the 'Polgon PG6' by Medelec Ltd., Old Woking, Surrey England) enables the angular displacement of each transducer to be determined from a fixed angular reference; this is determined by the position of a reference photocell (Mitchelson 1973). The polarised light goniometer makes it possible to record the angular displacement and the velocity and acceleration of limb segments and of body segments.

In Chapters 18 and 24, Mitchelson and Grieve each report on the application of polarised light goniometry to assess locomotor function in the lower limbs.

The polarised light goniometer can also be used with a force plate to calculate the forces (in muscles and across bones) at the knee joint during gait (Johnson 1977). In addition to the study of gait in patients with orthopaedic and neuro-logical disorders affecting the lower limbs, the method can also be used to evaluate arm/trunk coordination in the rehabilitation of patients with neuro-logical disorders.

The polarised light goniometer is used for two-dimensional spatial and temporal analyses of angular movements (Mitchelson 1977). However, Mitchelson (1974) is now developing a more complex opto-electronic technique termed 'CODA', for the purpose of three-dimensional spatial and temporal analysis.

(b) Cartesian opto-electronic dynamic anthropometer ('CODA', Mitchelson 1974). In Chapter 18, Mitchelson describes his new opto-electronic technique for spatial and spatio-temporal measurements of human subjects. In this technique small light emitting diodes (up to eight) are attached to selected parts on the surface of the body. These diodes emit infra-red pulses of light. Three electronic cameras are used to sense their position in three dimensions. The signals from the sensor (photodiodes) in each camera are used to calculate the x, y and z (Cartesian coordinates) of each light source. At the present time the results are shown in analogue form on a cathode ray oscilloscope or on paper.

This technique has been used in a pilot study of patients with orthopaedic and neurological disorders. CODA has also been used to record body contours.

16. Television/computer techniques. The fact that a television camera scans its field of view has been used to create a spatio-temporal reconstruction of movement in the limbs of human subjects (Jarrett et al 1976).

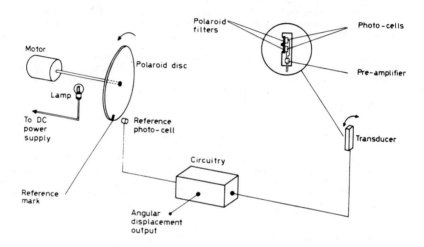

Figure 2 3   Polarised light goniometry.   Schematic diagram of the angle
              sensing apparatus. (Reproduced by kind permission of Dr. D.L.
              Mitchelson and the Editor of Medicine and Sport).

Up to six television cameras are used. Each camera scans its field of view
for a reference system which consists of reflective markers placed on the
subject, such as at the hip, knee, ankle and foot. Each television camera is
interfaced with a computer to produce x, y and z coordinates of the centres
of each marker placed on the subject.

17. Other recording systems. Body volume can be measured by the helium
dilution method. It can also be calculated by a water displacement technique;
this involves weighing the subject under water (with corrections for gas contained within the lungs and airways) and estimating the volume of water displacement by the body (Luft 1975). Body volume has also been calculated from
stereophotogrammetric recordings; the accuracy of the photogrammetric method
has been compared with that of the water displacement technique (Luft et al
1977). Blood volume is also of interest to orthopaedic surgeons in relation
to injury and surgical operations.

Measurements of total body fat, lean body weight and bone mass may also be
required in certain aspects of basic orthopaedic research.

VI. EXPRESSION OF BIOSTEREOMETRIC DATA.

In summary, the data collected by the recording systems outlined above can be
expressed as an image, mathematically, or as a model. The relationships are
shown as follows:-

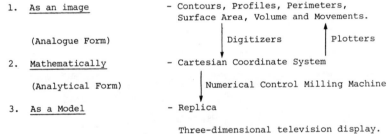

1. **As an image**   - Contours, Profiles, Perimeters,
                               Surface Area, Volume and Movements.

    (Analogue Form)   Digitizers   Plotters

2. **Mathematically**   - Cartesian Coordinate System

    (Analytical Form)   Numerical Control Milling Machine

3. **As a Model**   - Replica

                             Three-dimensional television display.

A more exact summary of the relationships is shown graphically in Figure 24.

VII. SHAPE REPLICATION

The use of plaster-of-Paris to produce casts of the body for the preparation of
orthoses and plaster beds has already been outlined.

The introduction of plastics which can be moulded directly onto the patient's
body surface, such as Plastazote for purposes of support or augmentation (such
as in the calf) has provided a more convenient means for replicating regions
of the body.

The technique of vacuum consolidation provides a further method for replicating
parts of the body, or the whole body, such as for contoured seating (Germans
et al 1975, Nelham 1975) and amputation stumps. In Chapter 42, Harris reports
the use of vacuum consolidation for the manufacture of specially-contoured seats
for the disabled, for limb replication and for whole-body orthoses for children
with osteogenesis imperfecta and cerebral palsy. Also, Crooks and Johnson
describe the application of the method to replicate the shape of the lower leg
prior to the production of an ankle/foot orthosis. Most recently, the technique
of vacuum consolidation has been used in conjunction with the structure of a
conventional chair to produce an item of furniture which is fitted to the
individual and is acceptable in a domestic setting (Wilson and Mitchell 1977).

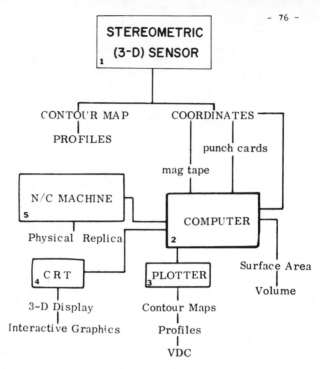

The scope of biostereometrics. (Reproduced by kind permission of Professor R.E. Herron and the American Society of Photogrammetry).

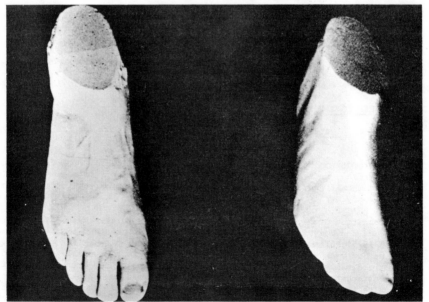

Figure 25 The original cast and machined envelope replica of a foot prepared using a numerical control milling machine. (Reproduced by kind permission of Professor J.P. Duncan and the American Society of Photogrammetry).

The use of a <u>numerical control milling machine</u> for replicating amputation stumps and parts of the limbs has already been discussed (Figure 25).

Finally, a <u>silicone foam elastomer</u> is being evaluated for the treatment of open granulating wounds as an alternative to the use of Eusol-gauze packing (Wood and Hughes 1975, Wood et al 1977). A multicentre trial of the method in patients with general surgical wounds has been undertaken recently in Cardiff, Leeds, Liverpool and York (Macfie 1977).

APPENDIX

In the stereocomparator, the coordinates are measured on both plates in stereoview. These coordinates are then transformed analytically into coordinates of a three-dimensional model. The model coordinates are then transformed to agree with the coordinates of known (reference) points in space (Manton, M., Department of Civil Engineering, City University, St. John's Street, London, EC1, Personal communication - 1977).

ACKNOWLEDGEMENTS

I am indebted to Mr. J.D. Harris and Dr. I.A.F. Stokes for introducing me to some of the publications relating to biostereometrics. I wish to thank the following experts for having read my comments relating to their work and for making suggestions: the vector stereograph (Mr. J.D. Harris); stereoscopic photography (Mr. L.F.H. Beard and Squadron Leader M. Whittle); the projected grid technique and Moiré contouring (Dr. E.J. Lovesey); laser holography (Professor J.N. Butters, Dr. E.J. Lovesey and Mr. N.J. Phillips); holographic radiography (Dr. E. Shuttleworth); morphanalysis (Dr. G. Rabey); ultrasound (Professor J. Anderson, Dr. G.B. Young); polarised light goniometry and CODA (Dr. D.L. Mitchelson); X-ray stereophotogrammetry (Dr. S. Willner); and stereocomparator (Mr. M. Manton). I am grateful to Dr. G. Rabey and Dr. F. Johnson for reading the entire text and for making helpful suggestions; and to Miss C.E. Frost for the typescript.

References

ABDEL-AZIZ, Y.I. and HERRON, R.E. (1974)
  The contour graph - a simple inexpensive method for measuring the fit
  of an artificial limb.
  p 386 In 'Biostereometrics 74'. Proceedings of the Symposium of Commission V
  International Society of Photogrammetry on Biomedical and Bioengineering
  Applications of Photogrammetry. Washington, D.C. 10-13th September 1974
  Virginia, U.S.A. : American Society of Photogrammetry.

AINSWORTH, H.J. and JOSEPH, M.C. (1977)
  A light-sectioning technique for contouring and measuring a child's face.
  Annals of Human Biology, 4, 331

ANDERSON, J. (1977)
  Department of Medicine, King's College Hospital Medical School
  Denmark Hill, London, England
  Personal Communication

ANDRY, N. (1743)
  Orthopaedia, or The Art of Correcting and Preventing Deformities in
  Children.
  London: A. Millar (English Facsimile)

ANSLEY, D.A. (1970)
  Techniques for pulsed ruby laser holography of people.
  Applied Optics, 9, 815

ARMSTRONG, G.W.D., BLACHUT, T.J. and VAN WIJK, M.C. (1974)
  Photogrammetric evaluation of the transverse loading system in surgical
  correction of scoliosis.
  p 564 In 'Biostereometrics 74'. Proceedings of the Symposium of Commission V
  International Society of Photogrammetry on Biomedical and Bioengineering
  Applications of Photogrammetry. Washington, D.C. 10-13th September 1974
  Virginia, U.S.A. : American Society of Photogrammetry.

ARONSON, A.S., HANSSON, L.I. and SELVIK, G. (1977a)
  Daily longitudinal bone growth in the rabbit determined with X-ray
  stereophotogrammetry.
  In press.

ARONSON, A.S., HANSSON, L.I. and SELVIK, G. (1977b)
  Roentgen stereophotogrammetry for determination of daily longitudinal
  bone growth: comparison with the tetracycline method.
  In press.

BALASUBRAMANIAN, N. (1976)
  Comparison of optical contouring methods.
  Photogrammetric Engineering and Remote Sensing.
  Journal of the American Society for Photogrammetry, 42, 115

BEARD, L.F.H. and BURKE, P.H. (1976)
  Evaluation of a system of stereophotogrammetry for the study of facial
  morphology.
  Medical Biological Illustration, 17, 20

BEARD, L.F.H. and DALE, P.F. (1976)
     A portable stereometric camera for clinical measurement.
     Medical and Biological Illustration, 26, 107

BENESH, R. and McGUINNESS, J. (1974)
     Benesh movement notation and medicine.
     Physiotherapy, 60, 176

BROWN, R.H., BURSTEIN, A.H., NASH, C.L. and SCHOCK, C.C. (1976)
     Spinal analysis using a three-dimensional radiographic technique.
     Journal of Biomechanics, 9, 355

BURKE, P.H. (1972)
     The accuracy and range of certain stereophotogrammetric measurements
     of facial morphology.
     Transactions of the European Orthodontic Society, 543

BURROWS, H.J., WILSON, J.N. and SCALES, J.T. (1975)
     Excision of tumours of humerus and femur, with restoration by internal
     prostheses.
     Journal of Bone and Joint Surgery, 57B, 148

BUTTERS, J.N.
     Department of Mechanical Engineering, University of Technology,
     Loughborough, Leicestershire, England
     Personal communication.

COBB, J. (1972)
     A projected grid method for recording the shape of the human face.
     Royal Aircraft Establishment: Technical Report, TR71184

COMPARETTI, A.M. and GIDONI, E.A. (1968)
     A graphic method of recording normal and abnormal movement patterns.
     Developmental Medicine and Child Neurology, 10, 633

DUNCAN, J.P., FOORT, J. and MAIR, S.G. (1974)
     The replication of limbs and anatomical surfaces by machining from
     photogrammetric data.
     p 531 In 'Biostereometrics 74'. Proceedings of the Symposium of Commission V.
     International Society of Photogrammetry on Biomedical and Bioengineering
     Applications of Photogrammetry. Washington, D.C. 10-13th September 1974
     Virginia, U.S.A. : American Society of Photogrammetry.

DUNCAN, J.P., GOFTON, J.P., SIKKA, S. and TALAPATRA, D. (1970)
     A technique for the topographical survey of biological surfaces.
     Medical and Biological Engineering, 8, 425

FOORT, J., COUSINS, J., VICKERS, G. and LEE, V. (1977)
     Automated Prosthetic Procedures.
     International Society for Prosthetics and Orthotics.
     New York, May 1977

FORSYTH, D.G., VICKERS, G.W. and DUNCAN, J.P. (1976)
     Replication of anatomical and other irregular surfaces.
     Proceedings of the Fourth North American Metalworking Research Conference.
     Edited T. Altan, May 17, 18 and 19, p 295

FREE, R.V. (1974)
Spinal examination using Moiré fringe photogrammetry.
p 634 In 'Biostereometrics 74'. Proceedings of the Symposium of Commission V.
International Society of Photogrammetry on Biomedical and Bioengineering
Applications of Photogrammetry. Washington, D.C. 10-13th September 1974
Virginia, U.S.A. : American Society of Photogrammetry.

GABOR, D. (1948)
A new microscopic principle. Nature, 161, 777

GERMANS, F.H., KOSTER, M.W., KWEE, H.H., MEY, N.v.d., SOERJANTO, R. and
WIJKMANS, D.W. (1975)
Vacuum dilantancy casting for the construction of individually molded seats.
Inter-Clinic Bulletin, 14, 1

GREGUSS, P. (1975)
Thoughts on the future of holography in biology and medicine.
Optics and Laser Technology, 7, 253

GRIEVE, D.W. (1969)
A device called the polgon for the measurement of the orientation of
parts of the body relative to a fixed external axis.
Journal of Physiology, 201, 70P

HALLERT, B. (1960)
Photogrammetry. Basic Principles and General Survey.
New York: McGraw Hill Book Co. Inc.

HALLERT, B. (1970)
X-ray photogrammetry. Basic Geometry and Quality
Amsterdam:Elsevier Publishing Co.

HERRON, R.E. (1972)
Biostereometric measurement of body form.
Yearbook of Physical Anthropology, 16, 80

HERRON, R.E. (1974)
Biostereometrics 74 - an epilogue.
p 635 In 'Biostereometrics 74'. Proceedings of the Symposium of Commission V.
International Society of Photogrammetry on Biomedical and Bioengineering
Applications of Photogrammetry. Washington, D.C. 10-13th September 1974
Virginia, U.S.A. : American Society of Photogrammetry.

HERRON, R.E. (1975)
Biostereometrics: modern, three-dimensional measurement of body form
and deformity.
Orthopaedic Review, 4, 19

HOUNSFIELD, G.N. (1976)
Picture quality of computed tomography.
American Journal of Roentgenology, 127, 3

HUGG, J.E., HERRON, R.E. and HARRINGTON, P.R. (1971)
Idiopathic scoliosis in 2, 3 and 4 dimensions.
Close Range Photogrammetry - Technical papers from ASP Symposium
January 1971, Urbana Illinois. University of Illinois

HUGHES, M. and STERNICK, E.S. (1974)
A method for obtaining body contours using an ultrasonic scanner and
transverse tomograms.
Medical Physics, 1, 72

JACOBY, R.K., SIMS-WILLIAMS, H., JAYSON, M.I.V. and BADDLEY, H. (1976)
Radiographic stereoplotting. A new technique and its application to the
study of the spine.
Annals of the Rhuematic Diseases, 35, 168

JARRETT, M.O., ANDREWS, B.J. and PAUL, J.P. (1976)
A television/computer system for the analysis of human locomotor.
Proceedings of the Institution of Electronic and Radio Engineers Golden
Jubilee Conference and Exhibition on 'The Application of Electronics in
Medicine'. Southampton University p 357

JOEL, H.C. (1974)
The corporograph - a simple photographic approach to three-dimensional
measurements.
p 622 In 'Biostereometrics 74'. Proceedings of the Symposium of Commission V.
International Society of Photogrammetry on Biomedical and Bioengineering
Applications of Photogrammetry. Washington, D.C. 10-13th September 1974
Virginia, U.S.A. : American Society of Photogrammetry.

JOHNSON, F. (1977)
Department of Medical Physics, University Hospital and Medical School,
Clifton Boulevard, Nottingham
Personal communication

JONASON, C-O. and HINDMARSH, J. (1975)
Stereo Xray photogrammetry as a tool in studying scoliosis.
p 245 In Symposium on Close-Range Photogrammetric Systems'.
Virginia, U.S.A. : American Society of Photogrammetry.

KEANE, B.E. and WRIGHT, L. (1977)
Department of Medical Physics, Royal Sussex Hospital, Brighton.
Personal communication

KENEDI, R.M., COWDEN, J.M. and SCALES, J.T. (1976)
Bed Sore Biomechanics.
London: The MacMillan Press

KETTLEKAMP, D.B., JOHNSON, R.J., SMIDT, G.L., CHAO, E.Y.S. and WALKER, M. (1970)
An electrogoniometric study of knee motion in normal gait.
Journal of Bone and Joint Surgery, 52A, 775

KOCK, W.E. (1972)
Lasers and holography. An introduction to Coherent Optics.
London: Heinemann. Science Study Series, No 39.

KRATKY, V. (1975a)
Digital modeling of limbs in orthopaedics.
Journal of the American Society of Photogrammetry, 41, 741

KRATKY, V. (1975b)
Analytical on-line systems in close-range photogrammetry.
p 167 In 'Symposium on Close-Range Photogrammetric Systems'.
Virginia, U.S.A. : American Society of Photogrammetry.

KRATKY, V. (1976)
Analytical on-line systems in close-range photogrammetry.
Journal of the American Society of Photogrammetry, 42, 81

LIPPERT, F.G. and HIRSCH, C. (1974)
 The three dimensional measurement of tibia fracture motion by photogrammetry.
 Clinical Orthopaedics and Related Research, 105, 130

LIPPERT, F.G., HUSSAIN, M. and VERESS, S.A. (1974)
 The application of photogrammetry to three-dimensional studies upon the musculoskeletal system.
 p 318 In 'Biostereometrics 74'. Proceedings of the Symposium of Commission V.
 International Society of Photogrammetry on Biomedical and Bioengineering
 Applications of Photogrammetry. Washington, D.C. 10-13th September 1974
 Virginia, U.S.A. : American Society of Photogrammetry.

LIPPERT, F.G., VERESS, S.A., TAKAMOTO, T. and SPOLEK, G.A. (1975)
 Experimental Studies on Patellar Motion using X-ray Photogrammetry.
 In 'Symposium on Close-Range Photogrammetric Systems'. Virginia, U.S.A.
 American Society of Photogrammetry.

LOVESEY, E.J. (1973)
 A simple photographic technique for recording three-dimensional head shape.
 Medical and Biological Illustration, 23, 210

LOVESEY, E.J. (1974a)
 The development of a 3-dimensional anthropometric measuring technique.
 Applied Ergonomics, 5, 36

LOVESEY, E.J. (1974b)
 The development of a simple 3 dimensional facial measuring technique.
 p 147 In 'Biostereometrics 74'. Proceedings of the Symposium of Commission V.
 International Society of Photogrammetry on Biomedical and Bioengineering
 Applications of Photogrammetry. Washington, D.C. 10-13th September 1974
 Virginia, U.S.A. : American Society of Photogrammetry.

LUFT, U.C. (1975)
 Specialised physiological studies in support of manned spaceflight.
 Annual Report on Contract NA59-12572
 Lovelace Foundation, Albuquerque, New Mexico.

LUFT, U.C., HERRON, R.E. and LOEPPKY, J.A. (1977)
 Body volume by stereophotogrammetry and by weighing underwater.
 Lovelace Foundation, Albuquerque, New Mexico
 Personal communication.

MACFIE, J. (1977)
 Department of Surgery, University of Leeds, England
 Personal communication.

MEIER, H.K. (1971)
 The StR 1-3 stereo X-ray comparator. A simple stereoplotting system for X-ray diagnosis.
 Bildmessung und Luftbildwesen, 3, 131

MEIER, H.K. (1976)
 News from Carl Zeiss of Oberkochen regarding computer-supported and computer-controlled photogrammetric plotting.
 In XIIIth International Congress for Photogrammetry, Helsinki 1976

MIKHAIL, E.M. (1974)
 Hologrammetry in biostereometrics.
 p 72 In 'Biostereometrics 74'. Proceedings of the Symposium of Commission V.
 International Society of Photogrammetry on Biomedical and Bioengineering
 Applications of Photogrammetry. Washington, D.C. 10-13th September, 1974
 Virginia, U.S.A. : American Society of Photogrammetry.

MILES, C.A. and SPEIGHT, B.S. (1975)
Recording the shape of animals by a Moiré method.
Journal of Physics, Series E, 8, 773

Ministry of Technology (1969)
Laser Systems - Code of Practice

MITCHELSON, D.L. (1973)
An opto-electronic technique for analysis of angular movements.
Medicine and Sport, 8, 181

MITCHELSON, D.L. (1974)
CODA: Instrument for 3-D recording.
Internal Publication. Department of Ergonomics and Cybernetics,
University of Technology, Loughborough

MITCHELSON, D. (1977)
Department of Human Sciences, University of Technology, Loughborough, England
Personal Communication

MORRIS, J.R.W. and HARRIS, J.D. (1976)
Three dimensional shapes
Lancet, 1, 1189

NELHAM, R.L. (1975)
The manufacture of moulded supportive seating for the handicapped.
Biomedical Engineering 10, 379

OLIN, T., OLSSON, T.H., SELVIK, G. and WILLNER, S. (1976)
Kinematic analysis of experimentally provoked scoliosis in pigs with
roentgen stereophotogrammetry.
Acta Radiologica Diagnosis, 17, 107

PHILLIPS, N.J. (1977)
Department of Physics, University of Technology, Loughborough, England

RABEY, G. (1968)
Morphanalysis
London: H.K. Lewis & Co. Ltd.

RABEY, G. (1971)
Craniofacial morphanalysis
Proceedings of the Royal Society of Medicine, 64, 103

RABEY, G. (1977a)
Current principles of morphanalysis and their implications in oral
surgical practice.
British Journal of Oral Surgery, 15 (2)

RABEY, G. (1977b)
Morphanalysis of craniofacial dysharmony.
British Journal of Oral Surgery, 15 (2)

RABEY, G. (1977c)
Bilateral mandibular condylosis - a morphanalytical diagnosis
British Journal of Oral Surgery, 15, (2)

RADOVICH, V.G. and HERRON, R.E. (1974)
Anthropometric golden shell models and their description by stereometric
measurements.
Society of Automotive Engineers, Automotive Engineering Congress
Detroit, Michigan. February 25-March 1. 740116

REED, D.J. and REYNOLDS, P.J. (1969)
A joint angle detector.
Journal of Applied Physiology, 27, 745

RIDYARD, J.N.A. (1977)
E.M.I. Ltd., Shoenberg House, Trevor Road, Hayes, Middlesex.
Personal communication

SCALES, J.T., LUNN, H.F., JENEID, P.A., GILLINGHAM, M.E. and REDFERN, S.J. (1974)
The prevention and treatment of pressure sores using air-support systems.
Paraplegia, 12, 118

SELVIK, G. (1974)
A roentgen stereophotogrammetric method for the study of the kinematics
of the skeletal system. Thesis. Lund (Quoted by Olin et al 1976)

SHORT, A., MUTCH, M., ANDERSON, J. and GROVER, R.D. (1974)
The direct measurement and display of human shape.
p 583 In 'Biostereometrics 74'. Proceedings of the Symposium of Commission V.
International Society of Photogrammetry on Biomedical and Bioengineering
Applications of Photogrammetry. Washington, D.C. 10-13th September 1974
Virginia, U.S.A. : American Society of Photogrammetry.

SHUTTLEWORTH, E. (1977)
Department of Medical Physics, Royal Postgraduate Medical School
Hammersmith Hospital, Ducane Road, London, W12

SHUTTLEWORTH, E., WILSON, A., REDMAN, J.D. and WOLTON, W.P. (1969)
Correspondence. British Journal of Radiology, 42, 152

STONE, B. and RAE, A. (1977)
WIRA Clothing Research and Services, Headingley Lane, Leeds
Personal communication

SUH, C.H. (1974)
The fundamentals of computer-aided X-ray analysis of the spine.
Journal of Biomechanics, 7, 161

TAKASAKI, H. (1970)
Moiré topography.
Applied Optics, 9, 1467

TAKASAKI, H. (1973)
Moiré topography
Applied Optics, 12, 845

TAKASAKI, H. (1974)
Moiré topography.
p 590 In 'Biostereometrics 74'. Proceedings of the Symposium of Commission V.
International Society of Photogrammetry on Biomedical and Bioengineering
Applications of Photogrammetry. Washington, D.C. 10-13th September 1974
Virginia, U.S.A. : American Society of Photogrammetry.

Texas Institute for Rehabilitation and Research (1976)
Texas A & M University, Baylor College of Medicine, Rehabilitation
Engineering Center. Annual Report. September 1, 1975-August 31 1976

THULBOURNE, T. and GILLESPIE, R. (1976)
    The rib hump in idiopathic scoliosis.   Measurement, analysis and response
    to treatment.
    Journal of Bone and Joint Surgery, 58B, 64

TOWNSEND, M.A., IZAK, M. and JACKSON, R.W. (1977)
    Total motion knee goniometry.
    Journal of Biomechanics, 10, 183

TUCK, W.H. (1967)
    New substances in orthopaedic appliances.
    Physiotherapy, 53, 368

TUCK, W.H. (1972)
    A new approach to orthopaedic footwear problems.
    Proceedings of the Royal Society of Medicine, 65, 739

TUCK, W.H. (1977)
    Shells made of Plastazote in cases of fragilitas ossium.
    Proceedings of the Institute of Surgical Technicians.
    Edited G.M. Down and Members of the Council.
    Printed by H.G. Waker, 203, King's Cross Road, King's Cross 1X9 DE

WHITTLE, M.W., HERRON, R.E. and CUZZI, J.R. (1976)
    Biostereometric analysis of body form: the second manned Skylab mission.
    Aviation, Space and Environmental Medicine, 47, 410

WILSON, B.E. and MITCHELL, J.C. (1977)
    Personal communication. Department of Three-Dimensional Design, Trent
    Polytechnic Nottingham and Department of Health Studies, Sheffield City
    Polytechnic, Sheffield.

WOOD, R.A.B., and HUGHES, L.E. (1975)
    Silicone foam sponge for pilonidal sinus: a new technique for dressing
    open granulating wounds.
    British Medical Journal, iv, 131

WOOD, R.A.B., WILLIAMS, R.H.P. and HUGHES, L.E. (1977)
    Foam elastomer dressing in the management of open granulating wounds:
    experience with 250 patients.
    British Journal of Surgery, 64, 554

YOUNG, G.B. (1977)
    Simpson Memorial Hospital, Edinburgh
    Personal communication.

INVESTIGATION OF CHANGES IN THE POSTURE OF THE SPINE, THE EFFECTS OF A HEEL RAISE AND THE WORKING DAY

R. Roger, B.A.,[1] J.W. Frymoyer, M.S., M.D.,[2] and I.A.F. Stokes, M.A., Ph.D.[3]

1 and 3   Oxford Orthopaedic Engineering Centre,
          Nuffield Orthopaedic Centre,
          Headington, Oxford. OX3 7LD.

2   University of Vermont College of Medicine,
          Department of Orthopaedic Surgery,
          Burlington, Vermont 05401, U.S.A.

INTRODUCTION

Posture is one of the factors affecting spinal loading. Patients with a progressive deformity such as scoliosis or an acute condition such as low back pain may undergo small postural changes, which can be measured to help describe the patient's condition. These small significant changes may be confused with changes unrelated to the deformity or clinical disease. We have investigated two such possible causes of postural changes in healthy subjects: the effect of fatigue, caused by normal day-time activities; and the effect of one type of shoeware.

Changes in posture classically are measured by alterations in lordosis and kyphosis. However, the importance of axial rotations and torsion forces, in the aetiology of low back pain, have been stressed. The axial rotations should not only be measured in scoliosis, but also in the assessment of lumbar pathologies. We have used a three-dimensional measurement system to enable us to make these important measurements.

METHOD

The three-dimensional measurements were made using one of the Moiré fringe contouring techniques. We used the projected grating method as described by Miles and Speight (1975), and more recently by Yoshino et al (1976), which requires an ordinary 35mm camera and slide projector. This gives contouring over a depth of at least 25cm. Using 400ASA speed film, good results were obtained using an exposure of 1/30 sec. at f4. It was felt that the method would be readily acceptable in clinics, as there is no need for high powered flash lamps, and the subject does not need any powder on his skin to improve its contrast.

The Moiré contour maps we obtained were printed at about quarter full size, and the centre lines of the fringes drawn in. These contour maps were digitised, the x-, y-, z-coordinates being stored on the disc memory in a PDP-11/34 computer. About 150 points of each surface were digitised.

Comparisons between Moiré photographs could only be made when these were both oriented identically in a three-dimensional frame of reference. This orientation of the experimental subjects relative to the measurement system was achieved by having them stand in an apparatus which was in a constant position relative to the camera and the projector. The apparatus includes a postural support frame, which positions the pelvis in a reproducible position. The pelvis is positioned by means of four pads which locate on the superior, anterior iliac spines and the left and right trochanters. Another pad rests

against the sternum, its purpose being to eliminate changes due to small
leans of the trunk. The initial positioning of these components was made with
the subject standing in his normal posture. The positions for the five pads
and supports were determined with a measuring device, which locates on, but
does not control the positions of, the same points of the body. These
measurements were subsequently transferred to the postural support frame. The
problem in such a location device is that achieving reproducible posture may
in fact impose significant postural restriction on the subject. This device
does not seem to inhibit pelvic tilts to the extent of limiting the postural
changes we were investigating.

THE STUDY

The study was concentrated on detecting changes in lordosis and axial
rotation, in a group of healthy volunteers, of whom seventeen were male and
ten female; their ages ranged from twenty-one to forty-nine years.

The shapes of the subjects' backs were recorded (see table):

    (1) in the morning
    (2) in the afternoon, a period of about seven hours separating
        the two

Both the recordings were made with the subject standing without shoes. In
the morning (3) a block of wood, height 45mm, was placed under the heels to
simulate high-heeled shoes, and the back shape was again recorded.

Two studies, on smaller groups of subjects, were made to assess (4) the
effects of breathing on the shape measured, and (5) the short-term
repeatability of the method.

ANALYSIS OF DATA

We have analysed the data obtained in two ways. In the first case the dorsal
profile in the sagittal plane was drawn. Profiles of the same subject, made
at different times, can be compared by drawing them on the same grid.

Figure 1a shows profiles of the same person in the morning (profile 1) and
the afternoon (profile 2). These indicate a slight increase in both the
lordosis and kyphosis of this subject between the morning and the afternoon.
The differences have been emphasised by exaggerating the horizontal distances
by a factor of two compared with the vertical distances.

The second method of analysis produced a map of the differences between the
two backs. The computer used the digitised points of one back as the basic
data points, then through an interpolation routine it calculated the heights
of the second back, at the same points. Using the differences in heights
between the two backs the computer drew out lines of equal height difference.
Figure 1b illustrates the type of result obtained. The difference map is
superimposed on an outline of the back and shoulders. This is similar to an
ordinary topographic map. In that case, the contours would represent the
lines of equal distances from a datum plane, but here the contours represent
lines of equal difference between the two shapes. The map in figure 1
shows that there has been very little change in the lumbo-thoracic area, but
there has been some change in kyphosis.

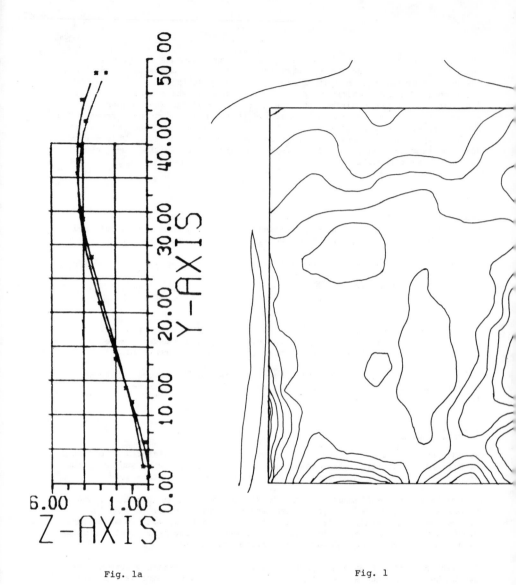

Fig. 1a

Fig. 1

Fig. 1   Contour map of the difference between the
         morning and afternoon back shapes. Lines of
         equal change marked in millimetres.

Fig. 1a   Profiles of the back (section in the sagittal
          plane). Curve 1 in the morning, curve 1a in
          the afternoon. The horizontal distance is
          magnified by a factor of two.

The contour map indicates changes in the shape of the lordosis and kyphosis, as can also be seen in the dorsal profiles. In addition, it shows changes over other parts of the back, especially axial rotations. A change in lordosis was indicated by a change of over 3mm, the accuracy of the method.

RESULTS

The results of the short-term repeatability and breathing tests were characterised by:

    (a) no change in lordosis
    (b) very small or no change in axial rotation (less than 1° at
        the lumbo-thoracic level)

In all subjects, the dorsal profiles showed no significant changes in shape.

The difference maps, for these two studies, were characterised by having few contours, and a difference range of less than 10mm. The pattern of changes in the breathing studies indicated a small lean of the trunk, between two positions, which is compatible with inflation of the lungs.

The results of the comparison of the morning and afternoon postures showed:

    (a) no detectable change in lordosis in the majority of subjects
    (b) no consistent change in the lordosis of the remaining subjects
    (c) the presence of small axial rotations, at the lumbo-thoracic
        level, mostly less than 3°, maximum 6°.

The comparison of the morning posture and that with the simulated high heels gives similar results when examined on a change-no-change basis. Results were:

    (a) no detectable change in the lordosis of the majority of subjects
    (b) a decrease in lordosis in ten of the elevent subjects who
        showed a change in lordosis
    (c) small axial rotations at the lumbo-thoracic level, again
        mostly less than 3°

It was thought that a change in posture, which caused a change in lordosis, would also be reflected in a change in axial rotation. No significant relationship between lordosis change and axial rotation was found. Similarly, a change in lordosis could be related to the overall change in posture. However, no relationship could be found between the lordosis changes and the overall differences between the two backs.

CONCLUSION

We have observed small changes in posture in some healthy subjects, occurring during the day, and resulting from raising the heel support. It seems that these changes cannot be attributed to the effects of breathing or to the measuring system. When looking for long-term changes in the shape of patients' backs associated with spinal pathologies, we must be aware of the small changes due to the other factors found in this study.

REPEATABILITY STUDIES

Change in Lordosis   Axial Rotation at Lumbo-Thoracic Level

	INCREASE	DECREASE	NO CHANGE
4 subjects 3 male 1 female	O	O	4

	LEFT	RIGHT	NO CHANGE (<1°)
4 subjects 3 male 1 female	1	O	3

BREATHING STUDIES

Change in Lordosis   Axial Rotation at Lumbo-Thoracic Level

	INCREASE	DECREASE	NO CHANGE
6 subjects 5 male 1 female	O	O	6

	LEFT	RIGHT	NO CHANGE (<1°)
6 subjects 5 male 1 female	O	O	6

MORNING/AFTERNOON

Change in Lordosis   Axial Rotation at Lumbo-Thoracic Level

	INCREASE	DECREASE	NO CHANGE
Male (17 subjects)	3	2	12
Female (8 subjects)	3	1	4

	LEFT	RIGHT	NO CHANGE (<1°)
Male (17 subjects)	7	3	7
Female (8 subjects	4	O	4

For 23 our of 25 rotations/angle of axial rotation/<6°

MORNING/HEELS

Change in Lordosis   Axial Rotation at Lumbo-Thoracic Level

	INCREASE	DECREASE	NO CHANGE
Male (17 subjects	O	7	10
Female (8 subjects)	1	3	4

	LEFT	RIGHT	NO CHANGE (<1°)
Male (17 subjects)	2	7	8
Female (8 subjects)	3	4	1

For 23 out of 25 rotations/angle of axial rotation/<3°

Details of four studies and summary of results of the investigations of changes in back shape

REFERENCES

MILES C.A., and SPEIGHT B.S. (1975)
    Recording the shapes of animals by a Moiré method
    Journal of Physics 'E', 8, p. 773

YOSHINO S., TSUKIJI M., and TAKASAKI H. (1976)
    Moiré topography by means of a grating hologram
    Applied Optics, 15, p. 2414

THREE-DIMENSIONAL MEASUREMENT OF TRUNK SHAPE
WITH MOIRE TOPOGRAPHY

B. DRERUP, Dr.(rer.nat.)

Sonderforschungsbereich 88/C1,
Hüfferstrasse 27, D-44 Münster, West Germany.

PRINCIPLE

The arrangement for Moiré topography, as it was described by Takasaki (1970) is well suited for three-dimensional surface measurement of larger bodies, when the required resolution is not too high.

Takasaki's arrangement consists of the following optical elements: light source, camera and grating. The grating constant is g and constitutes of lines with a width δ separated by slits of width σ. So by definition the equation holds: $g = \delta + \sigma$. The perpendicular distance of the light source as well as of the camera to the grating is ℓ. The mutual distance between light source and camera is d. The distance T_N of the Nth bright Moiré fringe to the grating then is given by the expression

$$T_N = \frac{\ell \cdot N \cdot g/d}{1 - N \cdot g/d} \tag{1}$$

which can be verified by simple geometrical considerations.

REQUIREMENTS

The selection of the parameters ℓ, d and g is governed by the requirements arising by the application. For medical purposes the requirements can be summarized under the following three topics:

1. Small Fringe Distance

The error of measurements in the direction perpendicular to the grating can be estimated to be smaller than half of the distance ΔT_N of two successive fringes: $\Delta T_N = T_{N+1} - T_N$. For the achievement of a small error therefore this distance has to be made small. Assuming a low fringe order N for ΔT, which is then nearly independent of N, then can be written:

$$\Delta T \approx g \cdot \ell/d \tag{2}$$

where the expression on the right hand side of (2) is the first term in a series development of the expression in (1). The ratio $(\ell/d)^{-1}$ equals the tangent of the angle between the directions of projection and observation. Considering formula (2) it is evident, that ΔT decreases with decreasing grating constant g and increasing angle projection/observation. For medical applications a fringe distance of some mm is sufficient.

2. Good Visibility of Fringes

Visibility or contrast is meant here as a quantity proportional to the difference in film density of the brightest and darkest area of a fringe

with given order. Without dealing the theory of visibility of the Moiré
fringes it is clear from that definition, that visibility diminishes, when
the shadows behind the grating lines are brightened. Therefore, for the
achievement of good contrast this brightening of the shaded areas should
be avoided.

3. Sufficient Measurable Volume

The size of the volume behind the grating, in which co-ordinate
measurements in all three dimensions can be done, should be selected
generously, so that positioning of patients behind the grating will not
become too critical. Especially, a minimum depth of 50cm seems desirable.

CONSTRAINTS

Unfortunately these three requirements: small fringe distance, good fringe
visibility and sufficient measurable volume cannot be fulfilled
independently, as they are linked by the following constraints.

1. Diffraction Effects

Due to diffraction effects at the grating slits, the grating constant
cannot be chosen arbitrarily small, as otherwise the shadows behind the
grating lines are brightened by the first order diffraction. The distance
T_D behind the grating, where the diffraction maximum is displaced half of
the grating constant and falling so into the shadow of the grating lines is
for parallel light of wavelength λ given by:

$$T_D = 1/3 \cdot g \cdot \sigma \cdot \lambda^{-1}$$

As an example assume $\lambda = 5000$ Å (green light), $g = 2mm$ and $\sigma = 1mm$ then for
T_D holds: $T_D \approx 1,3m$. As this distance is by far greater than the required
minimum depth and the intensity in the first diffraction order is much less
than the intensity of the not diffracted beam, the diffraction effects do
not represent severe limitations of the fringe visibility.

2. Finite Size of light source and entrance pupil of the camera. The
light source and the entrance pupil of the camera cannot be idealized to a
point, but they are of finite dimensions. As figure 1a shows, owing to the
width b_L of the light source, the depth behind the grating, up to which the
grating lines cast a complete shadow is limited, but a good contrast can
only be expected when there is a complete shadow. Thus the maximum depth
T_L is given by the formula

$$T_L = \ell \cdot \delta / (b_L - \delta)$$

Similar considerations hold for the camera (see figure 1b). Let Q be an
illuminated point behind the grating. All light emanating from Q and
falling into the camera may only pass one slit, which determines the fringe

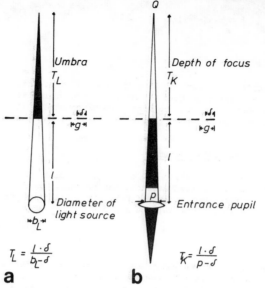

$$T_L = \frac{l \cdot \delta}{b_L - \delta} \qquad\qquad T_K = \frac{l \cdot \delta}{p - \delta}$$

a   **b**

Figure 1   Effect of finite dimensions of light source (a)
and camera entrance pupil (b) on the maximum
depth, up to which complete grating shadows
occur and fringes can be separated

Effect of light colour and skin treatment on fringe visibility

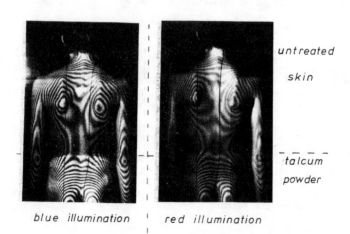

Figure 2   Visibility of Moiré fringes on human skin.
Topograms are shown from a patient, whose back
was partially rubbed in with talcum powder
(totally ≈ 0,5g). Photographs are taken with
blue and red illumination. (Schott
filterglass BGl and RG610)

order, to which Q belongs. If the light falling into the camera would pass different slits, the fringe order of Q cannot be determined. The entrance pupil p therefore must not be greater than the shadow of a grating line width. Under this condition the maximum distance T_K between Q and grating becomes

$$T_K = \ell \cdot \delta / (p - \delta)$$

The formulae for these two depths are identical, except the expressions for the width of the light source b_L and the entrance pupil p respectively. To take the best advantage of the arrangement, these two depths should have similar size, so that consequently also light source and entrance pupil should have similar size. It should be emphasized that in these two formulae only the line width, not grating constant, appears.

3. Optical Properties of the Skin

A severe limitation of the applicability of Moiré topography to medicine is the fact, that human skin behaves like a turbid medium. For light, incident on the human skin, following physical processes compete with another.

(a) Reflection: Reflections occur at boundaries. As there are many boundaries in the skin, reflections can occur in many places. The reflectivity at the surface boundary amounts to about 4% (Tronnier, 1977) and corresponds so to the reflectivity of a glass surface.

(b) Scattering: Scattering can occur at all inhomogenities of the skin tissue. In general, scattering of blue light disturbs much less than scattering of red light.

(c) Absorption: The absorption, e.g. by carotene or pigments, is wavelength dependent and is for blue light higher than for red light.

(d) Transmission is neglected here, as it becomes observable mainly in the infrared region.

(e) Fluorescence is neglected too, as it is noticeable only when the incident wavelength is shorter than about 4000 Å.

Reflection and backscattering can be summarised under the term: remission. Remission of white race skin amounts to about 60% for red light and 30% for blue light (Findlay, 1966), resulting mainly from stronger absorption of the blue light. Against that, remission of the epidermis is nearly wavelength independent and amounts to about 10% to 15%. Therefore, the fraction of light, remitted from the exterior parts of the skin, is higher for blue light than for red light, so that blue light is especially appropriate for the image formation of the skin surface.

If a pattern of light and shadow is projected on the skin, the contrast is flattened by scattering and reflection from deeper skin layers. The finer the pattern becomes, the more this flattening will disturb, so that the grating constant g cannot be made arbitrarily small. On the other side, also the magnitude of the expression ℓ/d cannot be chosen freely, as with greater angles between projection and observation the formation of shadows through prominent body parts, especially at patients suffering from scoliosis, will disturb. A solution to this problem could be the shadow free illumination with two light sources, as it was proposed by Takasaki (1970).

EXPEDIENCES

For Moiré topographic applications the following expediences seem suitable for a partly overcoming of the above mentioned handicaps.

1. <u>Projection with Blue Light</u> instead of white light. Hereby the brightening of the shadows on the skin by deeper reflections and backscattering is reduced. As a disadvantage of this method a twofold loss in intensity arises. First, the illumination is reduced, when using, e.g. a blue filter in front of the light source; second, as mentioned before, skin remittance is less for blue light than for white light.

2. <u>Reduction of the Ratio σ/δ</u>

Keeping the grating constant unchanged, the line width δ is enlarged at the expense of the slit width σ. Hereby the measurable depth is increased and brightening of the shadows in the skin reduced. On the other hand this measure deteriorates the ratio of illuminated to shaded area resulting in a loss in intensity. Against that a gain in intensity is reached by:

3. <u>Rubbing in the Skin</u> with talcum powder. The effect of this last expedience shows figure 2 for blue and red illumination at the example of a patient, whose back was partly rubbed in with talcum powder. It can be seen, that blue light gives better contrast than red light. Beyond that, talcum powder improves the contrast: that is for blue light more than for red light. Qualitatively this can be understood by Rayleigh scattering from the powder, which is for blue light more effective than for red light. Furthermore, even if there is for all colours an even increase of remission, due to the smaller remission from skin tissue for blue light the effect is relatively stronger than for red light.

REALISATION

APPARATUS

Under the above mentioned considerations an apparatus was built up with the following technical data.

Light Source

As an intense light source with a strong component in the blue wavelength region a 6 kW xenon high pressure arc lamp (Osram XBF 6000 W/1) was selected. The diameter of the radiating cylinder amounts to $b_L \approx 6mm$.

Photographic Equipment

For recording a Hasselblad camera, type 500 EL/M with a Zeiss Sonnar lens (f=150 mm) and a Kodak Royal X-Pan film (2500 ASA) were used. The entrance pupil of the lens at an f-number setting k=22 is about 7mm. Using talcum powder on the skin the resulting exposure time is t=1/15 sec.

Grating

The grating is formed by vertical lines printed on glass with a grating constant of 2mm and a line width of 1mm. The total size of the grating is 75cm high x 100cm wide. During the exposure the grating is moved for smearing the grating lines.

Geometry

Two different arrangements, one for mono, the other for stereo recordings are provided. The chosen distances are: for mono recordings l=300cm, d=150cm. The resultant fringe distance in the approximation of equation (2) is then T=4mm. For stereo exposures: l=300cm, d=60cm with $\Delta T=10mm$. In both cases the measurable depth amounts to about 50cm.

EVALUATION

As the Moiré fringes occur in planes parallel to the grating, they can be interpreted as height lines similar to those in a geographical map. Due to central projection from light source and camera however, the distance between two successive Moiré fringes is not constant, but increases with increasing depth. If therefore some extra calculation for the correction of the central perspective is made, the evaluation of the topograms can be done similar to the evaluation of maps by the establishment of profiles. For this purpose, all points of intersection between the fringes and a profile line, along which the profile shall be computed, are measured with a x-y co-ordinate reader and fed into a computer. The determination of the distance of the fringes from the grating is done by means of a plumb line, which casts a shadow on the object to be measured. The projection of the distance between the plumb line and its shadow is a measure for the fringe distance. These distances, at least of some distinct fringes are given as an extra information to the computer, so that a profile can be plotted.

MEDICAL APPLICATIONS

Positioning of Patients

As the grating plane, and with it the orientation of the planes, in which Moiré fringes occur, is fixed, the patient should be photographed in a standardised position. For that he is standing erect in a distance up to 50cm behind the grating with parallel oriented feet. For photographs in the frontal plane both frontal upper iliac spines should be oriented parallel to the grating plane. An occasional pelvic obliquety is corrected by compensating the different length of the legs. As examples, two cases, both with scoliosis, shall be shown.

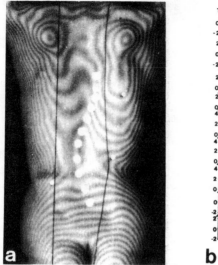
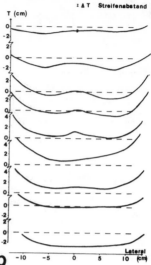

Figure 3   (b)

Topogram of a patient suffering from scoliosis.
The position of the centerpoints of the
vertebral bodies is indicated by white dots.
(b)
Profiles, corresponding to the topogram in (a).
The dashed lines specify the height of the
corresponding profile lines.

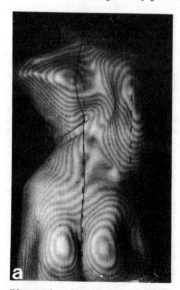
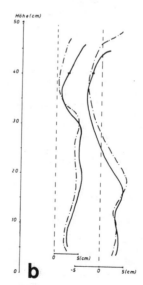

Figure 4   (a)

Topogram of a patient with severe scoliosis
(b)
Profiles from two different topograms. Solid
lines, patient without halo gravity traction as
shown in (a), dashed-dotted lines, patient
under traction.

Case 1

A fourteen year old female patient suffering from a left convex idiopathic lumbar scoliosis is presented. Two 90° radiographs and a Moiré topogram were taken in short succession, but with movement of the patient between X-rays and photograph. After evaluation of the radiographs (Drerup and Frobin, 1977) it was possible to project white dots into the topogram, indicating the positions of the centres of the vertebral bodies (L5 - T7), see figure 3a.

At nine different levels profiles were computed. These profiles are shown in figure 3b with the depth T plotted against the lateral extension. The dashed lines specify the levels of the corresponding profile lines (not drawn into the topogram). As the patient was not correctly positioned with the pelvis parallel to the grating, all profiles were rotated through 3°36', so that the lowest profile becomes nearly symmetrical.

The interpretation of the profiles gives following result: the lower profiles are symmetrical due to the symmetrical shape of the pelvis. In the height of the lower apex (L2) an asymmetry occurs, showing a peak on the left side. At the upper apex (T8) again an asymmetry occurs, this time with the peak on the right side. At higher levels this asymmetry is compensated, or as the highest profile shows, overcompensated.

Case 2

The effect of treating the scoliosis by halo gravity traction is shown at the example of a seventeen year old female patient with a right convex thoracic scoliosis and with a left convex compensatory curve. The weight of the patient was 37Kp, the traction force 14Kp.

Figure 4a shows a topogram of the patient without traction. Two vertical profile lines are indicated by dashed lines. In figure 4b the corresponding profiles (solid lines) as well as those measured under traction (dash-dotted lines) are shown. The comparison of the profiles taken with and without traction shows, that the kyphosis is fixed. The impression of a lifting up of the kyphosis arises, as the left pair of profiles clearly shows, only from a compensatory augmentation of the distal lordosis.

ACKNOWLEDGEMENTS

Financial support from "Deutsche Forschungsgemeinschaft" is gratefully acknowledged.

REFERENCES

DRERUP B., and FROBIN W. (1977)
        Objective measurements from 90°-radiographs
        Proceedings of the Orthopaedic Engineering Conference, Oxford, 28th -
        30th September, 1977. Published: Biological Engineering Society, London
FINDLAY G.H. (1966)
        The measurement of epidermal melanin by reflectance
        British Journal of Dermatology, 78, pp. 528-531

TAKASAKI H. (1970)
    Moiré topography
    Applied Optics, 9, pp. 1467-1472

TRONNIER H. (1977)
    Medizinische Wirkungen
    Ultraviolette Strahlen, 1st edition, editor Kiefer J., publisher
    Walter de Gruyter, Berlin.   pp. 567-598

A COMPUTERISED 3-D BODYSHAPE DESCRIPTION
LIGHT-SCREEN TECHNIQUE

Ir. J.W. SMIT, and Dr. L. SCHILGEN

Twente University of Technology, Enschede, Holland, and
Münster University of Medicine, West Germany

INTRODUCTION

In the co-operation between the Münster University of Medicine, West
Germany and the Twente University of Technology in Enschede, the
Netherlands, Professor Dr. H.H. Matthiasz, director of the Hüferstiftung,
orthopaedic surgeon, and Dr. L. Schilgen, orthopaedic surgeon, asked to
design a system for measuring the external shape of a human body.

Design Criteria

1. X-rays not allowed.
2. Low light-energy-level desired.
3. Body not to be touched during the measurement.
4. Shape to be followed during growth.
5. Body free for loading with external forces.

Criterion 1 is a consequence from criterion 4.

Criterion 2 forbids the use of a laser.

Criterion 3 is given, to be sure that only muscle forces define the
posture.

Criterion 4 is essential to be able to follow the alterations of posture with
age in healthy growth and in a growth under medical therapy. This implicates
a measurement of large numbers of individuals, starting at for instance an
age of five years and repeated every year or half a year.

Criterion 5 is given, to obtain the opportunity to measure the effect of
loading on the posture, especially to find information about the geometry of
the spine and about the muscles in the back.

A symmetric external shape can hide an asymmetric geometry of the spine and/
or the muscles. This hidden asymmetry can be found by applying symmetric
and asymmetric forces and/or torques onto the body. This technique has to
be developed as soon as the measuring system is available. This is a
medical diagnostic problem. A first step in solving this problem was
presented during a closed session of the Bio-engineering Conference in
Edinburgh in August 1975, by Dr. G.A. Barclay, Imanco, Melbourne, Royston,
Herts, using a report of Twente University, as an illustration of a possible
application of a computer. From then up till now, a few solutions are found
for a lot of problems.

LIGHT-SCREEN GEOMETRY

The external shape of a body can be described by means of the position of a
number of surface-points in a reference space (see figure 1).

In figure 1,b, one surface-point P is chosen to demonstrate the measuring system. This point P has the co-ordinates (xl, yl, zl) in an orthogonal system, figure 1,c. In figure 1,d this point P is shown as an intersection point of three orthogonal co-ordinate planes: x + xl, y = yl, z = zl.

In light screen geometry, these mathematical co-ordinate planes are replaced by light planes, one for each co-ordinate value wanted. When for instance a length of 100cm in each direction has to be defined in steps of 1cm, 100 light planes for each direction are to be used, 300 in total.

In figure 1,e one light plane x = xl is shown. To create this light plane a slide is used in a slide projector. The slide is a diapositive of a coded black line. This code represents the numerical co-ordinate value x = xl. The coding system will be shown in figure 2.

The light plane x = xl hits the body surface at a number of points, one of these being point P (xl, yl, zl) (see figure 1,e).

A short time after the projection of the plane x = xl, a plane y = yl is projected, giving a light-line y = yl at a number of surface-points, one of them being point P (xl, yl, zl) (see figure 1,f). Again a short time later a horizontal light-plane z = zl is projected, giving a light-line z = zl at the body surface at a number of points, one of them being point P (xl, yl, zl) (see figure 1,g).

To find the unique point P the intersection of the three light-lines has to be found (see figure 1,h). The three light-lines are projected in a dark room. Only these lines can be seen and can be photographed. It appeared that a photograph of the three line systems together is too complex for an easy and quick evaluation by a computer. A solution for this problem is to take photographs of the three light-line systems separately. This is the reason for the separate projection mentioned above. Of each light-line system a separate photograph is taken (see figure 1,i,j,k).

These photographs are analysed separately after conversion into a TV-image. This image consists of picture-points. The grey-level value in each picture-point is transported to an address in a computer memory, one address per picture-point. In this computer memory a scanning program finds the addresses belonging to an x-line, say xl, and this co-ordinate value xl is given to the addresses belonging to the x-line x = xl.

The same procedure is done with the y-lines and z-lines. Then certain addresses have obtained three co-ordinate values: in our example xl, yl, and zl. These addresses are in fact the intersections of an x-light-line, a y-light-line and a z-light-line, while the three numbers that are found on these addresses are the co-ordinates (xl, yl, zl) of a surface-point P (see figure 1,l). The problem to get enough intersection points can be solved by using light-lines with a width that is bigger than the free space between two lines. So when x-lines and y-lines are projected onto a vertical flat surface, so that the lines on that surface are parallel, a sufficient overlap will occur, so that "intersections" are found. The distance between two light-lines of the same system, the pitch (p) can preferably be chosen as 1,33 times the width (w) of the light-line. The number of intersections of the three light-line systems on a certain surface area, where each system projects (n) light-lines, is $(nw/p)^2$, when two systems are parallel, to $(nw/p)^3$ when two systems are not parallel on that surface.

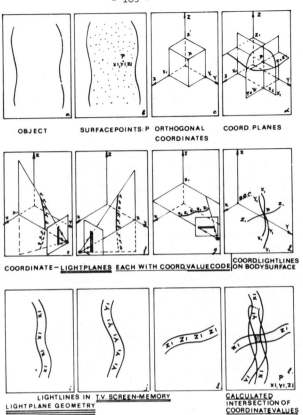

OBJECT   SURFACEPOINTS: P   ORTHOGONAL   COORD. PLANES
                         COORDINATES

COORDINATE–LIGHTPLANES EACH WITH COORD.VALUECODE ON BODYSURFACE
                                               COORDLIGHTLINES

LIGHTLINES IN T.V. SCREEN-MEMORY
LIGHTPLANE GEOMETRY   CALCULATED
                                  INTERSECTION OF
                                  COORDINATEVALUES

Figure 1   Light-plane geometry

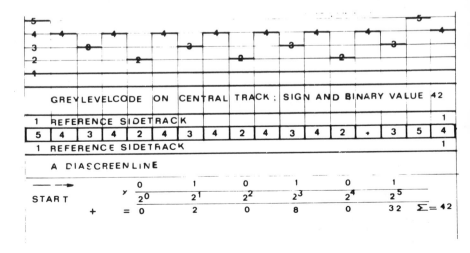

Figure 2   Three track screen lines and five gray level codes

CODING

The screen lines are coded by means of grey-level combinations (see figure 2).

A binary code is used: relative grey-level two for a zero, relative grey-level three for a one. These binary elements are separated by relative levels four. The code is repeated along the line as a number of binary blocks. The group five-four is used as a block separator. The sequence five-four indicates the positive (de)-coding direction, the element after the block-separator is used to indicate the sign: relative level three for plus, relative level two for minus. The code is situated on the central track of the line. Two reference side tracks present the unit grey-level, valid at the position covered on the body surface. The skin absorbs a great part of the light projected onto it, whereas the reflection of the skin can differ along the width and along the length of the light-line on the body.

By using the side tracks, that react on the local conditions, at each part of the central code track a local reference is found. In this way also the effect of the angle of attack on the reflection intensity is neutralised. Also the effect of changing distance between slide projector and object surface is neutralised by using the reference tracks. Skin colour or changes in it give no measuring problems, such as to select children with approximately equal skin colour for a certain type of photographic material. For the shape measurement of a large number of individuals this is very important. In figure 2 an example is given of decoding to find the co-ordinate value +42. When this code is found on a first picture out of three, it is understood as x = +42, if found on a second picture as y = +42 and if found on a third picture as z = +42. The code is repeated along the line, to be able to recognise each part of the co-ordinate line, also when it is split up into parts. This gives further the opportunity to neglect a binary block, disturbed due to body surface imperfections, or sharp alterations in density.

TRACING

Tracing of the light-lines on the TV-screen image can be done in several ways. One way is shown in figure 3, first four detail figures. First the trace of a light-line is found by following the side edge of the central track. The density step is shown under the first detail figure. This process of following the edge is done by means of a program that uses a small frame on the central track and a bigger frame on the side track. The small track uses nine picture-points, the bigger one eighteen picture-points. As soon as one of the two frames reaches the density edge, the other frame is used to continue. The two frames form a spiral, following the density step.

DECODING

As soon as the trace of a light-line is known, the decoding starts (see figure 3, detail figure 4). Picture-point A is a point of the traced edge. Square on this trace the points B, C and D are found. Along the trace the point E is found on a distance about equal to the distance BC. Then F, H and G are found, square to the trace AE and the centrepoint I. Then the densities on the picture-points in the three parts are measured. A summation

SDL is made of the density numbers in the left part ABFE. A summation SDR is made of the density numbers on the picture-points in the right part DHGC, and a summation SDM is made of the density numbers on the picture-points in the middle part AEHD. A mean reference level is found: $(SDL + SDR)/2$. The relative level of the middle part is now: $RDL = (SDL + SDR)/(2 \times SDM)$. By using this method the geometry of the light-line has no influence on the calculation, so the angle of attack has no influence. The number 2 has no influence and can be neglected. See figure 3, detail figure 6: $RDL = (SDL + SDR)/SDM$.

EVALUATION

After decoding the complete light-line the relative density-steps along the light-line are known. Following these steps the binary code can be derived and translated into a co-ordinate value (see detail figure 7 of figure 3). The co-ordinate value found is added to the addresses of all the picture-points belonging to the full length and width of that light-line, so also to those of the sidetracks. This is to ensure overlap with a parallel line (see detail figure 8 of figure 3).

INTERSECTION AND COMBINATION

The intersection of light-lines is found by looking for those addresses, that have obtained an x-value as well as a y-value as well as a z-value, as explained above (see detail figure 11 and 12 of figure 3).

TECHNICAL SET UP

A design of a technical set up as it can work in practice is shown in figure 4. This figure shows a top view of a measuring room.

APPARATUS

A force plate to carry the person to be measured; a few edges assure the correct position of the feet. The four load cells measure together the total weight and loading of the body.

A calculation device calculates the horizontal position of the body centre of gravity.

Three slide projectors, each projecting a group of light-planes, project a screen onto the object. Each separate light-plane is reflected on a small mirror, one mirror per light-plane. These mirrors are necessary to obtain parallel planes out of a diverging bundle of light-planes leaving the projectors. An important advance is, that the location of each light-plane can easily be adjusted by adjustment of the separate mirrors. This avoids very expensive curved mirrors.

A rotating wheel (LC) with one hole in it, is situated in front of each projector, chopping the three light-plane bundles after each other, to assure that only one system at a time can be projected onto the body surface.

- 106 -

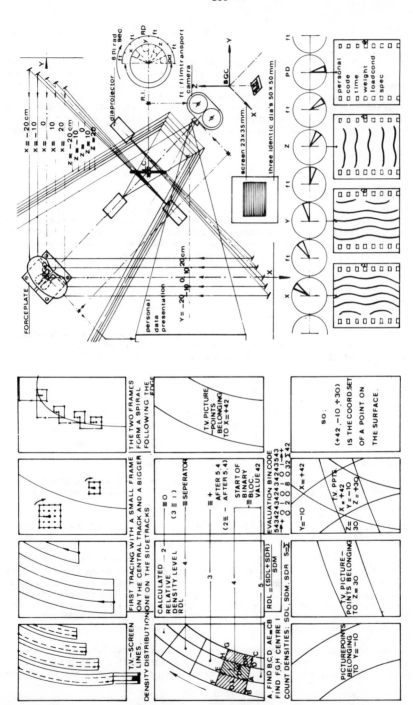

Figure 4   Light screen three-dimensional measuring technique

Figure 3   Scanning, decoding, evaluation, intersection combination

A camera, triggered by the rotating wheel, and activated to take four photographs in sequence, after command of the calculator that follows the position of the body centre of gravity.

A TV-screen, showing the personal data of the person measured, such as weight, loading, personal identification numbers, personal parameters known from measurements in the past.

A rotating mirror in front of the camera, to take photographs of the TV-screen with personal data, to be recorded on the fourth photograph. The four photographs are taken during 50% of an illumation cycle of the measuring room. During this half-cycle the room is in complete darkness, and the four photographs are taken. Nevertheless, this period of time is short enough not to be recognised by the eye, to avoid influencing the feeling of stable posture. The sequence of four photographs is kept together to assure the relative locations of the three line systems on these negatives. The eight actions during the dark half-cycle are shown. ft means film-transport in the camera. The size of the slides with coded screen-lines is shown. The position of the camera is not very important: even photographs by a hand-held camera are good enough. The camera only has to be directed to that part of the body, where all three light-screens can reach the body surface, because only there "inter-sections" can occur.

The slide projectors are so located that each optical axis passes through one point above the force-plate: the origin of the orthogonal system of co-ordinates. A special device is to be designed to adjust the height of the body in such a way that also the vertical position of the body centre of gravity matches with the origin of the co-ordinate system. A special device with inertia adjustable to zero is to be designed to load the body with forces and/or torques.

TOTAL BODY MEASUREMENT

Based on the same light-screen technique, a rotating system is designed, using orthogonal cylindrical co-ordinates, measuring the total external geometry of a body. This can be combined with a photograph taken of the load distribution under the two feet, by using a transparent force plate.

BODY MOVEMENT

The use of faster photographic material reduces the problem of movement of the body measured. A speed high enough to measure a free falling body could be useful for investigations where the influence of gravity on body shape has to be avoided.

ACKNOWLEDGEMENTS

I would like to thank Mr. J.H. Hesseling, photographer at the Twente University, for his help in developing the photographic technique.

I would like to thank the following persons and institutes for giving the opportunity to use their Quantimet-720 Image Analysing Computer:

Cambridge Instruments, Melbourne, Royston, Herts., England
Cambridge Instruments, Dortmund, West Germany - Drs. Polzin and Malkusch
The International Institute for Aerial Survey and Earth Science, I.T.C.
Enschede, Holland - Drs. D. Kovacs, Mrs. M.J.J. de Bruyn
Stevin Laboratories, Delft, Holland - Dr. ir. J. Luijerink

THE EFFECT OF SPACEFLIGHT ON REGIONAL BODY VOLUME, STUDIED BY A BIOSTEREOMETRIC TECHNIQUE

M.W. WHITTLE, M.Sc., B.Sc., M.B., B.S.

RAF Institute of Aviation Medicine, Farnborough, Hants., and
NASA Johnson Space Center, Houston, Texas

INTRODUCTION

The weightlessness experienced during spaceflight has two main effects on the body: it abolishes the normal hydrostatic pressure gradient from head to feet, and it permits posture control and locomotion to be accomplished by very much less muscular activity than would be required in a gravitational field.

On acute exposure to zero gravity the high venous tone in the lower limbs displaces blood into the upper part of the body, and causes an increase in the central venous pressure. A negative fluid balance ensues for two to three days, probably mediated by the Henry-Gauer reflex, and the central venous pool returns to its previous volume, in the presence of diminished intravascular and extracellular fluid volumes. Upon return to a gravitational field, pooling of blood again occurs in the lower limbs, with a reduced central venous pressure and a marked tendency to orthostatic hypotension. Positive fluid balance ensues, and the preflight pattern is restored in three to four days. The fluid changes resulting from spaceflight thus consist of a 'stepwise' loss of fluid in the two to three days immediately following orbital insertion, and a stepwise replacement of that fluid in the three to four days following return.

Much less muscular activity is required,when in space,for the maintenance of posture and for movement about the spacecraft. This could be expected to result in a partial atrophy of some muscle groups, and would also decrease the individual's caloric requirement, which could cause an alteration in his body fat.

Changes in gross body composition were studied in the nine astronauts taking part in the three Skylab flights. Due to the many demands on the astronauts' time around launch and recovery, and to the first two days postflight being spent on board ship, conventional techniques such as underwater weighing could not be attempted. Gross body composition was thus studied by isotope dilution (reported elsewhere) and by the relatively new technique of biostereometrics. An extensive background to the science has been given by Herron (1972).

METHOD

The biostereometric measurements of the Skylab crewmen were made by four-camera stereophotogrammetry, during the immediate preflight and postflight periods. Photographs were taken of each astronaut three times before flight, to establish a baseline, and postflight during the twenty four hours following spashdown. On the first two Skylab missions, a further set of photographs was taken one month later. On the final flight, photographs were obtained on recovery day, on recovery plus one and recovery plus four days, and again after two months. The subjects were weighed within a few minutes of taking the photographs.

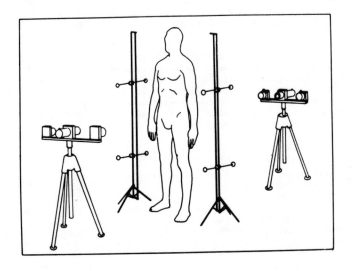

Figure 1: Diagram of photographic apparatus.

The layout of the apparatus is shown in Figure 1. The subject stood between two control stands, which provided dimensional information in the three orthogonal axes. He was photographed simultaneously by two cameras in front, and two cameras behind. The subject was nude except for an athletic supporter, and a skullcap to press his hair down. After development, the plates were analysed on a stereoplotter, which derived the three-dimensional coordinates of between 3000 and 5000 points on the body surface, punching them on IBM cards for subsequent computer analysis.

Body landmarks were located on frontal and lateral views of the subject, generated by computer from the coordinate data. These landmarks were used to define particular body segments, such as the chest, buttocks, and arms. A computer program then derived the area, shape and perimeter of between eighty and one hundred sections of different parts of the body. The volume and surface area of the body as a whole, and of the body segments, were derived by integration.

RESULTS

Preliminary results from the second Skylab flight have been previously reported (Whittle et al 1976).

Table 1 gives the preflight mean volume of the body and its segments for the nine Skylab astronauts, the change observed at the first postflight measurement, and the body weight. Although all the body segments examined showed a postflight reduction in volume, the changes observed in the chest and arms were small, and not statistically significant. The greatest absolute loss of volume was seen in the thighs, although the calves showed a greater proportional loss. The average loss in weight was 3.03 kg, and the loss in total body volume 3.02 litres, giving an average density of 1.00 g/ml for the tissues lost. This suggests either that the loss was predominantly water, or that a mixed loss occurred, with some loss of denser tissues, eg muscle, and some loss of less dense tissues, eg fat.

The rate of recovery of body volume was followed on the final Skylab flight. Table 2 gives the difference, for various body segments, between their mean preflight volume and the postflight measurements. The abdominal volume varies a great deal, as it is sensitive to food and drink intake. Nonetheless, a marked increase in volume was seen between recovery day and the other measurements. Buttock volume increased by 0.17 l during the postflight period. Both the thighs and the calves showed a rapid increase in volume, the rate of increase being greater in the thighs, which by recovery plus four days had exceeded their preflight volume, whereas the calves were still 0.13 l deficient.

DISCUSSION

The data provide some interesting information on the changes in body composition resulting from space flight. The rapid increase in volume in the first four days postflight clearly resulted principally from the 'stepwise' increase in fluid volume occurring on re-exposure to gravity. Body weight had generally levelled out by recovery plus four days, suggesting that rehydration was complete. The volume changes observed in the final crew during those four days probably consisted mainly of changes in fluid, although some changes in fat and muscle may have occurred.

Table 1: Mean preflight and first postflight measurements
of volume and weight - all Skylab crewmen (9 subjects)

	Preflight Mean Volume	Postflight Volume Change	Proportional Volume Change
	litres	litres	percent
Arms (both)	6.74	−0.15*	−2.2*
Chest	15.82	−0.16*	−1.0*
Abdomen	11.07	−0.59	−5.3
Buttocks	13.46	−0.52	−3.9
Thighs (both)	11.04	−0.76	−6.9
Calves (both)	5.91	−0.55	−9.2
Total body Volume	71.68	−3.02	−4.2
Body Weight (kg)	71.99	−3.03	−4.2

* Not statistically significant at 1% level.

Table 2: Change from preflight mean volume of body
segments (litres) - final Skylab crew (3 subjects)

	Recovery Day	Recovery + 1 Day	Recovery + 4 Days
Abdomen	−0.61	+0.12	−0.24
Buttocks	−0.13	0.00	+0.04
Thighs (both)	−0.46	−0.24	+0.05
Calves (both)	−0.41	−0.23	−0.13

The postflight change in volume of the buttocks for the nine Skylab astronauts correlated well with the postflight change in weight (correlation coefficient 0.88), suggesting, as might be expected, that the buttocks are a sensitive indicator of body fat. Changes in the volume of the buttocks may be used to estimate the change in body fat, and the relative changes in the different segments of the body during the first 4 days postflight may be used to estimate fluid changes. Changes in volume unaccounted for by fat or fluid are presumed to be due to changes in muscle bulk. Preliminary indications are that most of the observed changes in volume can be accounted for by fat and fluid, and that muscle loss was probably fairly small.

Buttock volume change also correlated fairly well (r = 0.78) with the inflight caloric intake, expressed per kilogram of lean body mass (LBM). A caloric intake of about 50 kcal/day/kg LBM appears to be necessary to preserve body fat at its preflight level.

Analysis of the coordinate information is continuing, and more detailed results will be available in the future. The data presented, however, amply demonstrate the value of biostereometric measurements.

ACKNOWLEDGEMENT

The photography and stereoplotting were performed by the Biostereometric Laboratory, Texas Institute for Rehabilitation and Research, Houston, Texas, under NASA Contract NAS9-11604.

REFERENCES

Herron, R.E. (1972)
    Biostereometric Measurement of Body Form.
    Yearbook of Physical Anthropometry, 16, pp. 80-121.

Whittle, M.W., Herron, R.E. and Cuzzi, J.R. (1976)
    Biostereometric Analysis of Body Form: The Second Manned Skylab
    Mission. Aviation, Space and Environmental Medicine, 47,
    pp. 410-412.

OBJECTIVE MEASUREMENTS FROM 90° - RADIOGRAPHS

B. DRERUP, Dr., and W. FROBIN, Dr.

Sonderforschungsbereich 88/Cl, Hüfferstrasse 27, D-4400 Münster

INTRODUCTION

90°-radiographs are bi-plane radiographs quasisimultaneously taken from two directions rectangular to each other. In this paper the reconstruction of three-dimensional structures from these radiographs is investigated, especially for the purposes of orthopaedics.

APPARATUS

The practical realisation of the bi-plane x-ray apparatus includes two tubes and two films at fixed positions. Hence for positioning, patients have to be moved up and down, which is done by a hydraulically-driven jack. The advantage of a fixed geometry is that the calibration has to be done only once. Exposures are taken one after the other. Because both of the films remain at the same positions all the time, they have to be shielded from scattered radiation. This is attained by movable lead shields, driven by linear motors within a time interval of 0.4 seconds. An arrangement of fast-movable shields offers a possibility to take quasi-simultaneous exposures without a special fixation of the patient. This is of importance to clinical applications, e.g. to the investigation of patients handicapped from deformities.

THEORY OF EPIPOLAR RAYS

The basic problem of evaluation of bi-plane radiographs is to find out corresponding images in the two radiographs. Ordinary stereophotogrammetry with its relatively small angles of convergence makes use of stereoscopic vision. However stereoscopic vision is not possible in the case of 90°-radiographs. On the other hand, the resolution in depth should be better, which makes this kind of configuration attractive. In favourable cases the localisation of corresponding points can be achieved by means of the so-called epipolar rays. However, a certain knowledge by the observer is indispensable.

Figure 1 shows the geometry of the x-ray apparatus. A is the object, A' and A'' by definition are corresponding points, which are the images of A projected by the tubes R' and R'' respectively. If the positions of corresponding points are known the position of an object point can simply be determined by the intersection of the lines A'R' and A''R''.

The main task of the observer is to find out corresponding points. As may be remembered in x-ray pictures the images are shadows projected from extended obstacles. Often then a correspondence of images is not one-to-one. In those cases the observer has to make a choice. To reduce the variety of choices and to draw the observer's attention to relevant regions of the picture are the important properties of epipolar rays.

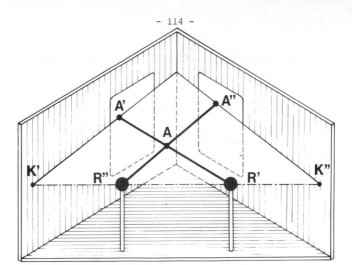

Figure 1   Configuration of the x-ray apparatus

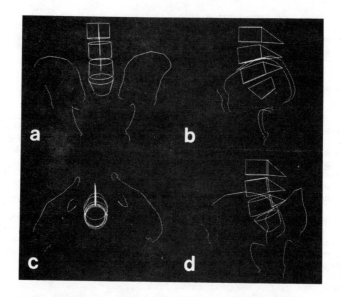

Figure 2   Reconstruction of contours of the pelvis and
            of vertebrae of the lower part of the spine.
            Radiographs were taken from a phantom.
            Projections of the reconstruction are to be
            seen from front (a), from aside (b), from
            top (c), and from an arbitrary direction (d).

The following theorems, which are known from photogrammetry (Hallert, 1960) hold for bi-plane radiography:

1. Every point A determines an epipolar plane together with the x-ray tube stations R' and R''.

2. The intersections of this plane in the image planes are lines, called epipolar lines.

3. The image points are lying in this plane, hence positions of corresponding points are reduced to a pair of lines. (This can be utilised for identification purposes.)

4. All epipolar lines form a pencil of planes through the line R'R''. This line is called the epipolar axis. The intersection points of the epipolar axis in the image planes are the epipoles K' and K'', which are the origins of the epipolar rays.

5. The epipolar rays can be thought of to have been generated by rotating a plane about the epipolar axis. (This property can be utilised for a nomographic procedure.)

NOMOGRAPHIC PROCEDURE

For a nomographic procedure there can be generated a set of scales by rotating epipolar planes about the epipolar axis K'K''. The intersections of the epipolar plane with the vertical picture edges form for each film a pair of scale marks. For a given image point in the first picture there is one and only one epipolar ray, which can be found by the help of a ruler. The ruler is to be rotated about the image point as long as it meets adjacent scales at corresponding marks. The readings, which determine the epipolar ray, have then to be transferred into the second picture. Now the possible locations of corresponding points are confined to this epipolar ray.

Especially for the evaluation of contours the concepts of epipolar rays are useful. For routine applications the nomographic procedure as described here is too slow. Therefore we are building now a mechanical apparatus with movable rulers. Their locations are congruent to those of the corresponding epipolar rays.

APPLICATIONS

As an application the three-dimensional reconstruction of contours of the pelvis and of the lower part of the spine is presented (see figure 2). In this reconstruction the contours of the pelvis were reconstructed point by point, whereas the vertebrae shown are models.

A model vertebra is described by a cylinder for the body and by a triangle for the spinous process. For this simplified description there are only a few points to be measured. By a slight modification of this model information can be provided about height, diameter, shearing, and wedge deformation of the body and also about the position of the spinous process.

A possible way of combining data taken from bi-plane radiographs with those taken from Moiré topographs is to project reconstructed parts of the skeleton (using an appropriate perspective) into Moiré photographs (Drerup, 1977). The right perspective can be calculated by evaluating the positions of leaden landmarks from both x-ray pictures and Moiré photographs.

ACKNOWLEDGEMENTS

The authors wish to acknowledge the assistance of Professor P. Brinckmann who developed and installed the movable lead shields.

We thank Dr. E. Hierholzer for helpful discussions.

This work was financially supported by the Deutsche Forschungsgemeinschaft.

REFERENCES

DRERUP B. (1977)
   Three-dimensional measurements of trunk shape with Moiré topography
   Proceedings of the Orthopaedic Engineering Conference, Oxford, 1977

HALLERT B. (1960)
   Photogrammetry
   McGraw-Hill Engineering Series, consulting editor H.E. Davis,
   pp. 27-28

THE DISPLAY-STEREOCOMPARATOR
APPARATUS FOR THE EVALUATION OF STEREORADIOGRAPHS

E. HIERHOLZER, Dipl.Phys., Dr.rer.nat.

Universität Münster, Sonderforschungsbereich 88/C1,
Hüfferstrasse 27, D-44 Münster

EVALUATION OF STEREOSCOPIC IMAGES: CONVENTIONAL APPROACH

The main objective of a numerical evaluation of stereoradiographs is to
obtain exact three-dimensional geometric data (i.e. co-ordinates) of body
structures. For example, in orthopaedics geometric data of the skeleton
are of interest, especially as input data for biomechanic calculations or
operation simulations.

The numerical evaluation of stereoradiographs is usually accomplished with
a stereocomparator. It consists basically of some type of a stereoscopic
viewing device (e.g. Wheatstone's or Helmholtz' mirror stereoscope). In
this instrument the two half-images composing the stereoscopic image pair
are reflected by several mirrors into the observer's eyes. If well
aligned, the two half-images may fuse and the observer gets the impression
of seeing a three-dimensional image in the space behind the mirrors .

In a stereocomparator the mirrors are semi-transparent. Thus if one brings
some illuminated object to the site of the three-dimensional image, the
observer can see a spatial superposition of this object and the structure
recorded on the stereoradiograph. In the case of the usual stereocomparator the illuminated object is a point-shaped target, which can be
moved in the three directions of space. By that it may be brought into
coincidence with any point of the three-dimensional image.

From the location of the target the co-ordinates of the point of the X ray
structure pointed at can be calculated. Thus by a point-by-point
measurement the object recorded on the stereoradiograph may be mathematically
reconstructed in three dimensions.

IMPROVEMENTS OF THE EXISTING PROCEDURE

Obviously, a complete reconstruction as described above is very tedious and
difficult and requires much experience. Therefore, in order to reduce the
measuring expense, it is useful to construct a simplified mathematical model
of the structure to be measured. This model body may then be fitted to some
properly defined points which are characteristic of the structure of
interest. Only these characteristic points have to be measured. For
example, a vertebral body could be approximated by a cylinder fitted to the
end-plates (Hierholzer, 1977/1).

Even though difficulties may arise in connection with the definition or
identification of the characteristic points in the stereoradiograph, a
considerable improvement would be achieved, if the model body could be fitted
directly to the three-dimensional image in the stereocomparator. That is,
instead of a single point shaped target a large number of points
constituting the model body is fitted to the spatial image at one and the

same time. Apart from time savings such a procedure might result in a much better perspicuity of the evaluation.

In earlier years Hasselwander (1954) proposed such a method to reproduce body organs according to stereoradiographs. He used an arrangement similar to a stereocomparator called stereoskiagraph, in which he formed the models from wax or clay.

THE DISPLAY-STEREOCOMPARATOR

Nowadays data handling with a computer is much simpler than model shaping by hand. So one may replace Hasselwander's real model body by a set of co-ordinates stored in a computer memory. From these co-ordinates a stereoscopic image of the model body may be calculated by a simulation program and may then be displayed on the screen of a cathode ray tube. If the screen is located in the reflected image plane (i.e. the plane in the three-dimensional image corresponding to the plane of the stereoradiographs), the observer can see both the radiograph and the model in a three-dimensional superposition. This device may be called a Display-Stereocomparator (DSC).

In the display-stereocomparator both the shaping and fitting of the model body to the X-ray-structures is accomplished by computer simulation. Motions and deformations of the model may be executed under program control by interactive data input into the computer. For example, the body as a whole may be shifted in the three directions of space; then it may be rotated about the three axes; and finally its shape may be altered by changing the size or by any other deformation.

In figure 1 the optical design of the DSC is shown schematically. The observer views the left and right stereoradiograph lying on a common support via the left and right set of mirrors respectively. At the same time he is looking through the large semi-transparent mirrors at the simulated image pair of the model body displayed on the left and right cathode ray tube (because of their higher performance two small tubes with flat screens are used instead of a single large one).

The data flow and computer control of the DSC is in principle as follows. At the beginning of the program the set of co-ordinates constituting the model body in its initial state is read from a magnetic disc. The processor computes the stereoscopic image pair, transfers it to the memory and - via a special interface and a control unit - to the display.

An analogue data input is provided for the interactive manipulation of the model body. A number of potentiometers is supplied for translations in the x-, y-, or z-direction, rotations about the x-, y-, or z-axis, and for several types of deformations of the model. The potentiometer settings are digitised by an analogue interface and are periodically read into the computer. Using these values the simulation program transforms the model body into the corresponding configuration and displays the proper image pair on the cathode ray tubes. Thus at any time the state of the model body as seen by the observer corresponds to the setting of the potentiometer array. The observer is enabled to handle the model much the same like a real deformable body in the three-dimensional space.

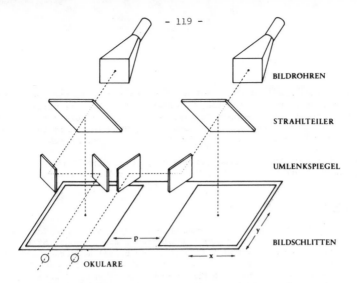

BILDROHREN

STRAHLTEILER

UMLENKSPIEGEL

BILDSCHLITTEN

OKULARE

Figure 1   Principle of the display-stereocomparator

       (bildröhren   - cathode ray tubes
        strahlteiler - semi-transparent mirrors
        umlenkspiegel - deflection mirrors
        bildschlitten - image support
        okulare   - oculars)

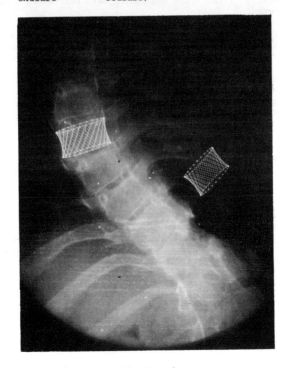

Figure 2   Measurement of a scoliotic spine

By these manipulations the model body can be fitted to the X-ray structures with respect to position, size, and shape. This being equivalent to a measurement, a lot of geometric parameters can be determined in a unique operation. The parameter values are represented in the potentiometer settings and are thus available for further computer processing.

More details of the construction and computer control of the DSC are given elsewhere (Hierholzer, 1977/2, Frobin and Hierholzer, 1974).

APPLICATIONS

Originally the display-stereocomparator has been developed for the measurement of scoliotic spines. Employing a simple model of a vertebra the position, rotation, and size of each vertebral body can be determined. Depending on the complexity of the model certain form parameters can also be measured, for instance torsion or wedge shape. Figure 2 gives an impression of what the observer is seeing during such a measurement, unfortunately in a two-dimensional representation only.

Once the best fitting of the model is achieved by turning the potentiometers, the individual geometric data of the vertebra are printed out or stored on magnetic media. Derived quantities such as the curvature of the spine in three dimensions can easily be calculated from these parameters. As an example, the geometry of the spine can be compared before and after an extension treatment.

Another application is the planning of operations, for example the fitting of endoprostheses. Using a simplified scaled model of the implant, the best choice of type, size, and position can be made in an "unbloody operation" in the DSC.

A future and more complicated operation might be the simulation of osteotomies directly in the three-dimensional image. The whole procedure should include the following steps:

1. Construction and fitting of models of the bones to be cut.
2. Selection and visualisation of the planes of osteotomy.
3. Simulation of the operation and representation of the bone models in their new configuration.
4. Data output.

It need not be pointed out, that the DSC is suited not only for the evaluation of stereoradiographs. Normal stereophotographs or even Moiré-stereophotographs can be measured as well. Only the model body and possibly the method of fitting (motion, deformation, etc.) has to be adapted.

Moreover, instead of a true model body any three-dimensional geometric structures such as auxiliary lines, planes, circles, and so on may be overlaid with the stereoscopic image to facilitate three-dimensional measurements.

ACKNOWLEDGEMENTS

I am greatly indebted to Dr. W. Frobin, Münster, for many helpful
discussions concerning the principles of the DSC.

This work was financially supported by the Deutsche Forschungsgemeinschaft.

REFERENCES

FROBIN W., and HIERHOLZER E. (1974)
     Application for patent no. DT 24 25 986 (30.5.1974)
     Offenlegungsschrift DT-OS 24 25 986 (18.12.1975)
     Deutsches Patentamt München

HASSELWANDER A. (1954)
     Die Objektive Stereoskopie an Röntgenbildern
     Thieme Verlag Stuttgart, 1954

HIERHOLZER E. (1977/1)
     Die Rekonstruktion der räumlichen Form der Wirbelsäule aus
     Stereoröntgenaufnahmen
     Fortschritte auf dem Gebiet der Röntgenstrahlen und der Nuklearmedizin,
     126, 1, pp. 22-28

HIERHOLZER E. (1977/2)
     Der Display-Stereokomparator, ein neues Gerät zur Auswertung von
     Stereoröntgenaufnahmen
     Interner Bericht Nr. 10, Sonderforschungsbereich 88/C1, Münster
     (Internal report, available by the author)

A KINEMATIC ROENTGEN STEREOPHOTOGRAMMETRIC METHOD
FOR STUDYING MOVEMENTS BETWEEN SPINAL SEGMENTS

S. WILLNER, T. OLSSON, and G. SELVIK

University of Lund, Lund and Malmö, Sweden

A kinematic roentgen stereophotogrammetric method has been developed in Sweden by Selvik (1974). This method permits a detailed description of the changes of the position of the vertebral column in all the three dimensions. Besides the lateral deviation of a scoliosis, even changes of the axial rotation and the flexion are described.

METHODS

The rotation and translation of the vertebrae studied about and along the co-ordinate axes of a Cartesian system are described in relation to a reference vertebra. If one vertebra has moved in relation to the reference vertebra between two examinations the displacement of the first vertebra is described in relation to the reference vertebra even if the latter is differently oriented at the two examinations. It is thus not necessary to place the patient in equivalent positions at the two examinations.

Three tantalum balls, 0.8mm in diameter, are inserted percutaneously or per-operatively into each vertebra to be studied. Then the patients are examined in supine and standing positions. Simultaneous exposures are made on one film from two röentgen tubes. On the same film a calibration cage with indicators, the mutual positions of which are known, is also double-exposed before or after the patient. The two-dimensional co-ordinates of the images of the tantalum indicators on the film are then measured by means of an instrument for cartography. This information is then treated in a computer so that the three-dimensional positions of the indicators are determined in a Cartesian co-ordinate system. Then the finite rotations and translations between the indicated segments are calculated.

With this method movements between different segments can be determined either between two positions (supine - standing) at the same date or between investigations in long-term studies, provided that the tantalum indicators have remained in a stable position.

The precision of the method is estimated to be 0.3°, 0.2° and 0.1° for the rotations about the transverse, longitudinal and sagittal axes, respectively. For a good accuracy:

    (a) The indicators must be placed well apart and not on a straight line.

    (b) The indicators must not move within a vertebra, i.e. the vertebrae have to behave as "rigid bodies" and the polygons formed by the indicators must be unchanged between different examinations.

The fusion healing in operated structural scoliosis has been followed up to 1100 days. The loss of correction and stability can be determined with high accuracy and a pseudarthrosis can be diagnosed without exploring the fusion area.

REFERENCE

SELVIK G. (1974)
    A röentgen stereophotogrammetric method for the study of the kinematics of the skeletal system
    AV-centralen, Lund

RECENT ADVANCES IN MORPHANALYSIS AND THEIR
IMPLICATIONS IN HUMAN ORTHOPAEDIC MEASUREMENT AND REPLICATION

G.P.Rabey M.B., B.S., B.D.S., L.R.C.P., M.R.C.S., F.R.A.C.D.S.
The Centre for Morphanalysis, Department of Anatomy, The University,
Manchester.

THEORY
Almost all modern approaches to technological three dimensional
measurement and replication (e.g. in engineering, physics and applied
mathematics) are essentially *analytic*, in that they entail indirect
relations via independent reference conventions in labelled environments.
Almost all current approaches to human measurement and replication (e.g.
in medicine and biology) are essentially *synthetic*, in that they entail
direct relations and dependent reference conventions in unlabelled
environments. The medical and biological sciences have been unable to
utilise the analytic methods initiated by Descartes in 1637, with three
dimensional validity. In consequence, most current techniques for the
clinical assessment of human shape are at least 340 years out of date.
The reason for this anomaly has been the lack of a suitable
rationale for the orientation of organic (e.g. human) forms to independent
reference frames. An appropriate solution to this difficulty was derived
in 1963 and called the Fixed Relations Theory. The theory has been
documented in detail elsewhere (Rabey, 1971) and may be summarised as
follows:
a)   A form may be defined as a set of recognisably related elements.
b)   In any family of two-dimensional forms, each of which contains at
       least two consistently recognisable elements, the forms may be
       analytically related to each other by orientation to a two-
       dimensional cartesian frame by means of the fixed relation of two-
       element symmetry (upon a cartesian axis and about the cartesian
       origin).
c)   In any family of three-dimensional forms, each of which contains at
       least three consistently recognisable elements, the forms may be
       analytically related to each other by orientation to a three-
       dimensional cartesian frame by means of the fixed relations of two-
       element symmetry (upon a cartesian axis and about the cartesian
       origin) and three-element planar freedom (within a cartesian plane).
PRACTICE
The foregoing theory provides a basis for the discipline called
Morphanalysis (Rabey, 1968). A recording machine called an Analytic
Morphograph (Figure 1) has been developed which converts the principle
into clinical practice (Rabey, 1977a). The records (analytic morphograms)
produced by the machine are graphic images such as radiographs and
photographs which relate with three dimensional validity in the same
patient and in all other patients. Thus, for instance, a frontal radiograph of a patient made in London would relate with three dimensional
validity to a lateral photograph of another patient made in Manchester.
ANALYSIS
In general, previous attempts to provide objective statements about
human shape have been either analytically invalid or mathematically
complex, or both. A new, graphic approach to this problem (called the
analytic histomorphogram) has been evolved to provide a simple,
analytically and statistically valid method which produces clinically
useful results without mathematical training (Rabey, 1977b). The method
involves the combination and comparison of analytic morphograms and may
be used to answer the two most common types of question asked about

clinical human shape, as follows:

a) <u>Inductive</u> questions such as 'What **is the variation in shape** of this organ throughout the population?' are answered by the assembly and interpretation of analytic histomorphograms. These records relate groups of forms to the same analytic reference frame. They are made by combining analytic morphograms (thus inheriting their analytic validity) but their main additional feature is their statistical validity. Appropriate curves from the morphograms are plotted in relation to the standard grid lines cut by them, by marking dots in standard millimetre squares according to a set of standard conventions. The array of marked squares associated with each grid line is a histogram, showing the distribution pattern of the chosen intersections together with the common measures of centrality and dispersion. A simple procedure of dot counting defines the mean cut and the first, second and third standard deviations about the mean. Adjacent mean, primary and secondary cuts are then connected to provide an analytic histomorphogram - a graphic representation of the variation in shape, size, position and orientation of the particular form.

b) <u>Deductive</u> questions such as 'How does the shape of this particular organ in this particular patient relate to the shape of the organ in the population?' are answered by the comparison of individual analytic morphograms with appropriate analytic histomorphograms. By means of such comparisons, a particular organ shape may be classified, for instance, as primary, secondary or tertiary.

Computer programs are being developed to enable both the inductive and deductive phases of the cycle to be carried out semi-automatically and eventually, automatically.

APPLICATIONS

A large amount of craniofacial research has been carried out using the morphanalysis method (e.g.Rabey, 1977c) and the approach is now spreading into the orthopaedic field. For instance, Hardy and Rabey (1977) have carried out analytic morphography of individual lumbar vertebrae and developed an analytic anatomy of lumbar intervertebral disc shape and size, in preparation for extension of the work into the intact spine. Studies have also been completed by the same workers on the evaluation of the sagittal and coronal capacity of the lumbar spinal canal, the morphanalysis of anterior compression of lumbar vertebral bodies, the changing relations of lumbar intervertebral articulations and the comparison of synthetic and analytic models for the assessment of the capacity of the lumbar spinal canal.

IMPLICATIONS

The principal benefits of morphanalysis are those of analytic validity, statistical validity, accuracy and improved communication.

<u>Analytic validity</u>. This is the most central benefit, because all of the others depend upon it. It is achieved by ensuring that every individual stage (choice of reference frame, fixation of reference frame, orientation of organ, imaging of organ, interpretation of images, manipulation of images) in the study of a problem in medical morphology is analytically valid in itself. It should be emphasised that five out of six will not do. One invalid stage invalidates the entire procedure.

<u>Statistical validity</u>. As a result of analytic validity, it is possible to combine groups of records to make statements about the distribution of normal and abnormal human forms within populations, with statistical validity. Further, for the same reason, it is possible to compare the records of an individual patient with those of the foregoing population distribution in order to assess dysharmonies and make diagnoses.

Figure 1   The analytic morphograph

Accuracy. As a result of analytic validity, the most important reason for inaccuracy in human morphological assessment (that of not comparing like with like) is removed, so that accuracy is immediately increased considerably.

Communication. As a result of the foregoing benefits, new levels of clinical communication are reached. Using the craniofacial example, every radiogram and photogram of every frontal, lateral and basal view, of every patient's head, at every age and in every normal and abnormal condition, relates with three-dimensional analytic and statistical validity and a high degree of accuracy, to every view of every other patient's head. The effect of this is that morphanalysis provides a structural language for recording, comparing and assessing human morphology which is not dependent upon national languages.

ORGANISATION

From the foregoing it will be clear that validity, accuracy and communication in morphanalysis depend upon careful standardisation and co-ordination, and the following arrangements have been made to ensure this.

The Centre for Morphanalysis, currently sited in the Department of Anatomy, The University, Manchester, England, is responsible for overall standardisation and co-ordination in morphanalysis.

REFERENCES

DESCARTES R. (1637)
    La Geometrie. Paris

HARDY P.A.J., and RABEY G.P. (1977)
    Journal of Anatomy, 124, pp. 266-267

RABEY G.P. (1968)
    Morphanalysis
    H.K. Lewis, London

RABEY G.P. (1971)
    Proceedings of the Royal Society of Medicine, 64, pp. 103-111

RABEY G.P. (1977 a,b,c)
    Journal of Oral Surgery, 15, (2)

CODA: A NEW INSTRUMENT FOR THREE DIMENSIONAL RECORDING
OF HUMAN MOVEMENT AND BODY CONTOUR

D.L. MITCHELSON, M.sc.

Department of Human Sciences,
University of Technology, Loughborough, Leics.

Introduction

Most of us are aware that all human endeavour is manifested only through patterns of physical movement but it does no harm to be so reminded. Viewed this way, it is slightly surprising that until very recent years there was no means of recording movements of limb and body segments and their patterns of co-ordination in a form which allowed immediate access to the mathematical parameters of the movement. Perhaps the most commonly used technique, cine analysis, requires a time-consuming intermediate stage of frame by frame measurement followed by off line computation to obtain three dimensional co-ordinates free of parallax. If one wishes to investigate how the central nervous system learns and controls the complex patterns of motor activity which characterise even simple everyday tasks, then a measurement technique is required which can record limb landmark co-ordinate data directly in computer readable form as the movements are carried out. Only then is it practicable to record and analyse movement data from the comparatively large number of subjects needed for statistical validity.

Of the available on-line techniques which are capable of recording more than the simplest of limited movement patterns only T.V. analysis or the use of ultrasonic techniques based on detection of doppler shift due to movement of sonic landmarks held any promise.   T.V. methods have a fairly low limit to their spatial and temporal resolution. There are also problems of contrast recognition for the landmarks which inevitably impose constraints on the illumination and visual content of the experimental situation. The ultrasonic technique suffers from problems associated with unwanted acoustic reflections from surfaces in the experimental area.

Against the background of these difficulties with existing techniques it was decided to design and build a new instrument based on optical sensing of light emitting landmarks. The initial design criteria were as follows:-

Minimum number of body landmarks	8
Movement sampling rate	1 KHz
Spatial resolution	1 in 4000
Linearity	.1%
3-D field of view up to a cube of side 2 metres	
Output as analogue or digital signals representing parallax free cartesian co-ordinates of each landmark to be produced concurrently with movement	

After intensive development spread over the five calendar years since 1972 the resulting machine called CODA (Cartesian Optoelectronic Dynamic Anthropometer) now substantially meets this specification.

General Description of CODA

The instrument is comprised of three major components; the subject worn landmark system, a set of electronic cameras and signal processing circuitry for transforming signals generated in the cameras to voltage analogues of the three dimensional cartesian co-ordinates of each landmark.

The landmarks are high power infra-red light emitting diodes (LED's) Circuitry required to pulse the LED's with 20 microsecond pulses of 4 amps. current is carried together with a lightweight rechargeable battery pack around the subject's waist. The general arrangement of subject, landmarks, cameras and processing circuitry is illustrated in Figure 1.

The two outside cameras A and B are sensitive to horizontal movement of the landmarks in the X direction. Because these two cameras are separated by a known distance (50 to 100 cms), it is possible to use the outputs from them to determine stereoscopically the position of the landmarks in the Y direction. The third camera C placed centrally between the other two is sensitive to vertical movement only, so that after electronic computation within the instrument to compensate for the effect of distance (Y co-ordinate) it provides the Z co-ordinate output. The outputs so produced are proportional to the true XYZ co-ordinates of the landmarks and do not contain errors equivalent to the parallax errors which occur in conventional photographic recording.

The computations which are carried out in the signal processing circuitry to produce the parallax-free XYZ co-ordinates of a particular landmark take less than 90 microseconds. The XYZ values which are computed following each flash of light from a particular landmark are held at the output of CODA in an analogue memory until the XYZ values resulting from the next flash from the same landmark are ready. The pulse repetition rate for each LED is 1 KHz and the duration of each flash of light is approximately 20 microseconds. The interval between light flashes from one LED and the next is 90 microseconds. This interval allows time for the XYZ computation for each landmark. To accommodate a total of eight landmarks and three co-ordinates for each landmark 24 output channels have been provided so that any or all landmark co-ordinates can be monitored or recorded on a multichannel analogue tape recorder. Synchronization of the light pulses with the three tier eight channel multiplexer in the main processor which routes signals to the appropriate output analogue memories is accomplished by means of a megahertz modulation signal which labels the number one landmark. This arrangement leaves the subject quite free of any electrical cables attaching him to static equipment.

The light from the LED landmarks is emitted into a solid angle of 2π steradians (i.e. a hemisphere) so that rotations within a 180 degree range are possible before the cameras lose the landmark signal.

The photograph shows the three cameras mounted on top of the signal processing module. Each camera has a cylindrical lens pair. Light from each LED landmark is focused into a line image in the focal plane of the camera. The position of the line is encoded by a set of eleven silicon planar photodiodes which are fabricated in a hybrid encoding pattern.

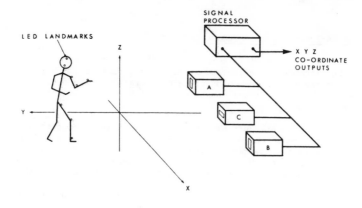

FIGURE 1 : Arrangement of CODA cameras in relation to subject and cartesian co-ordinate system.

FIGURE 2 : Photograph of CODA cameras and main signal processor unit.

Six of the photodiodes form a digital gray code to give the six most significant bits of resolution. The remaining five photodiodes form an analogue vernier which provides the balance of the resolution to the specified 12 bits (or 1 in 4096). The design of the photodiodes and the subsequent electronics is such that CODA is not sensitive to diffuse reflections of LED light from surfaces within the field of view. Even a sheet of white paper placed near on LED at an optimal angle for reflecting light into the cameras has no effect on the output of the instrument.

Applications

There are two principal modes in which CODA can be used. One is for direct monitoring of movement for applications ranging from biomechanics and bioengineering to the study of motor skills in physiological psychology. The other is for tracing body contours. By placing an LED landmark on a small wand the contours of any three dimensional surface can be traced and recorded on analogue magnetic tape. This stored infor mation could not only be used for analysis purposes, but also to control machinery for cutting moulds in prosthetic applications.

The first biomechanics application which is planned for CODA is the recording of all angular and translational movements about the knee joint. Placement of the three landmarks on convenient surface sites on the thigh and the calf in principle permits complete definition of the position of each segment in 3-D space. The problem of skin movement, however, makes it difficult to define the positions of femur and tibia. To reduce the effect of skin movement, four landmarks will be used on each segment and placed at different sites during a number of gait recording sessions. Artifacts due to skin movement may then be minimised by comparing records to identify the pattern and amplitude of elastic deformation of vectors connecting the various landmarks. A best estimate of the true movement of femur and tibia may then be extracted. Such an approach, using CODA linked on-line to a computer, will allow rapid comparison of the articulation of natural and prosthetic knee joints.

During the next two years the technique will be employed by the author and others at a number of medical rehabilitation centres in the U.K. dealing both with neurological and orthopaedic patients. Most of the neurological patients participating in the study have suffered a stroke. Their movements, recorded during therapy sessions and motor function and ADL assessments, will be analysed to gain information on the process of interaction between patient and therapist as aquisition of skill occurs. Measures of movement and functional capacity such as space-time trajectories, ranges and variances, phasing and total time will be computed in an attempt to identify criteria for assessment of these complex skills. It is hoped that application of these criteria to data from large numbers of therapy sessions will lead to identification of more effective therapeutic techniques, and to motor function assessment procedures which have predictive value for the ultimate profile of functional capacity which the patient can achieve.

The real-time nature of the output from CODA provides the means by which a wide variety of parameters of the patient's movements are available to be fed back to him via one or more of his sense modalities. One of the longer term aims of the research is therefore to investigate the possibilities of augmented feedback training to enable patients to practise movements on their own and reaquire lost skills more efficiently.

CLINICAL SHAPE MEASUREMENT AND REPLICATION

S.J. COUSINS, B.A.Sc., M.A.Sc., and M.F. NEIL, B.Sc., M.Sc.

Biomechanical Research and Development Unit,
Department of Health and Social Security,
Roehampton, London SW15 5PR.

APPROACH

Models made by hand, sculpted directly or by modifying a cast taken from
body shape have traditionally been used for manufacture of sockets for
residual limbs, lasts in shoe making, long leg braces and seats for disabled
children, to list a few examples. By replacing these artisan methods with
scientific procedures in defining, changing and replicating shape, some
aspects of clinical service in prosthetics, orthotics and the supply of
special devices, can be automated. The system described in this paper
developed at MERU[1] with improvements undertaken at BRADU gathers shape data
photographically from Shadow Moiré generated contour maps of a body part.
The photographs are hand digitised and displayed for shape changing purposes
in a computer. The computer outputs the shape to a paper tape for
automatic control of a milling machine. Useful information can be removed
from the computer directly or the shape can be machined and used in making a
device for one or more patients. The time consuming hand digitising of the
shape data is being replaced by a Television-Microprocessor system that will
allow live viewing of the computer displayed shape. This will allow the
shape changing process to be done while the patient is present which is
clinically more desirable. This process could be applied in medical and
industrial areas where shape is being measured, controlled and changed.

THE MERU SYSTEM

Hardware

The Mechanical Engineering Department and MERU at the University of British
Columbia collaborated to try TV Silhouette Scanning (TVSS), Close Range
Stereophotogrammetry (CRS) and Shadow Moiré Photogrammetry (SMP) as sensor
systems with the University's IBM-360 computer (smaller can be used) and
Mechanical Engineering's Superior Electric Numerically Controlled (NC)
milling machine as the shape changing/processing and replicating systems,
respectively (Duncan et al, 1974). TVSS did not allow us to sense re-
entrant shapes which we needed for replicating socket models. Although CRS
and SMP were about equal in our assessment criteria (clinical use, cost,
object size, resolution, acquisition time, portability, computer interface)
SMP was pursued allowing us to be independent of expensive commercial
equipment and giving us control over the amount and quality of data used
(digitisation, hand smoothing of moire contours, etc.).

A subtractive Shadow Moiré apparatus was built for shanks and residual limbs
(Takasaki, 1970, 1973). Three photographs were taken 120° apart through a
moving grid which improves the clarity of the Moiré fringes. The
photographs were enlarged and then hand digitised using a Grandicon digitiser.
This process takes approximately thirty to forty-five minutes per photo or
about one and a half to two and a half hours per complete shape. This is the
slowest part of the whole process and work on this is in the BRADU section of
this chapter.

Software

The computer programs, run in a few minutes, organise the raw surface data (from IBM cards obtained at the time of digitisation) into a rectangular matrix, correct for perspective, assign the appropriate heights to each fringe contour and format the data for acceptance into two other programs:

(a) PARTADJ (Lee et al, 1977) - Partial Surface Adjustment program allows us to change the shape of definable areas of the object's surface by raising or depressing dimples, ridges, patches and combinations of these.

(b) SUMAIR (Mair and Duncan, 1975) - Polyhedral NC Program - this program directs a spherical end mill cutter to visit the centre of each facet of a large polyhedron using the rectangular matrix of the data as its base. The program has a non-interference capability not allowing the cutter to enter an area where the radius of curvature is smaller than the cutter's radius.

Clinical Experiments

For each of the six below knee amputees (one bilateral) in this feasibility study control, prostheses were hand fabricated using modular components by Mr. James Foort[2]. At the time the prostheses were made alginate and plaster impressions were also taken of the residual limb and other leg. In the case of the bilateral; besides the residual limb impressions taken, donor shank shapes were taken to be used later for cosmetic cover fabrication. Plaster models were used as the input shapes to the Moiré apparatus to save the amputee making many trips while we worked out the problems with the equipment and the processes. These unchanged models allowed us to make comparisons for accuracy of shape replication (3 - 5%). For this limited sample then:

1. Five amputees had cosmetic covers made or shank models (used for making cosmetic covers) machined.

2. All the cosmetic covers made (except the bilateral's) were machined as mirror image.

3. One cosmetic cover shape was made by hand blending the contour Moiré patterns of the socket and shank to allow for alignment of the prosthesis.

4. One, the bilateral, had his donor shank shapes elongated by twenty-five percent and fattened by ten percent.

5. One had a stump model replicated (unmodified).

6. One had a socket model replicated (modified stump model).

7. One stump shape was computer manipulated into a socket shape using the interactive computer program PARTADJ.

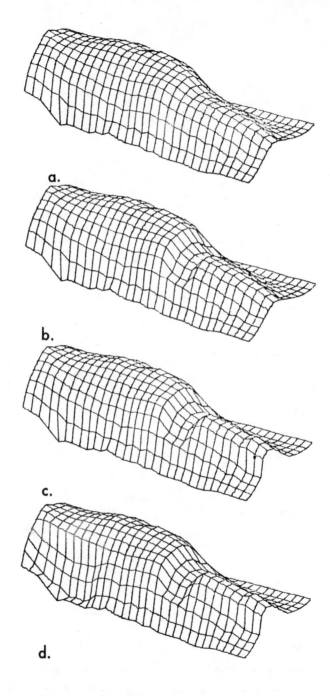

Figure 1   Computer sculpting

Figure 1 shows computer modification of one view (of the three) of a residual limb. The anterior view (a) shows the patella and tibial crest. In (b) a patella tendon bearing area has been created using the PARTADJ program. In (c) tibial crest relief was added followed by end relief. In (d) a medial supracondylar suspension area and necessary flares were imposed on the shape. The shape was rotated and a lateral area, as in (d), was added.

The replicating ability of the system has been tested on one of the amputees. Her socket model was hand shaped and then replicated with the Moiré-Computer-NC Machine system and used in fabrication of a leg. This leg was also dressed up with a cosmetic cover made from the automated process. This leg has been worked regularly for four months and is still being used. This does not make the system clinically viable (yet) but shows that the accuracy of replication is enough to be acceptable by an amputee. We have succeeded in using an automated system for clinically measuring shape, replicating a socket and creating a cosmetic cover for a prosthesis.

THE BRADU SYSTEM

The investigations (Foort et al, 1977, Forsyth et al, 1976) and trials of this automated system undertaken at MERU demonstrated the feasibility of automated shape replication. The current BRADU effort is being concentrated in the areas where the feasibility study revealed weaknesses such as interfaceability and clinical adaptability.

Up to two hours have been spent digitising a SMP photograph which first had to be developed and then enlarged to the correct format. In the BRADU system a video camera replaces the stills:camera and the photographs are replaced by quantised video pictures stored as matrices in a micro-processor's memory. The microprocessor becomes an adaptable interface and front end computer to any large computer system. The software of the microprocessor can determine the XYZ co-ordinates of the surface matrix and output them in a form acceptable to the system with the necessary facilities for the manual shaping using a graphics terminal (the PARTADJ program). Clinical considerations require the new design to have fast data acquisition, to view around the stump and to have the patient in a suitable position.

The schematic of SMP with its variations (figure 2), has footprints representing a person standing in front of two mirrors which give an all-round view of the front leg. A video camera sees this and passes it to the monitor where it is focussed and centralised (block 1 of figure 2). The interface unit is then switched in to display a quantified picture in two levels, no grey, with black and white transition adjustable to optimise the picture. The picture is stored in the microprocessing memory as a matrix of 256 points across a line by 128 lines. If the display matrix is acceptable the software produces contour lines at all the light/dark transitions, assigns Z co-ordinates values to each contour, and produces the XYZ co-ordinates in a form acceptable to the large computer.

We are evaluating three variations of shadow Moiré technique. Version A on figure 2 is a subtractive shadow Moiré arrangement. It has a large grid in front of the object and lamps in front of the grid. Version B has a

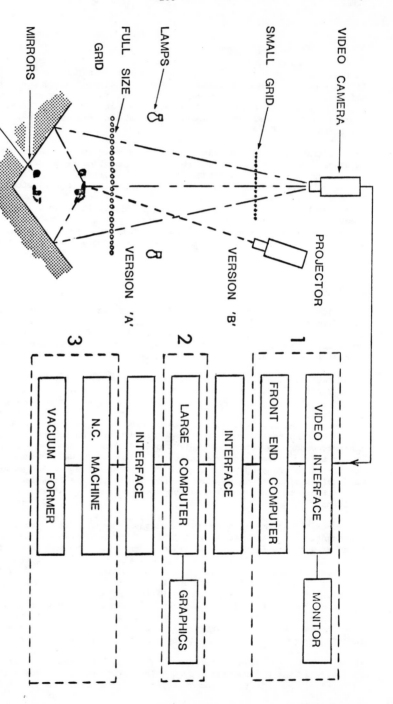

Figure 2   Schematic diagram of shadow Moiré photogrammetry

projected grid focussed on the object and the camera looks through a fine grid. Version C, (not shown) is similar to B except that there is no second mechanical grid; the TV raster will produce the effect.

Another approach, CRS, will use the same facilities as before but will have different software in the front end computer, a projected dot grid to generate reference points on the surface of the shape and a stereo pair of video cameras connected to the interface unit. The mathematics for the reconstruction of shapes is known (Kratsky, 1975).

The accuracy of the sensing system will be proportional to the matrix size and to the viewed area size. For a view 50cm by 25cm and a matrix of 256 by 128 the device can resolve position to 2mm. The interface can handle a matrix as large as 1024 by 512 and the resolution would be 0.5mm. The amount of detail on the surface is dependent on the number of Moire fringes and experience to date with the MERU system gave about 5% accuracy.

Block 2 of figure 2 represents a computer carrying three programs. The first program orders, smooths and then displays the data in a three-dimensional form on the graphics terminal. The second (PARTADJ) allows adjustment to the co-ordinates via the graphics terminal while the third directs the end mill cutter of the NC machine.

Block 3 of figure 2 refers to the production side of the system. The NC machine mills the shape out of rigid polyurethane foam which is then suitable for use as a mould for the automatic vacuum former developed by BRADU. This machine takes cone shaped thermoplastic blanks and moulds them into sockets, cosmetic covers, etc., for direct use with modular parts in rapid assembly of artificial limbs.

1 Medical Engineering Resource Unit, Division of Orthopaedics, University of British Columbia, Vancouver, Canada.

2 Director of Prosthetic/Orthotic Research, Medical Engineering Resource Unit.

REFERENCES

DUNCAN J.P., FOORT J., and MAIR S.G. (1974)
    The replication of limbs and anatomical surfaces by machining from
    photogrammetric data
    Proceedings of the Symposium of Commission V, International Society
    for Photogrammetry, Biostereometrics, 1974, p. 531

FOORT J., COUSINS S.J., VICKERS G.W., and LEE V.T.Y. (1977)
    Automated prosthetic procedures
    Proceedings of ISPO, New York, May 1977

FORSYTH D.G., VICKERS G.W., and DUNCAN J.P. (1976)
    Replication of anatomical and other irregular surfaces
    Proceedings of the Fourth North American Metalworking Research
    Conference, p. 295

KRATSKY V. (1975)
    Digital modelling of limbs in orthopaedics
    Photogrammetric Engineering, 41, (6), pp. 741

LEE V.T.Y., VICKERS G.W., and DUNCAN J.P. (1976)
    Program PARTADJ, partial surface adjustments
    Internal Report of the Department of Mechanical Engineering,
    University of British Columbia

MAIR G.G., and DUNCAN J.P. (1975)
    Polyhedral NC program documentation
    Report published by the Department of Mechanical Engineering,
    University of British Columbia

TAKASAKI H. (1970)
    Moiré topography
    Applied Optics, Vol. 9, no. 6, p. 1467

TAKASAKI H. (1973)
    Moiré topography
    Applied Optics, Vol. 12, no. 4, p. 845

MEASUREMENT OF THE LUMBAR SPINAL CANAL
BY DIAGNOSTIC ULTRASOUND

R.W. PORTER, F.R.C.S., D. OTTEWELL, Ph.D., M.Inst.P., and M. WICKS

Doncaster Royal Infirmary, Doncaster

The lumbar spinal canal can be measured radiographically using a
magnification factor. In the coronal plane the interpedicular distance is
easily measured. The mid-sagittal diameter,however, which is probably of
more clinical significance, is difficult to measure because overlapping
shadows obscure the posterior boundary of the canal. Jones and Thomson (1968)
and Eisenstein (1977) describe methods of identifying the posterior boundary
of the canal, but this is not easy in practice. Rothman and Simeone (1975)
agree that the mid-sagittal diameter is the most significant and state that
it can be measured accurately only by direct measurement (Verbiest, 1977).
Gargano (1974) has shown that transverse axial tomography can demonstrate
the cross-sectional shape of the lumbar canal, but has not used the method
to measure the canal. This paper describes a method of measuring a ten
degree oblique sagittal diameter of the lumbar canal by pulsed echo ultrasound.

METHOD

A Nuclear Enterprise diasonograph, a machine now widely available for
obstetric diagnosis, was used to measure the spinal canal. The 1.5MgH
transducer was placed one centimetre lateral to the spinous process at L.1,
inclined at an angle of ten degrees to the sagittal plane, and moved
longitudinally to L.5. Olive oil was used as a coupling medium. With
repeated movements a two-dimensional B-scan display recorded echoes from the
laminae and vertebral bodies (figure 1). The echoes were lost by
moving the transducer medially over the spinous processes and lost if moved
laterally over the facet joints and thickened lateral lamina, because of the
high absorption of sound by bone. The echoes were recordable only through a
narrow longitudinal band (figure 2). At any particular vertebral level a
simultaneous A-scan display showed three major echoes from the posterior and
anterior lamina and from the posterior surface of the vertebral body
(figure 3). The time interval between the second and third echoes is
proportional to the distance between the reflecting surfaces of the canal
and is measurable in millimetres on a digital read-out. The identification
of the echoes was aided by electronic calipers which were displayed
simultaneously on the B and A-scan. The canal was measured at each lumbar
level.

A cadaveric vertebra was immersed in saline. Direct and ultrasound
measurements were identical,confirming the identity of the major echoes.

The lumbar spinal canal was measured by ultrasound in one hundred male mining
recruits between fifteen and eighteen years, and in fifty female nurses of
the same age range.

RESULTS

The mean, tenth and ninetieth percentiles for the miners and nurses are shown
in tables 1 and 2, and diagramatically in figures 4 and 5.

Figure 1   B-scan display of asymptomatic subject

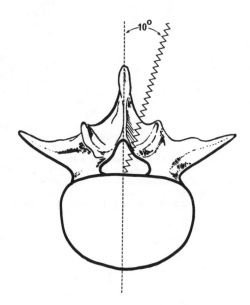

Figure 2   Canal diameter measured by ultrasound

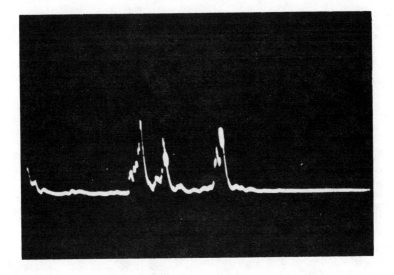

Figure 3   A-scan of asymptomatic subject

Ultrasound measurements of the lumbar spinal canal have been remarkably repeatable to within O.2mm.

There was no difficulty in obtaining measurements from the asymptomatic miners and nurses, but it was occasionally impossible to obtain reliable echoes from the vertebral body in very obese subjects, and following posterior spinal fusion.

DISCUSSION

The repeatability of ultrasound measurement of the spinal canal is understandable when it is recognised that the bony "window" of the lamina through which sound enters and is reflected back is extremely small. A two centimetre beam of sound from the transducer covers this "window" and it is the average measurement between the second and third echoes that is recorded. The measurement will thus be repeatable for any particular vertebra.

It is apparent that ultrasound provides a safe, simple and very accurate means of measuring a ten degree oblique sagittal diameter of the spinal canal, which is probably a highly significant diameter clinically.

REFERENCES

EISENSTEIN S. (1977)
    The morphometry and pathological anatomy of the lumbar spine in South
    African negroes and caucasoids with specific reference to spinal
    stenosis
    Journal of Bone and Joint Surgery, 59B, pp. 173-180

GARGANO F.P., JACOBSON L., and ROXOMOFF H. (1974)
    Transverse axial tomography of the spine
    Neuroradiology, 6, pp. 254-258

JONES R.A.C., and THOMSON J.L.G. (1968)
    The narrow lumbar canal
    Journal of Bone and Joint Surgery, 50B, pp. 595-605

ROTHMAN R.H., and SIMEONE F.A. (1975)
    The spine
    W.B. Saunders and Company

VERBIEST H. (1977)
    Results of surgical treatment of idiopathic developmental stenosis of
    the lumbar vertebral canal
    Journal of Bone and Joint Surgery, 59B, pp. 181-188

MEAN VALUES AND PERCENTILES FOR 100 YOUNG ASYMPTOMATIC MALES

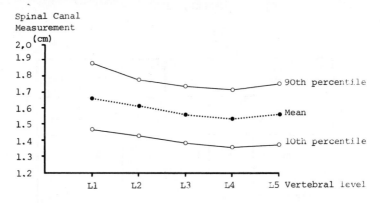

Figure 4   Lumbar canal measurements in one hundred
            male mining recruits

MEAN VALUES AND PERCENTILES FOR 50 YOUNG ASYMPTOMATIC FEMALES

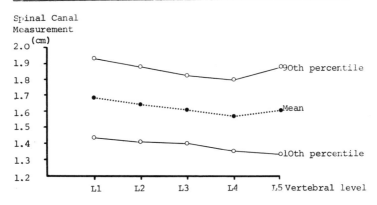

Figure 5: Lumbar canal measurements in fifty female nurses.

MINING RECRUITS

Vertebral Level	L1	L2	L3	L4	L5
10th Percentile	1.47	1.43	1.39	1.36	1.38
Mean	1.66	1.62	1.56	1.54	1.57
90th Percentile	1.88	1.78	1.74	1.72	1.75

Table 1   Mean and percentiles of canals in
one hundred male mining recruits

NURSES

Vertebral Level	L1	L2	L3	L4	L5
10th Percentile	1.45	1.42	1.41	1.36	1.34
Mean	1.69	1.65	1.62	1.58	1.62
90th Percentile	1.94	1.89	1.83	1.81	1.89

Table 2   Mean and percentiles of canals in
fifty female nurses

GAIT ANALYSIS, INTERPRETATION AND APPLICATION

GAIT ANALYSIS

J.P. PAUL, B.Sc., Ph.D., A.R.C.S.T., C.Eng., F.I.Mech.E., c.F.B.O.A.

Bioengineering Unit, University of Strathclyde, Glasgow

In a normal presentation of a subject, one would review the history, the intentions of the studies, their achievement, and then go on to outline areas requiring further study with predictions of the development of instrumentation or analysis which might be expected. In the topic of gait analysis, however, the achievements of the investigators have been conditioned very largely by the equipment available to them and also constrained by the objectives of their study at the time. I am therefore going to present in an apparently disorderly fashion my own view of problems of gait analysis, jumping about in history and also in area of study in an apparently random manner.

The characteristics of human gait are frequently assessed subjectively by, for example:

1. A member of the clinic team watching the locomotion of a patient.

2. By recognition of the characteristics of the sound of approaching footsteps, allowing identification before vision.

3. By response to the stimulus of a sexually provocative gait and in other ways.

In my view, the first significant contribution to the scientific measurement of gait was that of Muybridge (1882), whose studies indicated the possibilities of development of the photographic method. Muybridge's multiple cameras comprised effectively the rudiments of a ciné-photography system and the studies of Elftman (1938a) and the University of California's Biomechanics Research Group (Eberhart et al, 1947) led naturally to the investigations known to us all at the present day and generally too numerous to mention individually. The multiple exposure on a single photographic plate technique is known principally for the studies by Fischer (1908), Bernstein (1935), Eberhart and the California Group (1947) and Murray et al (1966), as exemplified in figure 1. All of the photographic methods involve the production of film or prints from which the analysis or measurement is performed; although there have been two developments of systems for automated analysis from ciné film, Kasvand et al (1971) and Pepoe (1970) - these are not largely used. The major problem is of course the interposition of the human at some point in the transcription of the data from the photographic record to numbers for analysis. This involves generally many hours of eyestraining work with the inevitable worry of diminishing accuracy. It was a natural step therefore for the development of non-photographic optical systems, since they preserve the freedom of the individual from gross hardware connections and yet allow the acquisition of information in analogue or digital form for subsequent analysis. In this category comes Grieve's POLGON (1969), Lindholm's SELSPOT (1974), Mitchelson's CODA (1974) and

Strathclyde's television/computer system, Jarrett et al (1976). Subsequent contributors will deal with the characteristics of these systems and the extent to which each has achieved the objective of full three dimensional displacement data acquisition in computer compatible form and the freedom of the test subject from the requirement of carrying heavy hardware or having an umbilical connection to the instrumentation.

Admitting to my own prejudice against spatial information acquisition systems involving considerable mechanical connections such as multiple axis goniometer systems, it has to be agreed that in some cases very useful and interesting information can be obtained in this way; as for instance, allowing the production of the angle/angle diagrams, of which mention is made in the chapter by Dr. Grieve. There have of course been other methods used for the acquisition of spatial information but they are not currently in general use. Examples might be the flexible cord electric generator system for velocity measurement, Drillis (1958), Ganguli and Datta (1975), sonar (Wirtar et al, 1970) and Chronocyclograms, Drillis (1965).

Although not strictly speaking a displacement measurement, it is convenient here to refer to systems such as that of Morris (1973) where multiple accelerometers mounted on a limb segment allow the determination of the spatial displacements of the segment and of course give the most accurate information relating to the three dimensional accelerations, linear and angular, to which the segment is subjected. It would appear that these systems are most effective when used in association with other displacement measurement systems, since the effective dynamic analysis of the "inertial navigation" problem for one body segment requires considerable computer resources.

It must be remembered that the objectives of research groups differ and the techniques appropriate to the analysis of the gait of a racehorse may not be appropriate to the problems of the geriatric, nor are the characteristics of the signals obtained during athletic performance necessarily a guide to the problems of data acquisition for the leg amputee.

Another major parameter of the kinetics of human gait is the pattern of forces developed by the environment and acting on the individual. The early studies of Braune and Fischer and Bernstein suffered from the inability to measure forces by the environment and; as a result, they were unable to analyse the dynamics of the double support phase and the loading of the leg had to be inferred from assessments of the summations of the mass properties of body segments and accelerations derived from displacement data with the inevitable inaccuracies of these procedures.

Elftman had some information relating to ground to foot force, although reservation may be expressed with regard to the dynamic characteristics of his instrument and it required the major activities at the University of California Berkeley Group before Cunningham and Brown (1952) gave the world its first six quantity force measurement platform with acceptable dynamic characteristics, figures 2 and 3. In my view, fundamental knowledge of the mechanics of locomotion took a large step forward with the availability of this measurement system. This instrument has been copied and alternative designs produced, to the extent that gait laboratories can be thought to be incomplete without this equipment.

It is interesting at this point to recall a little referenced

Figure 1   Lateral view of test subject walking on level surface.
The multiple exposure on a single negative shows the
trajectories of markers on the pelvis, knee, ankle and
foot.
From Eberhart et al (1947)

Figure 2   Exploded view of force platform of the Cunningham and
Brown type (1952), used by Harper et al (1961)

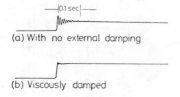

(a) With no external damping

(b) Viscously damped

Figure 3   Dynamic response of
Cunningham and Brown's
(1952) force platform.
Electrical output from
circuits measuring lateral
shear force on application
of an impulsive load

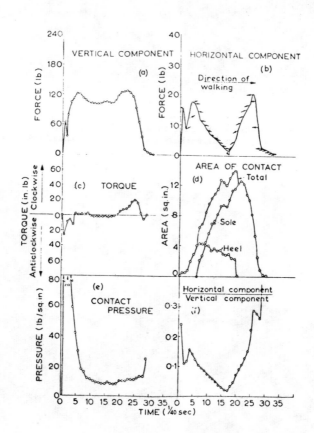

Figure 4   Ground to foot force actions for test subject
walking at normal speed in a straight line on
a level surface from Harper et al (1961).
Torque is defined as moment about a vertical
axis through the centre of pressure and
cannot therefore be related to a single set
of anatomical axes

publication containing a lot of useful work. As mentioned before, most gait analysis studies refer to athletic or clinical situations and therefore the work of Harper et al (1961) aimed at determining the required force transmitting characteristics of flooring materials is a useful reminder to be broad in the work of abstracting literature references. Some of their data is shown in figure 4. The force platform is of course a most awkward instrument to use, requiring for a useful measurement that the appropriate foot of the test subject land within a very constrained area. Ideally, the transducer within the shoe is the appropriate solution but, although Carlsoo (1972) and others have produced some devices of this type, there has been none which can give the full six quantity information required to define with precision the magnitude and direction of the resultant force being measured. The problem is of course compounded if one wishes to be aware of the part of the resultant load transmitted by different fractions of the surface area of the foot. In this connection, since it is the privilege of the reviewer to express bias, I personally feel that few walking activities of the western human are conducted without the restraint of footwear. It appears therefore that analysis of the gait characteristics of an individual should be obtained when he is wearing his own footwear and special sandals or barefoot locomotion must be recognised as fundamentally altering the characteristics of the phenomenon. The problem of the mechanics of the foot in its normal and disabled condition will therefore require transducers within the shoe.

Another major tool in the armamenta of the gait researcher is the measurement of the phasic EMG signals of muscles relevant to the activity and the work of Joseph and Battye (1966), Basmajian (1962) and Bauman (1974) in this field needs no further mention. There have been studies attempting to relate some function of EMG to the force being developed by particular muscles or groups of muscles. Unfortunately they have not yet produced a solution which can deal with the presence of agonistic and antagonistic muscles during a dynamic situation and the technique appears to be most useful as an indicator of the periods in time in the activity cycle in which particular muscles are active or quiescent, although there is still great scope for a multiple interpretation with regard to the criterion for activity or quiescence. Figure 5 compares the average phases of muscle activity demonstrated by EMG studies.

Another basic technique relating to gait analysis involved the determination of the metabolic energy cost of locomotion. Once again the "classic" reference is to the University of California, Berkeley and the work of Ralston (1965, 1958). In some situations the overall metabolic energy cost of locomotion may be very relevant. Similarly, studies of the kinetic and potential energy changes in limb segments during function, University of California, Berkeley (1953), Winter et al (1972) and Cappozzo et al (1976), may be of interest.

In many attempts to analyse the mechanics of locomotion a function is specified and the basic characteristics of the human performance in walking are derived from a minimisation of this function. For instance, Nubar and Contini (1961), Seireg and Arvicar (1975) and Chao et al (1976), optimise on a basis of minimum "muscular effort" and others utilise the concept of a minimum total muscular force. I think one should be aware that the human functions under a range of constraints with different priorities on different occasions. Gait during a long walk naturally differs from that

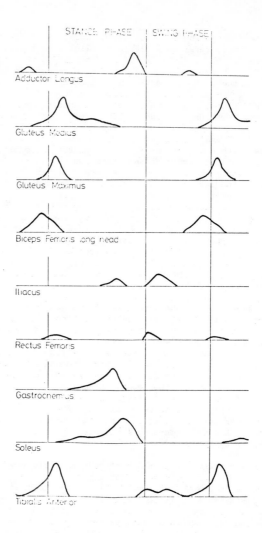

Figure 5   Average of periods of activity of certain leg muscles
            from needle electrodes in six test subjects during
            normal speed level walking. From University of
            California (1953). The magnitudes of the curves have
            no relative significance one to another

while hurrying for a bus and both are equally and significantly different from the movement pattern adopted in the presence of personable members of the opposite sex. Correspondingly, the arthritic patient is continuously being required to minimise some function of joint force, joint angulation and velocity and the amputee will, in many situations, be attempting to minimise contact pressures in specific areas of the stump socket interface. It is important to recognise therefore that analytical attempts to interpret the characteristics of human locomotion, while interesting, will rarely be able to reflect the multiple characteristics and natural optimisation of our response to daily life. Narrowing the discussion towards clinically related gait analysis, it appears that, taken separately, displacement analysis systems or force measurement systems or EMG systems must be recognised as of themselves providing information which has the characteristic of being symptomatic rather than relating to the basic disability causing the gait abnormality. For instance, Grieve's angle/angle diagrams show that angular movement is reduced in pathological cases but do not indicate whether the restriction is because of inability to carry load or because of contracture or muscle malfunction. Similarly Jacobs et al (1971) in their ground to foot force measurements on patients following hip surgery showed the difference in force between left and right foot, but did not relate this to pain or muscle weakness or involvement of other joints. For a full interpretation of the mechanics of the relevant structures the desirable situation is a combination of displacement, force measurement and EMG recording. Even the very valuable and classical data produced by Rydell (1966) and illustrated in figure 6, using a strain gauged implanted femoral head replacement would have been much more valuable in conjunction with information on the relative angulation between femur and pelvis in three dimensions. Possibly the only exception to this situation relates to pylon force transducer tests of amputee locomotion. If the interest is primarily in the loads transmitted at the socket stump interface, this can usually be inferred with sufficient accuracy from the transducer information, possibly supplemented by a knee goniometer information channel.

The basic problem in all instrumentation systems relates to the required dynamic characteristics. In my view there has not yet been a clear definition of the sampling frequency required for displacement measurement. The studies of Smith (1974), Winter et al (1974), Cappozzo et al (1973) and Gustavsson and Lanshammar (1977) are so much at variance that, in my view, the question of required dynamic characteristics is still open. Similarly, with regard to force measurement, there is little hard information on required dynamic characteristics to reproduce not only the fundamental ground to foot force wave form but any transients occurring at first contact. It would appear useful for someone to investigate a range of normal and pathological cases to determine the desirable recording and digitisation frequency, so that the transients as well as the fundamental characteristics could be established for particular activities conducted at prescribed speeds.

In conclusion, a review of gait analysis indicates that it is very much a developing field and, with the present concentration of interest and scientific expertise, it is hoped that progress will continue to be made and that, in the future, they may look back to the seventies as we now look back to the fifties and the major advances by the Berkeley investigation team.

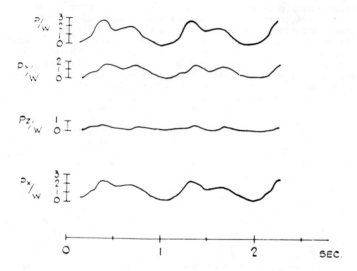

Figure 6   Cyclic variation of resultant hip
joint force P and components Px, Py,
Pz expressed as multiples of body
weight W for a female test subject
walking on the level at a speed of
1.34 m/s from Rydell (1966)

REFERENCES

BASMAJIAN J.W. (1962)
   Muscles Alive, their function revealed by electromyography
   Williams and Wilkins, Baltimore

BAUMANN J.U., and BAUMGARTNER R. (1974)
   Synchronised photo-optical and EMG gait analysis with radiotelemetry
   In Neukomm P.A., Biotelemetry II, Karger, Basel

BERNSTEIN N.A. (1935)
   Issledovania po biodinamike lokomotiij
   Moscow

BRAUNE W., and FISCHER O. (1890)
   Ueber der Schwerpunkt der Menshchen Koerpers
   Abh d Koenigl. Saechs. Gessellsch. d. Wissensch. Bd. 26, 561

CAPPOZZO A., FIGURA F., and MARCHETTI M. (1976)
   The interplay of muscular and external forces in human ambulation
   Journal of Biomechanics, 9, 35-43

CAPPOZZO A., LEO T., and PEDOTTI A. (1973)
   A general computing method for the analysis of human locomotion
   Report R72-12 Istituto di Automatica, Universita di Roma

CARLSOO S. (1972)
   How man moves
   Heinemann (Wm) Limited

CHAO E.Y., OPGRANDE J.D., and AXMEAR F.E. (1976)
   Three dimensional force analysis of finger joints in selected
   isometric hand functions
   Journal of Biomechanics, 9, 387-396

CUNNINGHAM D.M., and BROWN G.W. (1952)
   Two devices for measuring the forces acting on the human body during
   walking
   Proceedings of the Soc. Exp. Stress Analysis IX, 2, 75

DRILLIS R.J. (1958)
   Objective recording and biomechanics of pathological gait
   Annals of the New York Academy of Science, 74, 86

DRILLIS R.J. (1965)
   The use of gliding cyclograms in the biomechanical analysis of
   movements
   Human Factors, 1, 2, 1

EBERHART H.D., INMAN V.T., and SAUNDERS J.B. de C. (1947)
   University of California Berkeley
   Fundamental studies of human locomotion and other information relating
   to design of artificial limbs
   Eberhart H.D., Editor

ELFTMAN H. (1938a)
   The measurement of the external force in walking
   Science 88, 2276, 152

FISCHER O. (1908)
    Theoretische grundlagen fur eine mechanik der lebenden korper
    Leipzig

GANGULI S., and DATTA S.R. (1975)
    Prediction of energy cost from peak heart rate in low extremity
    amputees
    Biomedical Engineering, 10, 52

GRIEVE D.W. (1969)
    A device called the POLGON for the measurement of the orientation of
    parts of the body relative to a fixed external axis
    Journal of Physiology, 201, 70

GUSTAVSSON L., and LANSHAMMAR H. (1977)
    ENOCH - An integrated system for measurement and analysis of human
    gait
    Doctoral Thesis, Institute of Technology, Uppsala University

HARPER F.C., WARLOW W.J., and CLARKE B.L. (1961)
    The forces applied to the floor by the foot in walking
    National Building Studies Research Paper 32, HMSO London

JACOBS N.A., SKORECKI J., and CHARNLEY J. (1971)
    Analysis of the vertical component of force in normal and
    pathological gait
    Journal of Biomechanics, 5, 11-34

JARRETT M.O., ANDREWS B.J., and PAUL J.P. (1976)
    A television computer system for the analysis of human locomotion
    IERE Conference Proceedings, no. 34

JOSPEH J., and BATTYE C.K. (1966)
    An investigation by telemetering of the activity of some muscles in
    walking
    Medical and Biological Engineering, 4, 2, 125

KASVAND T., MILNER M., and RAFLEY L.F. (1971)
    A computer based system for the analysis of some aspects of human
    locomotion
    Institute of Mechanical Engineerins Conference on Human Locomotion
    Engineering, University of Sussex

LINDHOLM L.E. (1974)
    An opteoelectronic instrument for remote on line movement monitoring
    World Congress Montreux

MITCHELSON D. (1974)
    CODA Instrument for 3-D movement recording
    Loughborough University of Technology, England, Report No. 145

MORRIS J.R.W. (1973)
    Accelerometry - a technique for the measurement of human body
    movements
    Journal of Biomechanics, 6, 729-736

MURRAY M.P., KORY R.C., CLARKSON B.H., and SEPIC S.B. (1966)
Comparison of free and fast speed walking patterns of normal men
American Journal of Physical Medicine, 45, 8-24

MUYBRIDGE E. (1882)
The horse in motion as shown by instantaneous photography
London

NUBAR Y., and CONTINI R. (1961)
A minimal principle in biomechanics
Bulletin of Mathematical Biophysics, 23, 377

PEPOE R. (1970)
Manual for automatic film scanner developed at Children's Hospital
in Iowa City, Iowa, USA

RALSTON H.J. (1958)
Energy speed relation and optimal speed during level walking
Internationale Zeitschrift für angewandte Physiologie 17, 277

RALSTON H.J. (1965)
Effects of immobilisation of the knee on energy expenditure during
level walking
Ergonomics Proc. 2nd IEA Congress, Dortmund

RYDELL N.W. (1966)
Forces acting on the femoral head prosthesis
Acta Orthopaedica Scandinavica Supplement 88

SEIREG A., and ARVIKAR R.J. (1975)
The prediction of muscular load sharing and joint forces in the
lower extremities during walking
Journal of Biomechanics, vol. 8, 89-102

SMITH A.J. (1974)
Balance and kinetics of the fingers under normal and pathological
conditions
Clin. Orthop. 104, 92-111

UNIVERSITY OF CALIFORNIA (1953)
The pattern of muscular activity in the lower extremity during walking
Prosthetic Devices Research Report Series II, Issue 25

WINTER D.A. et al (1972)
Television computer analysis of kinematics of human gait
Computer and Biomedical Research, 5, 498-504

WINTER D.A. et al (1974)
Kinematics of normal locomotion - a statistical study based on TV data
Journal of Biomechanics, 7, 479-486

WIRTA R.W. et al (1970)
Laboratory for Kinesiologic Analysis
Bulletin of Prosthetics Research, 10 - 13, 165-172, Spring

MEASUREMENT OF KNEE TORQUE/ANGLE CHARACTERISTICS
DURING THE SWING PHASE OF GAIT

G. JUDGE, B.Sc.(Eng.)

Biomechanical Research and Development Unit,
Roehampton Lane, London SW15 5PR.

INTRODUCTION

During 1976, five in every eight of the 4700 new leg amputees in England, Wales and Northern Ireland were amputated above the knee (Department of Health and Social Security, 1976). Whether or not the lost function was replaced in the artificial legs prescribed for their rehabilitation depended on a clinical assessment of the amputee's ability to cope, both physically and mentally, with a moveable hinge jointed knee; the 64.3% who could not were given knees which remained locked straight unless manually released for sitting. A further 15.4% had knees which were completely free to flex between stops at full extension and maximum flexion; and 20.3% had some form of device at the knee for modifying the swing of the leg during walking.

Walking with a "free" knee tends to produce excessive heel rise just after the beginning of the swing phase and excessive impact on the extension stop at the end of it, more so at faster cadences. Greater control of the lower leg swing and a more natural gait can be achieved by using a suitable knee swing control device, particularly for the more active amputee who needs an effective gait over a range of speeds. Of such devices fitted in 1976, three-quarters used friction to absorb the energy acquired by the shank during swing; another 15% used resistance to the flow of a fluid, mainly air. Pneumatic devices have a potential for energy storage as well, due to the compressibility of air.

It is the eventual aim of the present work to find out what characteristics are required in a knee swing control device so that it shall allow the above-knee amputee to walk with "good" gait at any reasonable speed without conscious control and with minimal energy cost to his body.

MEASUREMENT OF KNEE TORQUE/ANGLE CHARACTERISTICS

Philosophy

It is reasonable to assume that for the active unilateral amputee to have a "good" gait the motion of the amputated leg with its prosthesis shall match that of the sound leg as closely as possible. Indeed, the hypothesis used by all previous workers (Radcliffe, 1957, Moffatt et al, 1966, Wallach, 1966, Maillardet, 1975) is that the required swing control characteristics are those of the natural knee of an adult male non-amputee.

However, it has been shown that loss of the natural foot/ankle action in an amputee generates compensating adaptations during gait by the remaining natural leg segments (Breakey, 1975); and more specifically that the natural ankle is actively extended just before toe-off by the calf group

of muscles, helping to drive the knee forwards into the swing phase - a
function not provided by the passive foot/ankle components of standard
artificial legs (Eberhart et al, 1945).

Therefore, the philosophy of the present work at the Biomechanical Research
and Development Unit (BRADU) is that desirable knee swing control
characteristics for above-knee amputees are best derived from analysis of
the gait of below-knee amputees, as they have a natural neuromuscular knee
control system in combination with an artificial foot and ankle. Further,
because their knee musculature will have been modified by amputation,
selection of below-knee amputees for the work must be made by an experienced
prosthetist in conjunction with a doctor, and confined to those with
subjectively judged "good" gait.

Techniques

Previous Work Elsewhere

In California, Radcliffe (1957) twice differentiated existing displacement
data describing the level gait of four normal adult males wearing shoes.
He then determined the knee swing torque needed to make a prosthetic shank
match the recorded gait kinematics, using measured values of the inertial
properties of an actual above-knee prosthesis and shoe.

At New York (Wallach, 1966) acceleration data had similarly been obtained
by two differentiations of limb displacement data, this time based on
results from sixty normal adult males wearing shoes. He then computed
the force required in a linear-acting control device across the knee of a
typical above-knee prosthesis/shoe combination to give the observed normal
motion patterns. However, in developing his equations from free-body
diagrams he omitted to take account of the linear acceleration of the knee
during swing.

In New Orleans another group (Moffatt et al, 1966) described a two-
accelerometer method requiring an additional measurement; the absolute
angular velocity of the shank. Unfortunately what they actually measured
was the angular velocity of the shank relative to the thigh, not to a
fixed datum.

Recently a worker at Brighton (Maillardet, 1975) has made a analogue
computer model of the leg in the swing phase of locomotion and used it
to find out what hip and knee muscle forces were needed to control the
leg in such a way that its swing pattern lay within the envelope of
published kinematic data relating to normal adult males wearing shoes. He
then did a similar simulation for an above-knee prosthesis. In such
models, compromises are usually unavoidable, the usefulness of the results
depending on the validity of the assumptions. For example, Maillardet's
assumption of zero shank angular velocity at toe-off is not corroborated
either by the early Californian work (Eberhart et al, 1945) or by recent
BRADU recordings. In fact the shank is still rotating backwards at toe-
off: in non-amputees it may go a further five degrees or so; in below-
knee amputees, ten to fifteen degrees; and in above-knee amputees it may
rotate up to twenty degrees before it begins to swing forward again.

The BRADU Three-Accelerometer Technique

For the BRADU work with below-knee amputees, therefore, techniques were
sought which permitted direct measurement of the knee torque/angle
characteristics of the affected limb while walking, without significant
disturbance of the gait and without modification of the prosthesis. In
fact both measurements were readily accomplished: Knee angle, by means
of a polarised light goniometer system, one receiver being mounted on
each thigh and shank, with the projector pushed by an assistant on a
trolley parallel to and 2.8m from the 13.5m x 1.24m walkway; and knee
torque, by a new three-accelerometer technique whose theoretical basis
has been described elsewhere (Judge, 1976).

Figure 1 summarises the technique: each of the three accelerometers is
applied so that its sensitive axis is perpendicular to the KC line by
means of a special alignment frame (figure 2), graduated to allow direct
readout of the co-ordinates of each accelerometer's seismic mass (h_1, h_2,
d_1, d_2, x). The inertial properties (mass, centre of mass position,
moment of inertia about the knee axis) of the stump are estimated from
stump measurements, assuming it to be a right conic frustum of specific
gravity 1.1; and corresponding values for the prosthesis/sock/shoe
assembly are obtained by simple measurements of weight, distance and
period. Totalling these two sets of data gives values for m, r, k^2: hence
the values of the three constants A, B, C can be computed and set up on
the analogue computer as indicated in figure 1.

At each accelerometer mounting site a piece of double-sided adhesive tape
is stuck to the prosthesis and a blob of a thick mix of plaster of paris
is applied. Then, using the alignment frame a dummy accelerometer is
pushed into the plaster to form, when set, a shallow "seat". These form
accurate locations for the three accelerometers (A1, A2, A3 in figure 3)
when they are fitted and taped to the prosthesis after it has been donned
by the amputee. Figure 3 also shows two of the four polarised light
goniometer receivers (P1, P2), applied with double-sided tape.

EXPERIMENTAL WORK AND RESULTS

An experiment in which a specially built below-knee prosthesis, strain-
gauged to measure knee-swing torque directly, was additionally instrumented
for the BRADU three-accelerometer technique,has been done to validate the
accelerometric method against direct measurement. The prosthesis was used
by an amputee during fast, slow and normal level walking. In all cases
excellent agreement was obtained throughout the swing phase except during
a decaying oscillation in the accelerometric record, initiated at toe-off.
The cause is believed to be oscillation of the foot following its rapid
unloading at the end of the stance phase. Results for normal level walking
are plotted together on figure 4.

One problem is the definition of the knee axis K. The natural knee has no
fixed axis, so the position of K can only be estimated. Work has therefore
been done with the three-accelerometer technique applied to a pendulum rig,
swung by a shaft strain-gauged to measure the applied torque. This has
shown that if the accelerometers are set up, and measurements made, with

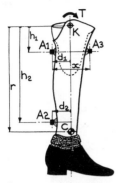

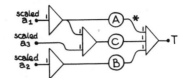

$T = Aa_1 + Ba_2 + C(a_3 - a_1)$
where
$A = m(rh_2 - k^2)/(h_2 - h_1)$
$B = m(k^2 - rh_1)/(h_2 - h_1)$
$C = (Ad_1 + Bd_2)/x$
and
a_1, a_2, a_3 are the linear accelerations recorded by accelerometers A_1, A_2, and A_3 respectively;

Point K is the approximate centre of knee rotation.
Point C is the centre of mass of the whole shank assembly; stump + prosthesis + sock + shoe.

k is the radius of gyration of the shank assembly about the knee axis;
m is the mass of the shank assembly.
(❋ extra inverter here if A is negative).

Figure 1   The BRADU three-accelerometer technique

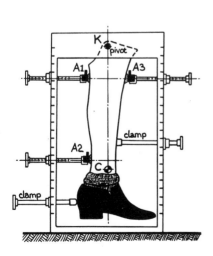

Figure 2   Accelerometer alignment frame

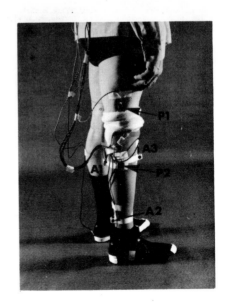

Figure 3   Below-knee amputee instrumented for knee swing torque/angle measurement

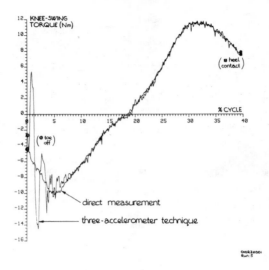

EXPERIMENTAL BELOW-KNEE PROSTHESIS: VALIDATION OF THE
BRADU THREE-ACCELEROMETER TECHNIQUE

Figure 4   Three-accelerometer technique compared to
direct measurement of knee swing torque

KNEE-SWING TORQUE/ANGLE CHARACTERISTICS FOR A
UNILATERAL BELOW-KNEE AMPUTEE

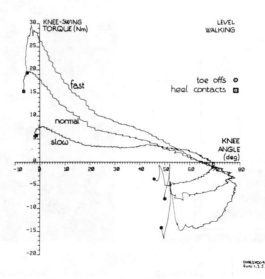

Figure 5   Knee swing characteristics for a
unilateral below-knee amputee

respect to an axis 15mm away from the true centre of rotation, an error of up to 5% may be introduced, depending on the direction of the discrepancy.

Having thus proved the technique, it has recently been applied to the unmodified prostheses of six male below-knee amputees aged between thirty and sixty-one years in order to obtain their knee swing torque/angle characteristics. Results for one of them at three walking speeds are plotted as figure 5. Maximum torque values achieved by this group were:

     23.5Nm resisting knee flexion
     35.0Nm resisting knee extension

It is hoped to extend the work to include some female subjects and to apply the technique to "good-gait" above-knee amputees fitted with a commercial swing control device; and eventually to predict the desirable characteristics for a specific above-knee prosthesis, make a device to provide them, and test the quality of the resulting gait. The gait pattern information built up by these experiments should also allow some form of definition of what is "good" gait for an amputee.

CONCLUSIONS

The knee swing torque/angle characteristics of six below-knee amputees have been obtained for a range of walking speeds using polarised light goniometry and the BRADU three-accelerometer technique of knee swing torque measurement.

ACKNOWLEDGEMENTS

The contribution of colleagues at BRADU, Roehampton in terms of ideas, assistance, construction, and provision of services is gratefully acknowledged, as is the willing co-operation of the amputee test subjects.

REFERENCES

BREAKEY J.W. (1975)
    Gait of unilateral below-knee amputees - a kinesiologic and
    electromyographic study
    Ph.D. Thesis, Queen's University, Ontario, Canada

DEPARTMENT OF HEALTH AND SOCIAL SECURITY 1976
    Amputation Statistics for England, Wales and Northern Ireland
    DHSS Statistics and Research Division, Blackpool

EBERHART H.D., et al (1945)
    Fundamental studies of human locomotion
    University of California, Berkeley, Prosthetic Devices Research
    Project, Final Report

JUDGE G. (1976)
    Measurement of knee torque during the swing phase of gait
    Engineering in Medicine, $\underline{4}$, 3, pp. 13-17

MAILLARDET F.J. (1975)
   The swing phase of locomotion
   Ph.D. Thesis, Brighton Polytechnic, Brighton, Sussex

MOFFATT C.A., HARRIS E.H., and HASLAM E.T. (1966)
   An experimental determination of prosthetic knee moment for normal
   gait
   American Society of Mechanical Engineers, paper no. 66-WA/BHF-8

RADCLIFFE C.W. (1957)
   Biomechanical design of an improved leg prosthesis
   University of California, Berkeley, Institute of Engineering Research,
   Report Series II, Issue 33

WALLACH J. (1966)
   Control mechanism performance criteria for an above-knee leg
   prosthesis
   Ph.D. Thesis, Rensselaer Polytechnic Institute, Troy, New York

CALCULATION OF THE LOADS TRANSMITTED BY THE JOINTS OF THE BODY

N. BERME, B.Sc., M.Sc., Ph.D.

Bioengineering Unit, University of Strathclyde,
Glasgow, Scotland.

INTRODUCTION

The joints which provide the body with the desired range of movement also transmit loads from one segment to the other. The tensile components of the loading are mainly transmitted by the tendinous and ligamentous structures, while the compressive components are taken by the articulating surfaces. A knowledge of these forces is relevant in developing means of treatment for various categories of patients. One of the major areas which benefit from this information is joint replacement surgery. Loading values are utilised in establishing endoprostheses design parameters, and surgical techniques. Joint force analyses carried out on patients who already have undergone surgery yield additional information regarding design criteria and fixation and also add to the very limited data bank of information on the loading patterns developed during activity. This information eventually could be utilised as a clinical tool for assessing the progress of the patients. The design of other orthopaedic implants such as fixation plates, nails etc., is also facilitated by the knowledge of the joint loading patterns. If the loads transmitted by two adjacent points are known then the load distribution in the segment between the joints can be calculated. Thus, information relating to the requirement of implants can be obtained. Yet another area where the calculated joint loading values can be used for the benefit of the patient is orthotics. Loads transmitted by the relevant joints help to study the function and effects of orthoses and facilitate design improvements.

This paper discusses the various techniques involved in assessing the loads transmitted by the joints of the body, and illustrates some of these concepts with an analysis of the forces in the metacarpophalangeal joint of the index finger.

RESULTANT LOADING AT THE JOINTS

Determination of the resultant loading at a given cross-section of the body is a straightforward calculation provided that the external loading on the body segments and their spatial configurations are known. In the analysis the segments distal to the cross section are treated as parts of a free body. The loading on the free body consists of the loads transmitted between the environment and the body, the inertia forces and moments, and the resultant loading at the cross section. The loads transmitted to the body from the environment are measured by utilising appropriate load transducers. A suitable kinematic recording system such as ciné cameras is used to collect information on the spatial configuration of the body segments with time. Anatomical landmarks where skin movements are minimal are highlighted using markers attached to the body. The positions of the relevant joints and centres of gravity which are predetermined relative to these landmarks are then readily calculated during activity. Linear acceleration and angular velocity and acceleration components of the segments are determined from this information.

Kinematic data are then combined with the body segment parameters to establish the inertia loads on the free body. Then the equilibrium equations are solved for the resultant force and moment acting at the cross section.

JOINT LOADS

Determination of how the resultant load is shared by the various structures of a joint is a more difficult task. The main difficulty arises from the fact that the number of structures that transmit the load is usually far greater than the number of available equilibrium equations. Thus, the problem is indeterminate. In various other applications of mechanics indeterminate problems are solved by making use of the stress strain relationships. The load displacement information relating to the structures involved are either included in the analysis or experimental methods of determining the unknowns are used. Both of these techniques have very severe limitations in in vivo applications. However, reference should be made to Rydell (1966) who employed instrumented hip prostheses to obtain joint loading information from two patients. No such reports are yet available from other centres involved in instrumenting endoprostheses. Although these tests provide very valuable information, it is unfortunate that they only relate to patients who have undergone major surgery.

There have also been attempts of using optimisation techniques to infer joint forces. Minimisation of a weighed sum of all the lower limb muscle forces and the residual unbalanced moments at all the joints have been carried out by Seireg and Arvikar (1975). However, justification for such a minimisation criteria is still debatable.

The generally accepted methods of calculating the joint forces only make use of the anatomical and physiological constraint conditions together with the equilibrium equations. The constraint conditions applicable to all joints include that the tendinous and ligamentous structures only transmit tensile loads, compression is carried by the articulating surfaces, and electromyographic data give an indication of activity in the respective muscles. The different techniques used by various researchers mainly vary on the method of applying these conditions to the equilibrium equations. At one extreme all unknowns are included in the equilibrium equations. A number of tendon forces are then assumed zero to make the system determinate and the equations are solved. This is repeated for all possible combinations of the unknowns, and the values for the joint forces are obtained after discarding the inadmissible solutions (Chao et al, 1976). At the other extreme first the primary functions of all the structures are identified and the equations are simplified as much as possible before they are solved (Paul, 1967). A combination of these two techniques can be successfully applied to solve many of the joint loading problems.

Regardless of the method employed an additional difficulty is in establishing the lines of action for forces in many of the structures involved. This is due to the generally large origin and insertion areas of these structures and the variations in their relative orientations during activity. In some of the structures such as the collateral ligaments of the knee, the problem is not very severe and it is possible to infer the line of action of the force with reasonable accuracy. However, in most short muscles this is not the case, and one is left with the option of investigating the effects of this

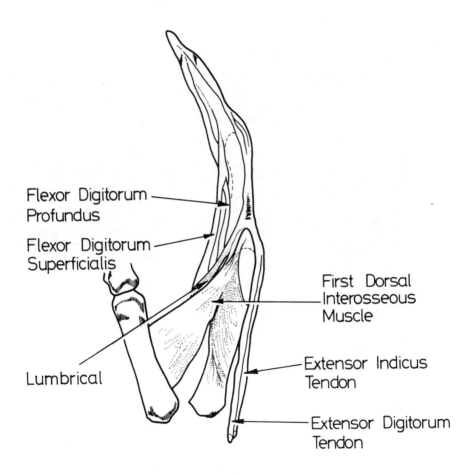

Figure 1   A lateral view of the index finger
showing the anatomy

uncertainty on the magnitude of the loading in the remaining structures.
The line of action of the compression force acting on the articulating
surface is much easier to determine. As the coefficient of friction on
the joint surface is negligibly small, the joint force can be taken acting
normal to the surface.

THE METACARPOPHALANGEAL JOINT

One of the least complicated joints of the body to illustrate some of the
above concepts is the metacarpophalangeal joint of the index finger. The
joint surfaces are ellipsoid and are capable of transmitting all three
components of the compressive loading. The tensile forces are shared by
the two extensor and two flexor tendons, a lumbrical muscle, the first
dorsal interosseous and the second palmar interosseous muscles, and the
two collateral ligaments. Thus, the total number of unknowns are twelve.
However, it is seen from figure 1 that some of these elements can be
combined in groups of two to simplify the problem. These are the two
extensors and the two flexors, and the lumbrical which can be considered
together with the dorsal interosseous. This way the number of unknowns to
carry the tensile loading are reduced to six. These are shown in figure 2.
The joint capsule can be assumed not to be transmitting any load. This
way the joint force calculated will be the lowest possible in any situation,
For example, in hyperextension the capsule will be transmitting some load,
but it can be assumed that the flexor tendon is the only relevant structure.
Since the effective radius of the tendon from the joint centre is greater
than that of the capsule the lower value of joint force will be obtained.

During activity one of the main components of the external loading on the
finger is the flexion/extension moment about the z axis (figure 2). When
extensor activity is required the magnitude of the force is determined
directly. However, if flexor activity is required, then there are three
load sharing elements, and it would be impossible to determine how tension
is distributed among the flexor and the interossei simply from the z
moment balance equation. In this example it is possible to consider the z
moment balance equation about an adjacent joint, the proximal interphalangeal joint, to determine the magnitude of the flexor force. The
interossei together with the ligaments also contribute to the abduction/
adduction and rotation moments (x and y moments respectively). The
solution of these two moment equations therefore involves four unknowns.
Here the combination principle of assigning zero values to two of the
unknowns and solving the remaining two can be utilised. The contribution
of the interossei force to the flexion moment must then be added to the
contribution of the flexor itself and compared with the external z moment.
Any unbalance must be taken by the extensor activity or simultaneous
activities of the interossei depending on its sign. If extensor activity
is required its value and the value of the modified flexor force can be
determined by the simultaneous solution of the flexion/extension moment
equations about the metacarpophalangeal and the interphalangeal joints.
Once the loads transmitted by the tensile elements are determined, then the
force balance equations can be solved to calculate the joint force
(Berme et al, 1977).

As illustrated above during an analysis it is usually necessary to go back
and reassess the values of some of the forces on the basis of more recent
findings. Sometimes several iterations are necessary before the results

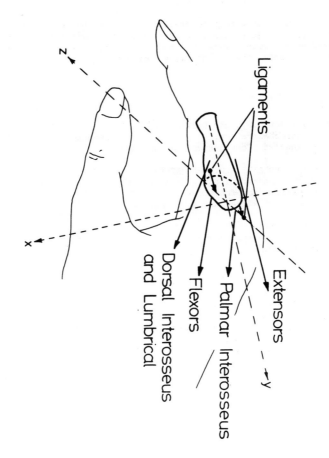

Figure 2   The main load bearing elements of
the metacarpophalangeal joint

Ligaments

Extensors

Palmar Interosseus

Flexors

Dorsal Interosseus
and Lumbrical

x

y

z

converge. It is also possible to find that the solution to the problem is not unique and the external loads can be transmitted by several different combinations of muscle and joint forces. Thus, for each component a range for the force is calculated rather than a single value.

Another limitation of these calculations is that usually antagonistic muscle activity can not be determined, as opposing muscles can be active without influencing the external loading.

In interpreting the results of joint analyses the philosophy of the calculations must always be considered. The joint forces should never be viewed as absolute values, but accepted within the range of uncertainty that accompanies the respective assumptions.

REFERENCES

BERME N., PAUL J.P., and PURVES W.K. (1977)
    A biomechanical analysis of the metacarpophalangeal joint
    Journal of Biomechanics, 10, pp. 409-412

CHAO E.Y., OPGRANDE J.D., and AXMEAR F.E. (1976)
    Three dimensional force analysis of finger joints in selected
    isometric hand functions
    Journal of Biomechanics, 9, pp. 387-396

PAUL J.P. (1967)
    Forces transmitted by joints in the human body
    Proceedings of the Institute of Mechanical Engineering, 181, pp. 8-15

RYDELL N.W. (1966)
    Forces acting on the femoral head prosthesis
    Acta Orthopaedica Scandinavica, Supplement 88

SEIREG A., and ARVIKAR R.J. (1975)
    The prediction of muscular load sharing and joint forces in the lower
    extremities during walking
    Journal of Biomechanics, 8, pp. 89-102

OBJECTIVE ASSESSMENT OF LOCOMOTOR FUNCTION IN THE LOWER LIMB

D.W. GRIEVE, M.Sc., Ph.D.

Biomechanics Laboratory, Royal Free Hospital School of Medicine, London

Knowledge of a patient's body movements is only part of the information relevant to routine clinical practice. Semi-quantitative information may be generated by clinicians through muscle testing, measurement of joint ranges and by ADL rating. These assessments are not clearly related to each other, certainly not in severe disability.

Measurements are only resorted to if they can be done quickly and cheaply, although the demand for objective evidence of a patient's physical status, and change of it, exists. Satisfactory and defective locomotor performance is today assessed in a traditional subjective manner by clinicians who are essentially acting alone and relying upon their own remembered experience, At the same time, much effort is devoted to the development of devices with which the clinical team would be able to record selected features of locomotor performance. Bringing clinicians and devices together for routine clinical application is most likely to succeed if the marriage develops from existing clinical experience. Since the experience relies upon visible movements, movement analysis should be developed in preference to other techniques which deal with invisible phenomena whose place is more appropriate to research. Although a wide range of devices exist for movement analysis, immediacy and economy in routine work dictates a current choice of electro-goniometry and polarised light goniometry, the latter being more flexible than the former.

Many clinics will possess movement recorders in the immediate future and it is appropriate to consider what may be expected from their use. I anticipate that we will recognise that the patient's movements contain information which can not only supplement but supplant the formal tests of muscles and joints and; if a suitable locomotor task is chosen, the patterns obtained will be indicative of basic abilities in domestic and working environments.

Progress will be slow if the clinicians remain isolated from each other; if communication is to be fruitful some standardisation of approach is necessary together with effective means of presenting the data. The angle diagram is finding favour as a means of presentation, which emphasises the coordinates between (usually adjacent) parts of the body and yields shapes which are useful for examination and discussion. The relationships between the analytical approach to the shapes and the subjective impressions of directly observed movement deserves investigation. Only a few types of angle diagrams have been explored so far. Exchange of information between groups or with a data bank may or may not be best achieved by transmission of the angle diagrams themselves and must obviously be accompanied by other information.

At an international level (figure 1), the need for exchange and collation of locomotor data is recognised. Proposals for an international data bank for gait (IDBG) were put to Congresses of International Society of Biomechanics in 1973 and, in more detail, in 1975. Personnel from 60 Institutes expressed an active interest and, if funding can be found, the opportunity exists to develop a data exchange scheme concerning normal and pathological movements which cannot be provided by the normal channels of publications.

Standardisation is as important in assessment through movement analysis as it is in muscle testing or electrocardiography. We tend to think that movement analysis and analysis of walking gaits are synonymous in clinical work but it is worth asking whether walking is the most suitable task for

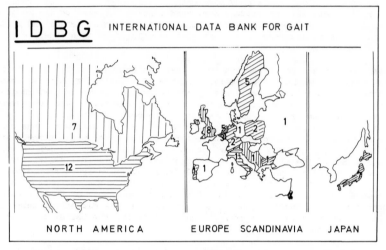

Figure 1   Geographical distribution of those
            interested in an International
            Data Bank for Gait

assessment. The mobile patient is one who can get in and out of a chair, walk and negotiate stairs and obstacles. Rather than assess each separately it is possible that a test based upon one familiar activity (figure 2) would yield as much information as a battery of tests.

Sit-stand movements are easily standardised and may be graded in difficulty by choosing the seat height. Space requirements are minimal. However, the angle diagrams from the lower limb have little information content because the movements are largely dictated by anthropometric dimensions, relatively few components of the locomotor system are required, left-right assymetries do not greatly affect them and sit-stand ability is not predictive of other abilities.

Walking movements have the benefit of much research effort. The angle diagrams are rich in information because many components of the neuromuscular and articular systems are necessary and the movements are sensitive to left-right assymetry. Unfortunately, walking cannot readily be standardised or graded in difficulty without interfering with the patient's free choice of solution and the space requirement and walk away facility is often not available.

Stepping movements have received little attention. They require minimal space and are highly suitable activities for monitoring with the Medelec Polgon. The movements are sensitive to left-right assymetry and require function of many components of the locomotor system. The tasks are readily standardised and graded in difficulty. The ability to negotiate a step is probably predictive of the abilities to walk and sit-stand whereas the converse is not true.

There are eight ways in which a person may employ a limb when mounting or dismounting a box. The limb may be leading or trailing and the movement may be upwards or downwards and forwards or backwards. The eight movements (illustrated by strobe flash photographs on left of figure 3) divide into four conjugate pairs of movements. Each conjugate pair has associated thigh-knee angle diagrams of similar shape but generated in opposite directions. Although normal performance involves similar sets of postures, the similarities must reflect normal locomotor function since anti-gravity, flexor and backward movements (for example) in one movement are gravity-assisted, extensor and forward movements in the conjugate manoeuvre. The set of stepping manoeuvres are a rich source of within-subject comparisons by which normality, or departure from it may be judged and possibly rich enough to have differential sensitivity to a range of pathologies. It is suggested that stepping movements merit consideration as a suitable single set of tests for purposes of routine assessment.

Let us suppose that standardisation was achieved between clinics and data was transmitted to a data bank together with clinical assessment and value judgement concerning each patient. Typical movement patterns associated with particular pathologies would begin to emerge and the central bank would become the means of benefiting objectively from the collective experience. Such a development depends upon research in a new area. Most research effort into movement analysis has been devoted to devices and descriptions of normal movement and these studies have outstripped the use that can be made of them. Norms for stepping activities are now available from which numerous comparisons of conjugate movements may be made. It is salutary to remember that norms of walking movements, intended for clinical use, were published about twenty years ago and we still have little idea how to attach importance to departures from the normal patterns.

LOWER LIMB ACTIVITIES ESSENTIAL FOR MOBILITY:	1 SIT-STAND	2 WALK	3 UP/DOWN STEPS
ECONOMY OF PREDICTION			
Does ability in one imply ability in the others ?		?	✓ 1&2
TESTING WITH MEAS^T			
• Can task be standardised	✓		✓
• Graded in difficulty ?	✓		✓
• Done quickly ?	✓	✓	✓
• In limited space ?	✓		✓
SENSITIVITY OF MOV^TS			
• To several components of musculo-skel^tl system		✓	✓
• Spatially to dysfunction		✓	✓
• Temporally " "	✓	✓	✓
• To L/R assymmetry		✓	✓

Figure 2 Some relative merits of using three common locomotor tasks for assessment purposes

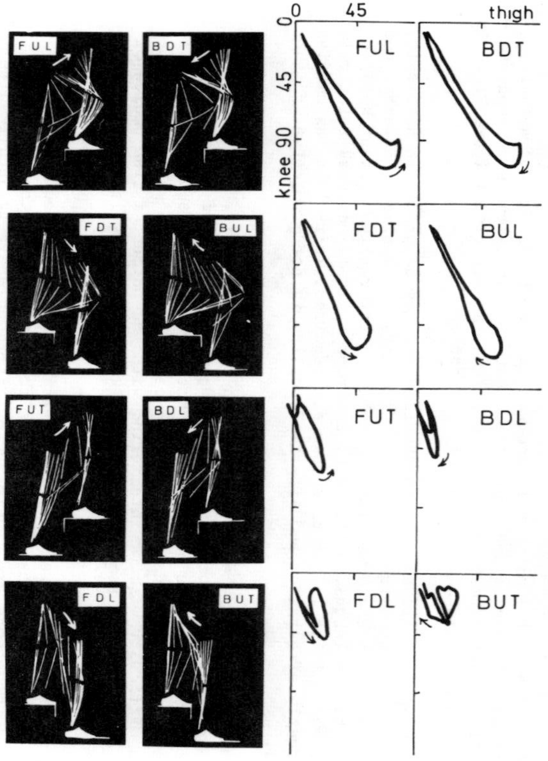

Figure 3 Left: Strobe-flash photographs of thigh and shank in stepping movements (one subject). Right: Corresponding thigh-knee-diagrams of the same stepping movements (another subject). F,B,U,D, L,T in titles refer to Forward, Backward, Upwards, Downwards, leading limb and trailing limb

Our research effort should therefore concentrate on how to associate value judgements with records of movement. The answers presumably lie in techniques of pattern recognition and, to a lesser extent in improvement in our biomechanical knowledge of locomotion. Conventional pattern recognition does not improve its discriminatory power when more than about ten parameters are used. A set of stepping movements generates at least forty parameters and we must find how to pick our way through data of that complexity before simpler and acceptable tests emerge. Secondly, data for 200 patients in one category is by no means excessive for purposes of reliably distinguishing one set of patterns from another. Data in this quantity can only come from collaborative effort and the use of international data banks.

THE CLINICAL ASSESSMENT OF GAIT USING THE POLARISED LIGHT GONIOMETER

D.L. MITCHELSON, M.Sc.

Department of Human Sciences, University of Technology, Loughborough

Diseases which cause impairment of motor function often involve long periods of rehabilitation in which the skills of clinicians, therapists and biomedical engineers are required. All of these people are concerned to help patients achieve recovery to a functional state which is as close as possible to the normal condition they enjoyed before the illness. Where this is not possible, the aim is to assist the patient in making the best use of a more limited set of abilities, both with orthotic or prosthetic devices designed by the engineers and by therapy and by training provided by medical rehabilitation staff.

Although the clinicans and the engineers are concerned to achieve a similar end result, the exercise of their respective skills demands very different sorts of information about the patient. The engineer engaged in prosthetic design wants highly detailed information about forces, torques, and articulation in joints. To obtain this information he is prepared to undertake research which involves much tedious and time consuming measurement and analysis. Correspondingly, the benefit from this work is often applicable to comparatively large numbers of patients.

The clinician, on the other hand, must treat many individual patients on a day to day basis. He requires information which will help him in the following areas:-

a) To assess and to predict the rate of recovery of motor function.

b) To quantify the effect of different forms of treatment on functional capacity.

c) To form better understanding of individual patients functional pathology in order to choose the most suitable forms of treatment or motor skill therapy.

d) To give feedback to the patient which will help him to re-learn lost motor skills or acquire new ones more quickly and efficiently.

Clinical assessment of movement function in gait or any other activity is mostly done by subjective observation on the part of clinical staff. This recognises that the appearance of the patient's patterns of movement are what he and other people rely on to form judgements about how much he departs from the 'normal'. For clinical purposes, however, observation on its own suffers from the problems of validity, repeatability and accuracy inherent in any subjective technique. Instrumented forms of recording which give an objective record of movement function can overcome these difficulties and provide the information which clinicians need, but they must be quick and easy to use and interpret. Also, where possible, they should attempt to quantify aspects of the movement which clinicians and patients alike have tried to assess by direct observation.

These considerations imply that:

a) the number of parameters of movement which are measured should be the minimum necessary, and

b) they should be displayed in a form which facilitates rapid appreciation of both minor and major changes in the pattern of movement and how it differs from normal.

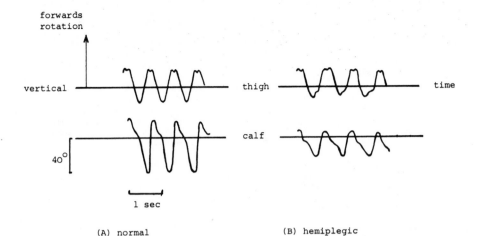

forwards
rotation

vertical   thigh   time

calf

40°

1 sec

(A) normal   (B) hemiplegic

Figure 1   Thigh and calf angles with respect to the vertical
            plotted against time for the right leg in
            (A) normal gait at 1.3 M.S.$^{-1}$ (3 m.p.h.)
            (B) hemiplegic gait

each division = 10 degrees

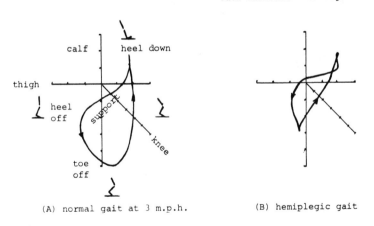

calf   heel down

thigh

heel
off

support

knee

toe
off

(A) normal gait at 3 m.p.h.   (B) hemiplegic gait

Figure 2   Data from the same gait records as figure 1 but
            with calf angle plotted against thigh angle for
            the normal and hemiplegic gaits

For gait assessment, measurement of thigh and calf angles and their display in the form of angle-angle diagrams appear to satisfy these criteria well. Figure 1(A) shows thigh angle and calf angle plotted against time for the right leg of a normal healthy subject walking at 1.3 M.S^{-1} (3 m.p.h.). Figure 2(A) shows the same angles plotted against each other for one gait cycle. The stick figures indicate the actual thigh and calf angles at various stages through the gait cycle. The knee angle at any point in the gait cycle is the difference between thigh and calf angles. For the right leg, increasing knee flexion is indicated by the diagonal axes which progress away from the origin towards the bottom right of the graph.

Figures 1(B) and 2(B) show data recorded from the affected leg of an elderly patient with hemiplegia following a stroke. From a comparison of the angle vs. time records of figure 1 the only difference which is readily seen is the reduction in angular range for the thigh movements of the hemiplegic. The angle vs. angle graphs of figure 2 not only show the difference in angle but also an interesting and dramatic difference in phasing following toe off. It is clear from Figure 2(B) that the thigh lags behind the calf in moving forward at the start of the swing phase compared to the normal pattern of Figure 2(A). The result is a sharp discontinuity at this point in the hemiplegic gait. Whilst the phase information is present in both the angle vs time and angle vs angle graphs, it is clearly much easier to perceive in the latter.

Functional pathologies of the locomotor apparatus appear to affect gait in one or all of three important ways: as changes in angular range, as changes in phasing of limb segment movements or as changes in speed of movement. Angle vs. angle graphs are undoubtedly the most helpful way to display information about range and phasing, but they do so at the expense of temporal information. One way of displaying speed of movement which is complementary to the angle vs. angle graph is the angular velocity vs angle graph. This allows the velocity of limb segment movement to be seen at each point in its angular range. Alternatively, the angular velocity of a joint such as the knee may be plotted against the angular position of a segment such as the thigh throughout the gait cycle as in Figure 3(A).

The Polarised Light Goniometer is well suited for these measurements in the clinical situation. The instrument manufactured by Crane Electronics Limited is based on the author's design and provides facilities for recording up to four limb segment angles with respect to vertical, or three joint angles and the corresponding angular velocities. Experience in recording gait patterns of some 120 orthopaedic patients at Harlow Wood Orthopaedic Hospital and hemiplegic stroke patients at Charing Cross and Northwick Park Hospitals has shown that the instrument enables gait records to be obtained quickly and easily, and with little or no discomfort to patients. The time required for each patient varies from five to ten minutes depending on the severity of the patient's condition. Angle vs. angle graphs are normally produced by an X-Y pen recorder concurrently with the gait movements, and they are available for immediate inspection by staff and patients. Often this means that aspects of some abnormal feature of the gait pattern can be identified and the patient helped to understand how he departs from normal. In some cases this has enabled therapists to select what may be most appropriate instructions and training exercises for patients. Figure 3 illustrates how recovery of gait function can be monitored over a period of months in orthopaedic patients. Figure 3(A) shows a series of records of a rheumatoid arthritic. Each record has right and left leg angle vs angle graphs. The sense of angular movement for the left leg is opposite to that of the right leg, since the

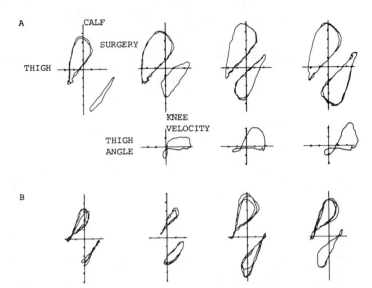

FIGURE 3   (A) The four records at top show right and left leg angle diagrams for an elderly rheumatoid arthritic man. The first record, taken before knee joint replacement surgery, shows 40 degrees of fixed flexion of the right knee. The three post-operative records indicate improvement towards a normal pattern. Knee angular velocity vs thigh angle graphs also show increase in speed of movement over the two month post-operative period.

(B) A similar series for an elderly rheumatoid woman showing gradual improvement during a two month period of conservative treatment as an in-patient.

All of these records were plotted concurrently with the gait.

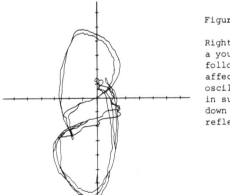

Figure 4

Right and left leg records for a young female patient following a mild stroke. The affected right leg shows oscillation of knee and ankle in support phase after heel down due to hyperactive reflexes.

patient walks in the opposite direction acorss the field of view of the
polarised light projector. The graphs for the left leg are thus reversed
about both the horizontal and vertical axes compared to the right leg.
In practice, this is a useful circumstance because it allows the symmetry
of range and phase to be directly compared on the same graph. The first
record of Fig. 3(A) shows the patient's gait prior to surgery in which he
was given a Freeman knee arthroplasty in his right knee. The right leg
record is compressed almost to a straight line at forty five degrees to the
axis and displaced from the origin by an amount equivalent to forty degrees
of fixed knee flexion. The three post operative records show that the
extreme fixed flexion disappears immediately following surgery and the range
and phasing of movement gradually improves towards the normal pattern over
a period of two months. Post operative knee angle velocity vs. thigh angle
records of Figure 3(A) show a progressive increase in knee angle velocity
for the right leg.

    This set of records is typical of data from a one year series in
which   knee arthroplasty patients who undergo surgery at Harlow Wood
Orthopaedic Hospital are having their gait monitored before and during
the months following surgery. Rate and extent of recovery, as well as other
features of gait will be related to severity of the initial disability and
to the type of arthroplasty used.

    Figure 3(B) shows a series of records of an elderly female patient
with generalised rheumatoid arthritis. The first three records were taken
over a two month period during which she was receiving in-patient treatment.
No surgery was carried out. The treatment consisted of a conservative
regime of bed rest, physiotherapy and anti-inflammatory drugs (ACTH).
The first record taken shortly after admission shows severe limitation of
both thigh and calf range of movement, in particular the knee joint range
in both legs is limited to less than twenty degrees. The next two records
show the increase in angular ranges and the increased openness of the trace
indicating an improvement towards a more normal phasing of thigh and calf
angles and the corollary increase in dynamic range of knee joint movement
throughout the gait cycle. The last trace was obtained one month after the
patient was discharged from hospital. It can be seen that after living
alone at home for this period the range of movement has slightly deteriorated.

    The pattern of hemiplegic gait seen in Figure 2(B) is typical of about
30% of the stroke patients recorded in our Northwick Park and Charing Cross
studies. Since the discontinuity feature arises from a delay in hip flexion
following toe-off, it seems reasonable to hypothesise that hip extensor
muscles may be active at this point in sympathetic (though abnormal) co-
contraction of the homonymous hip extensors of the contralateral good leg.
This possibility is currently being examined by the author and others in
studies linking EMG and Goniometer measurements on normal and hemiplegic
patients.

    Figure 4 shows a gait pattern not uncommon in patients with very mild
hemiplegia after a slight stroke. The overall range and phasing of thigh
and calf movements are quite normal. The one peculiarity in the pattern is
an oscillation of knee angle which ranges in amplitude from five to ten
degrees and occurs in the support phase following heel down. It appears
that either the transient force which is transmitted up the leg at the moment
of heel contact, or the imposition of gravity induced stretch of knee extensors
as the limb takes the body load triggers a fast alternating sequence of knee

extension and flexion. It is known clinically that these patients often show an apparently lower threshold for reflex activity whether elicited by passive muscle stretch or cutaneous stimulation.

This paper has tried to illustrate that in addition to the research engineering applications of the Polarised Light Goniometer, the instrument is well suited to a variety of clinical purposes. Apart from the direct clinical benefits of using an objective instrumented movement recording technique which were listed at the beginning of this paper, there is another benefit. That is, once clinical records have been taken they can also be used by researchers for retrospective or longitudinal studies of movement function and treatment methods in various categories of patients.

Results of such research may then help to raise our general under-standing of the nature of various functional pathologies of movement and lead to improved forms of treatment for chronic motor dis-abilities which may promote more rapid and cost - effective rehabilitation.

Acknowledgements

Some of the clinical trials reported in this paper were conducted in hospitals associated with the Ridgeway Group. The Ridgeway Group is an informal association of British centres concerned with developing multi-disciplinary approach to problems of stroke rehabilitation.

This work has been funded by M.R.C. grant G. 975/122/N.

THE CALCULATION OF THREE-DIMENSIONAL POSITIONS
FROM OPTICAL DATA

L.J. HUNTINGTON, B.A., and B.R. TIETJENS, M.B.Ch.B., F.R.C.S.(Ed.)

Oxford Orthopaedic Engineering Centre,
Nuffield Orthopaedic Centre, Oxford.

This paper describes a photographic method of obtaining the three-
dimensional positions of markers placed on a subject. These results are
then utilised to give a description of the kinematics of the knee joint.

In the study the body segments are assumed to be rigid and to be adequately
described by markers placed on the surface. It is thus the positions of
these markers that are determined by the method.

The principles of vector algebra are employed. In particular, if two known
line vectors intersect, their point of intersection can be found. The case
of two known, non-parallel vectors, AF and BG on figure 1, which do not
intersect is considered. The distance between them is a minimum when the
line joining them is perpendicaular to both; this is the line RQ on the
diagram. It is possible to calculate the position of points R and Q, the
position vector of the normal, RQ, and its length.

The principles are used to make three-dimensional measurements of the
markers using ciné cameras. Points A and B are given by the co-ordinates of
the camera lenses relative to some fixed origin. Directions AF and BG are
the directions of the marker from the cameras given by the position of its
image on each film.

Owing to experimental error, the line vectors from the two cameras do not
necessarily intersect. If this be the case the mid point of the normal, P,
is taken to be the position of the marker. The length of the normal, RQ, is
a measure of the error in this position.

This method has two main advantages; first, the error is divided between all
three co-ordinates. Secondly, there is no longer an advantage in having
orthogonal cameras in order to simplify the calculations.

The lack of restriction in camera positioning is very useful. For example,
the marker positions for a study of knee joint stability during walking is
shown in figure 2. For these markers to be in the view of both cameras
during several walking steps, the cameras are placed with their optical
axes at an angle of 45°. Even with this arrangement the oblique camera
does not see the markers on the medial side of the leg and so a third
camera is needed, or alternatively, a mirror, which is the system we use
(see figure 3).

The marker positions were chosen to define:

1. A set of three orthogonal axes in the femur.

2. The position of the tibia.

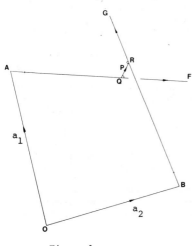

Figure 1

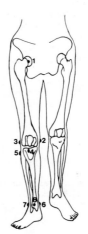

Figure 2

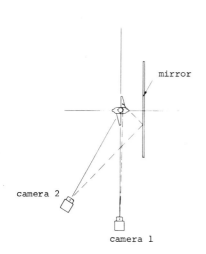

Figure 3

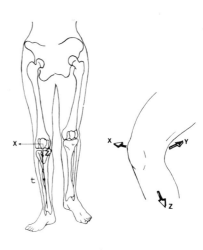

Figure 4

The origin of the femoral axes is taken as the mid point of markers 2 and 3 (on the femoral condyles). The long axis of the femur (-Z) is defined by the position of marker 1 (over the femoral head) relative to the origin. Any medio-lateral movement of the knee joint, abduction or adduction is assumed to occur about an axis (Y) through the origin and normal to the plane containing markers 1, 2 and 3, while the axis for flexion and extension (X) is perpendicular to the other two in the plane of markers 1, 2 and 3 (see figure 4).

The tibia is described by two vectors, one joining marker 4 (over the tibial tubercle) to the mid point of markers 6 and 7 (on the malleoli) and one perpendicular to the first on the plane defined by markers 4, 6 and 7.

In our work so far, we have described the movement of the knee joint during walking as rotations about these three axes. At each time instant that measurements are taken, the axes are set up in the femur, and the angles made by the tibia vectors with these axes are calculated.

This system is being used for the assessment of functional stability of the knee joint. We hope to demonstrate characteristic patterns of abnormal motion for different types of medio lateral and rotary instability of the knee.

KINEMATIC ASSESSMENT OF ARTHRITIC KNEES

A. MUKHERJEE , M.S., D.Phil.(Oxon.), G. DEANE, M.B., M.Sc., F.R.C.S.,
N.D. GREW, B.Sc., M.Sc., and J.R.W. MORRIS, B.Sc.(Eng.), D.Phil.

Oxford Orthopaedic Engineering Centre, Nuffield Orthopaedic Centre, Oxford

INTRODUCTION

The functional state of a walking patient with joint disease is frequently assessed on the basis of static measurements of joint angle and stability. This is the traditional physical examination made by the clinician and has many shortcomings, particularly its relationship to function, as it in no way demonstrates the dynamic situation.

This kinematic study of gait has shown that there is little association between quasi-static joint movement and dynamic performance for patients with osteoarthrosis and rheumatoid arthritis of the knee.

MATERIALS AND METHOD

The positions of markers on a subject's lower limbs were recorded by cinematography at fifty frames per second in both the frontal and sagittal plane (figure 1). These markers were placed to delineate the links in the lower limb so that measurement was able to be made of thigh, knee, and ankle angle (figure 2). The marker positions were measured by hand frame by frame using an analysing projector and then digitised for analysis by a PDP-11 computer. The data was presented as angle/time graphs 'stick man" representations, (figure 3), and angle/angle graphs of knee angle against thigh angle (figure 4).

Measurements were made of three groups of twenty middle-aged subjects:

    (a) A control group with no symptoms or signs of disorders
        affecting the lower limbs.

    (b) A group of patients with osteoarthrosis of the knee.

    (c) A group of patients with rheumatoid arthritis of the knee.

For quantitative analysis ten subjects with unilateral joint disease were chosen from each of the patient groups. These sub-groups were matched for mean age, height and weight with the normals.

RESULTS

The results indicated quite distinct differences in the three groups. Considering the knee angle/thigh angle graphs, a reduction in knee excursion and functional flexion deformity is seen in disease compared with the normal (figures 4, 5 and 6).

LAYOUT OF CINE CAMERAS

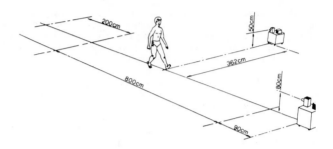

Figure 1

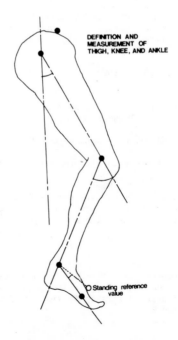

Figure 2   Definition of thigh, knee and ankle
angles. Thigh angle defined relative
to a vertical

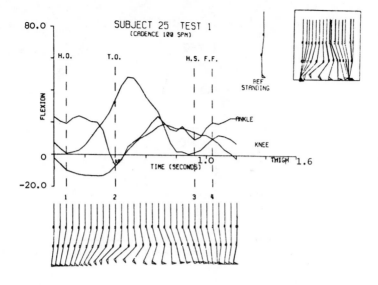

Figure 3   Angle/time graphs and "stick man"
            representations

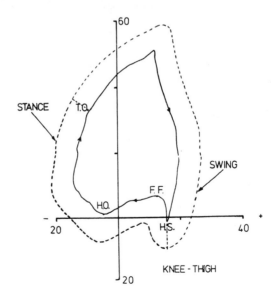

Figure 4   Knee angle (ordinate) plotted against thigh
            angle for a typical normal subject. The dotted
            lines delineate the stance and swing phases

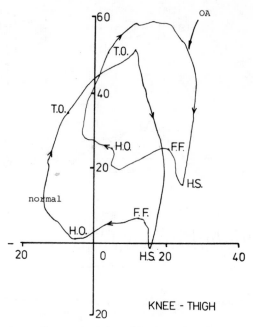

Figure 5   Typical knee/thigh angles for a normal
            subject and patient with osteoarthrosis

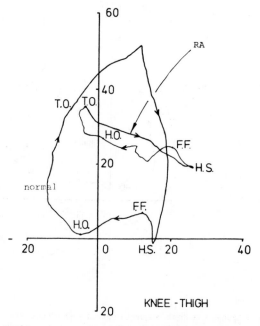

Figure 6   Typical knee/thigh angles for a normal
            subject and patient with rheumatoid arthritis

Table 1 shows the angular excursions of the three groups and also highlights the difference between clinical assessment and dynamic assessment.

Table 1   Mean of the total knee movements and percentage of movement used during level walking in normals and patient groups

Subjects	Clinical assessment, total knee movement	Biomechanical assessment, total knee movement	Percentage of movement used during walking
Normal	130.0°	52.5°	40.4%
Osteoarthrosis	108.0°	39.3°	39.4%
Rheumatoid arthritis	94.0°	20.2°	21.5%

No increases in thigh and ankle excursions were found to compensate for the reduced knee excursion in disease. Thus step and stride lengths were reduced as shown in Table 2.

Table 2   Step and stride lengths: normals and patient groups

	Step Length (cms)		Stride Length (cms)	
	Normal Side	Affected Side	Normal Side	Affected Side
Normal	62.7 (7.0)		124.8 (14.4)	
Osteoarthrosis	51.2 (13.0)	51.0 (8.5)	102.0 (20.6)	102.5 (20.7)
Rheumatoid arthritis	40.0 (15.0)	38.2 (13.1)	75.3 (28.7)	77.2 (27.6)

Standard deviations given in brackets

An increasing degree of disability through osteoarthrosis to rheumatoid arthritis is again seen and reflected in trends to lower cadence velocity of walking and an increased time in stance phase as demonstrated in Table 3.

Table 3   The temporal changes (normal and abnormal)

(Mean ±SD)

	Velocity (met/sec.)	Steps per minute	Percentage of the total cycle				Swing phase
			HS-FF	FF-HO	HO-TO	Stance	
Normal	1.1 (0.2)	109.9 (10.2)	11.3 (2.0)	28.0 (3.8)	23.4 (2.6)	62.7 (3.3)	37.3 (3.3)
Osteo-arthrosis	0.8 (0.3)	94.6 (12.8)	8.0 (3.2)	38.3 (15.4)	21.1 (10.4)	67.4 (9.8)	32.6 (9.8)
Rheumatoid arthritis	0.5 (0.2)	81.6 (12.6)	7.5 (2.1)	42.5 (9.5)	19.9 (4.3)	69.9 (7.3)	30.1 (7.3)

HS - heel strike; FF - foot flat; HO - heel off; TO - toe off
standard deviations given in brackets

DISCUSSION

The results of dynamic testing showed an increasing degree of disability
through osteoarthrosis to rheumatoid arthritis. Quasi-static clinical
examination did not demonstrate the same functional differences.

The most striking changes which appeared to be characteristic for the two
pathologies considered were the almost total absence of knee movement in
rheumatoid arthritis and the reduced and displaced knee movement in osteoarthrosis. These differences, which were not evident on passive physical
examination, suggest that the rheumatoid knee is particularly characterised
by movement pain as well as a greater inherent instability. During walking
the knee is splinted by muscle action into as stable and comfortable a
position as is possible and retained thus through the entire gait cycle.
By contrast, the osteoarthrotic knee has predominantly load bearing pain
with relatively little movement pain, and is also characterised by rather
less inherent instability. Thus, the knee movement is diminished largely as
a result of adopting a functional knee flexion deformity during stance phase
with a relatively normal swing phase.

The ratio of stance phase to swing phase is increased with both pathologies
and is evidence of greater caution being taken by patients to load the joint
more gently and check on stability before committing themselves to the single
support phase of the gait cycle. The shortening of step and stride length
is also predictable for the same reasons.

CONCLUSIONS

1. Routine clinical examination by passive movements reveals little of the
   dynamic function of the knee joint.
2. The kinematic measurement made revealed marked differences which appear
   to be characteristic for osteoarthrosis and rheumatoid arthritis.
3. Objective studies such as this help in both understanding normal and
   pathological function and in the assessment of treatment.
4. Kinematic data should be more and more included in the design criteria
   for newer treatments to lower limb disability, both internal and external.

THE MEASUREMENT OF FOOT CONTACT PATTERNS

J.C. WALL, B.Sc., M.Sc., Ph.D., J. CHARTERIS, B.A., M.Sc., and J.W. HOARE

Department of Human Kinetics, College of Biological Science,
University of Guelph, Ontario, Canada

INTRODUCTION

The literature is replete with studies aimed at elucidating the temporal/
distance factors involved in human gait (Gardner and Murray, 1975).
Continued interest in methods of monitoring the duration of floor contact
attests to the ongoing search for improved techniques for the collection
and clear presentation of the complex interactive factors concerned with
gait.

Our purpose here is to introduce an innovative technique for measuring the
temporal/distance factors of gait which has the following advantages: (a)
it is less restrictive, in that it eliminates need for trailing wires,
adhesive taping, etc.; (b) the technique is on-line and data collection
and reduction is significantly improved by the aid of a minicomputer; (c)
the resulting graphic displays are easy to interpret, and readily stored
(in the case of clinical applications) with the patients' files. Test-
retest applications are permitted by storage files. The method herein
described was inspired by progress made in solving problems involved in
hemiplegic gait analysis.

METHOD

The technique is based on the temporal/distance factors walkway described
earlier (Wall et al. 1976). The basis of the walkway is an electrical
circuit containing a power supply connected in series with several
resistances. Conducting rods are connected between these resistors to form
a grid as shown in Figure 1. When two rods are shorted-out, the circuit
is completed and a current will flow. The current depends on the number
of resistors in the circuit and therefore on the position in the grid where
the short is occurring. The connecting rods are set into ribbed rubber
matting and are shorted-out by means of self-adhesive conducting tape,
attached to the patient's own shoes.

If more than two rods are shorted-out, then the current recorded is that
passing through the path of least resistance. In Figure 1 this would be
through the lowest numbered resistors in the circuit. Thus, if one were
walking completely flat-footed from R_1 towards R_{14}, then the position of
the toe would be indicated. Therefore, when walking in the direction of
increasing resistance, the most proximal point of foot/floor contact is
indicated. In the direction of decreasing resistance, it is the most
distal position that is recorded. By walking once in each direction, it
is possible to determine the rearmost and foremost parts of the foot that
are in contact with the ground at any given part of the support phase of
gait.

The two traces shown in Figure 2 were obtained for a normal pattern of
foot contact. The upper trace, Figure 2a, was obtained for a walk in
the direction of increasing resistance and, therefore, the maximum value
indicates the position of the heel. As soon as the heel is removed, the
next most proximal position of foot/floor contact is indicated. In
Figure 2b, the most distal part of the foot that is in contact with the
floor is indicated, since the trace was obtained from a walk in the
opposite direction. Hence, the position of the heel is indicated only as
long as no other part of the foot is in contact, as soon as the ball comes

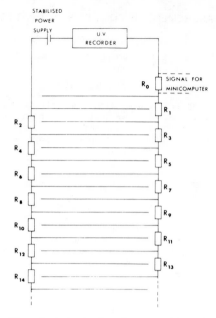

Figure 1   The electrical circuit upon which the technique
            for measuring the patterns of foot contact is based

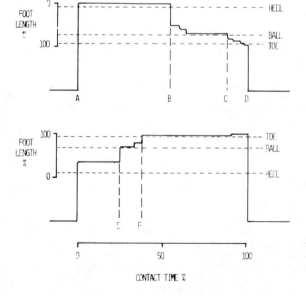

Figure 2   Traces of the voltage output from the walkway mat.
            The upper trace, 2a, was obtained from a walk in the
            direction of increasing resistance.   Trace 2b was
            obtained for a walk in the direction of decreasing
            resistance

down this is indicated. Between the two graphs, therefore, one can
determine when the various parts of the foot both make and break contact
with the floor.

For the purposes of this analysis, three parts of the foot are considered,
the heel, ball and toe. The heel is defined as from 0-25% of total foot
length. The ball is the 60-80% region and the toe, 87-100% of foot length.
The maximum on the trace in Figure 2a is the hindmost part of the foot,
the heel. This equals 0% of total foot length. Knowing the length of the
foot (by previously measuring it) and the relationship between the voltage
measured and distance on the walkway, one can calculate the voltage
level corresponding to 100% of foot length, i.e., the position of the toe.
The selected levels for heel, ball and toe can, therefore, be marked off
as horizontal lines as shown in Figure 2. Where the traces intersect
these lines indicates the times of contact with or removal from the floor
of that part of the foot. Thus, in trace 2a, which always shows the
rearmost part of the foot in contact, one can determine the following:

        Time of heel strike   = A
        Time of heel off   = B
        Time of ball off   = C
        Time of toe off   = D

From trace 2b, which always indicates the foremost part of the foot in
contact with the ground, the following can be calculated:

        Time of ball on   = E
        Time of toe on   = F

Knowing the times of initial and final contact of a foot part, one can
easily calculate the duration of contact.

All the data collection and the calculations described above are carried
out automatically by the minicomputer.

RESULTS

It was felt important that the results should be presented in a form which
is both easy to comprehend and suitable for inclusion with the patients'
notes. This underlying principle had earlier been applied to the results
from the temporal/distance factors walkway. The clinicial acceptance of
the graphical presentation of those results prompted us to consider a
similar format for the patterns of foot/floor contact. The results from a
normal subject are shown in Figure 3 as an example of the method of
presentation. The subject details are given at the top of the page and
these are followed by the graphical representation of the results. The
times that the three selected parts of the foot are in contact with the
ground are shown by the X's on the graph which has support time as ordinate
and foot length as abscisa. The graph shows that initial contact is made
by the heel alone and that the heel remains in contact for about 57% of
total contact time. The times that the ball makes and breaks contact with
the ground are approximately 20% and 80% of total contact time respectively.
The toe is the final part of the foot to remain on the ground after making
contact at about 35% of the total contact time. The actual times of
contact (start) and removal (stop) of the foot parts, together with the
duration of contact are given in the table below the graph. These
times are all calculated as a percentage of total contact time. The 100%
figures in the table show the total contact time in seconds and the foot
length in centimetres.

GAIT LABORATORY: UNIVERSITY OF GUELPH

NAME : M.T. JONES   DATE : 77 08 25

HOSPITAL NO. : NIL   GAIT LAB. NO. : 123M

CONDITION : NORMAL   VISIT : 1

CONTACT PATTERN OF RIGHT FOOT

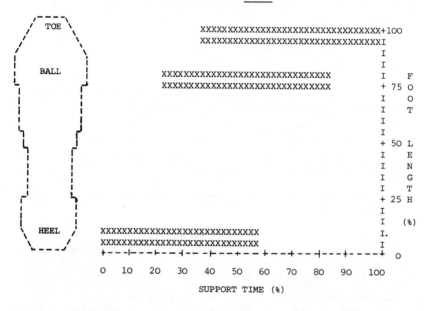

SUPPORT TIME (%)

	START (%)	STOP (%)	DURATION (%)
HEEL	0.0	55.2	55.2
BALL	20.6	80.3	59.7
TOE	34.0	100.0	66.0

100% CONTACT TIME = 0.58 SEC.   100% FOOT LENGTH = 31 CM.

Figure 3   Results sheet from a normal subject

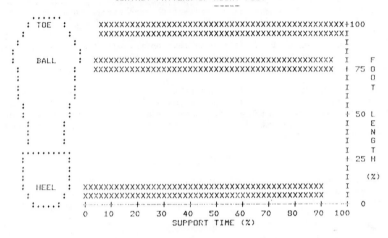

(a)

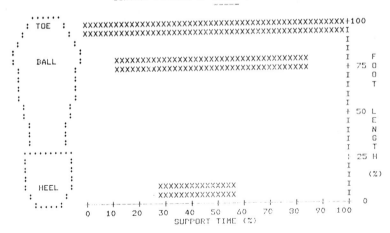

(b)

Figure 4   The graphical results obtained from two subjects with abnormal
patterns of foot-floor contact
(a) flatfoot
(b) drop-foot

The graphs can also be used to demonstrate abnormal patterns of foot contact as shown in Figure 4. The upper graph shows a pattern in which essentially the whole foot is in contact for the entire duration of the support phase, i.e., flat-foot. The lower graph shows a condition where initial contact is made with the toe followed by the ball and finally the heel. The sequence of the foot breaking contact with the ground is near normal, i.e., heel first followed by ball and finally toe. This drop-foot pattern is common among hemiplegic patients with lower limb spasticity.

It is hoped to further develop this technique so that it can be used in conjunction with the results from the temporal/distance factors walkway. Together, these two, which use the same raw data, should prove extremely useful in the assessment of disability in those pathologies where locomotor function is affected.

ACKNOWLEDGEMENTS

Sincere thanks to Mr. L. Klenerman and Ann Ashburn of Northwick Park Hospital, London, for their invaluable advice during the initial stages of this project.

REFERENCES

GARDNER G.M., and MURRAY M.P. (1975)
A method for measuring the duration of foot-floor contact during walking
Physical Therapy, 55, pp. 751-756

WALL J.C., DHANENDRAN M. and KLENERMAN L. (1976)
A method for measuring the temporal/distance factors of gait.
Biomedical Engineering, 11, pp. 409-412

SKELETAL TRANSIENTS ON HEEL STRIKE IN NORMAL WALKING

L.H. LIGHT, G. McLELLAN, and L. KLENERMAN

Clinical Research Centre and Northwick Park Hospital,
Harrow, Middlesex.

Walking on soft ground feels different from walking on hard, and the "feel" of different footwear can likewise be distinguished. The sensation associated with heel-strike in particular varies greatly, yet conventional gait analysis instrumentation barely differentiates between the impact of soft and hard heels (Hull and Perkins, 1977).

As part of an investigation of whether shock-absorbing footwear may ameliorate symptoms in sufferers from joint or back pain, we have studied the transients associated with heel strike. Günther (1968) has shown that peak acceleration of ∿300m/s² (30g) can be measured on shoe heels, but simultaneous measurements at hip and head level were taken through soft tissue and are therefore difficult to interpret. We have investigated the effect of walking barefoot, with normal and with shock-absorbing footwear, on the accelerations observed in a normal subject with lightweight transducers of extended frequency response, one of which was mechanically coupled to the tibia: two stiff pins (Kirschner wires of 1.14mm diameter) were driven into the tibia of one of the investigators (G. McL., age 31 years, weight 72Kg) through vertical slits in the skin 4 and 6cm below the tibial tubercle. An aluminium framework bonded to the pins carried a "Kulite" accelerometer type GYN 155-50 (resonant at 2.8kHz). Another transducer was attached to a moulded spreader plate of high-density Plastazote which was glued and strapped to the skin 15cm further down the shin. Vertical acceleration at head level was recorded from a transducer mounted on a bite-bar.

Figure 1 shows simultaneous tibia/shin-surface and tibia/bite-bar recordings which were obtained when the subject walked on a hard (vinyl-on-concrete) laboratory floor. The observed transient depended strongly on the footwear, though all leg recordings were in the range of 2 - 8g for peak deceleration and 10 - 25 mS for duration of the deceleration phase. The shape of the tibial transient was characteristic of the heel construction - the hard leather heel giving a short transient of very abrupt onset and the two compliant heels showing smoother and lower deceleration waves, with the shock-absorbent construction (which incorporated a high-hysteresis polymer) showing less reverberation after the initial transient than the crepe rubber.

Comparison between simultaneous observations at the different sites showed that the transient suffered more than five-fold attenuation, loss of high frequency components and ∿10mS delay in passage to the head. Shin-surface recordings differed from those from the tibia mainly in the loss of high frequency components. Although details of the skeletal transient (in particular the rate of loading) are not reproduced in the non-invasive shin measurements, they do serve to give a rough indication of its magnitude.

As the vigor of walking could not be adequately controlled in the above study - so that the amplitude of transients with different footwear could

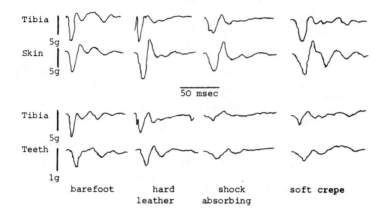

Tibia

Skin

50 msec

Tibia

Teeth

barefoot   hard   shock   soft **crepe**
                  leather   absorbing

Figure 1   Vertical acceleration transients on heel strike
            in normal walking with different footwear.
            Top pair: simultaneous tracings from tibia/shin
                      surface
            Bottom pair: simultaneous tracings from tibia/
                         bite bar

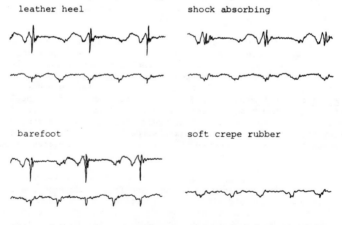

leather heel   shock absorbing

barefoot   soft crepe rubber

Figure 2   Acceleration transients recorded during steady
            walking on rubber-covered walkway of treadmill
            at. 5.3 km/hr.
            Top: from shin-surface transducer
            Bottom: from bite-bar transducer

not reliably be compared - further recordings were taken from the skin-
surface and bite-bar transducers after the subject had been walking for
several minutes in each pair of shoes (and barefoot) on a treadmill at a
set speed (5.3 km/hr) - figure 2.

The constancy of the transients then seen in each condition suggests that
valid inter-shoe comparisons can be made from these tracings. The lower
amplitude observed when the compliant heels were worn is in agreement with
the subject's sensory impression of the heel strike impact.

We conclude that:

1. Instrumentation of extended frequency response is required to
   register the transients experienced on heel strike in
   everyday walking. (In addition, measurements from body-
   mounted transducers are preferable to ones by force-plate, as
   the latter reacts primarily to the impact of the shoe heel
   and does not give direct evidence of the shoe-leg interaction.)

2. The heel strike transients observed in the tibia, though brief,
   are of considerable amplitude compared with the forces exerted
   in locomotor activity. The rates of loading are particularly
   high, especially when hard heels are worn on hard surfaces.

3. Surface recordings from the shin are of broadly similar
   magnitude to those from the tibia, but waveform details are
   lost. The difference may be important if rate-of-loading
   turns out to be significant in, for example, inducing or
   exacerbating joint damage.

4. As the "feel" of different footwear suggests, the transients
   depend strongly on the composition of the shoe heel. Their
   biological effect can thus be studied in trials with different
   shoes.

These results, although obtained on only one subject, form a background to
the design of experiments to find out more about heel strike transients:
In particular, we wish to establish whether (as suggested by some anecdotal
evidence) they play a part in the genesis of joint disease or the
aggravation of symptoms. Should they be shown to have clinical
significance, shock-absorbing heels of the kind used in these experiments
may offer a practical way of reducing their impact.

We are grateful to several of our colleagues and to Kulite Limited, for
the loan of some of the instrumentation.

REFERENCES

GÜNTHER R. (1968)
    Über stosserschütterungen beim gang des menschen
    Internationale Zeitschrift für angewendete Physiologie, 25, pp. 130-141

HULL W., and PERKINS P.J. (1977)
    Effect of heel hardness on contact forces during wear
    Internal Report 687, Shoe Research Association, Kettering, Northants.

A DIRECT TELEMETRIC METHOD FOR MEASURING HIP LOAD

T.A. ENGLISH, F.R.C.S.E., and M. KILVINGTON

Department of Orthopaedic Biomechanics,
Hull Royal Infirmary, Humberside

HIP FORCES

The force acting on the hip joint is important in relation to stress on cartilage affecting arthritis and on ageing bone affecting femoral fructure incidence. These are long-term problems but recently the hip forces have been of more immediate importance since they affect implant failure due to loosening, fatigue and wear.

GAIT CYCLE

Gait cycle studies by Paul (1976) give a clear current analysis of the variation in hip load against time expressed as a percentage of the cycle and showing load increase with walking speed. The peaks vary in magnitude between four and eight times body mass. The first peak is 7% after heel strike and the second peak at 47% just before toe off.

ANGULAR LOADING

Paul also calculates the important angles of 12° extension for the first load peak and 7° of flexion for the second peak. In the A.P. view he gives 21° adduction at the first load peak and 12° of adduction at the second. It must be remembered that these angular loads are in relation to the femur and *not* to any implant within it. Thus posture and design of the implant is all important. Rydell (1966) gauged and implanted a Moore neck component without telemetry and Carlson (1974) placed fourteen gauges in a Moore head with the object of measuring and analysing the angular loads and angles in vivo. At the time limited walkpath and telemetry technology and the difficulties of multi-channel analysis limited the potential of this invasive method.

PHILOSOPHY

The simple philosophy which we have adopted to obtain direct readings while not endangering the patient has been made possible by employing a new design of femoral neck replacement which lies on the theoretical calculated axis at peak loads. Telemetric output is used.

FATIGUE

The upper femur is a loaded curved beam with a high offset from hip rotation centre to the trochanter (y, figure 1.1) of about 72mm. We know that most medullary cavities will not accommodate metal stems of sufficient sectional area to withstand cyclical loads of 4903N or more indefinitely without deformation or fatigue fracture at high offsets.

Our implant neck is designed to lie on the theoretical load axis 15° to
the A.P. vertical and mid-way between the two peak load angles. In the
lateral view the neck angle depends upon its anteversion posture of 10° to
25°. Zero anteversion tends to cause a torsion effect on the upper stem
when the hip is loaded in flexion. It is probably no coincidence that this
theoretical calculated load axis is observed to coincide with the thickened
long axis of the femoral calcar.

DESIGN

Within the sealed implant axis loaded neck we have placed a piston attached
to the head. The piston recess has four platinum   tungsten gauges at 90°
stations on its circumference.

CIRCUIT

The direct output from the gauges is balanced by wiring into a Wheatstone
Bridge circuit so that angular side loads are compensated to give a mean
true axis reading. The bridge output modulates a reed-switched F.M.
transmitter, totally sealed against corrosion, with seventy hours active
life and infinite shelf life. The resulting signal, a square wave, is
filtered and smoothed to modulate the amplitude on a chart recorder.

BENCH TESTS

The gauged implant is bench tested in a fatigue rig at cyclic reference
loads up to 9810N (fourteen times body weight) at rates varying from 1Hz
up to 20Hz in a saline medium. The implant is calibrated for loads up to
20° off the axis. This approximates the load angles imposed on the implant
derived from the work of Paul, Rydell and others. The cosine effect gives
a theoretical 6% loss which is compensated by the bridge circuit and the
ultimate resolution has been found to be + or -3.7% up to loads of 9810N.
The 316L steel implant behaved elastically within this range during short
periods of cyclic loading at 1Hz up to twenty-four hours. Tests for
sealing against the corrosive environment and thermal effects due to
cement setting are nearing completion.

CLINICAL APPLICATION

How can this axis load design of implant be used safely in patients
without risk of dislocation? The low offset necessitates shifting the
femur shaft towards the body centre line (English, 1975). This shift
causes risk of dislocation if the trochanter moves inwards with it by
reducing muscle tensions (figure 1.2). The implant can only be inserted
safely by using the muscle balanced trochanter detachment shown in
figure 1.3. The trochanter is displaced outwards to its former offset by
using a spacer graft cut from the femur head shown in figure 2. If no
graft is available a spacer insert is used instead. The technique has been
used in over six hundred hip replacements including thirty with the low
35mm offset design shown in figure 2 and earlier with a modified high 50mm
offset design. Under adverse vertical loading our low offset model showed
a lateral tensile stress of 48300 x 10^3 Nm -2 compared with 78600 x 10^{-2} Nm^{-2}

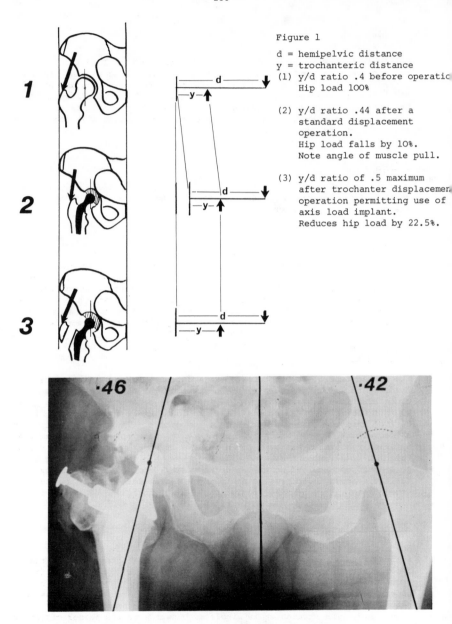

Figure 1

d = hemipelvic distance
y = trochanteric distance
(1) y/d ratio .4 before operatic
    Hip load 100%

(2) y/d ratio .44 after a
    standard displacement
    operation.
    Hip load falls by 10%.
    Note angle of muscle pull.

(3) y/d ratio of .5 maximum
    after trochanter displacemen
    operation permitting use of
    axis load implant.
    Reduces hip load by 22.5%.

Figure 2   Radiograph of the axis load implant without
            instrumentation showing the trochanter spacer
            graft and the raised y/d ratio of .46 compared
            with .42 on the unoperated hip

as for the standard design, measured 80mm vertically from the top of the implant. The photoelastic model of the low offset model loaded at 15° to the long axis showed equal compressive loading on both sides of the neck.

RESULT ANALYSIS

The operation itself, when combined with the inward shift of the rotation centre by 10mm at operation, is calculated to reduce the vertical component hip load J by 10% (figure 1.2) since J falls as y increases in relation to d. If the trochanter is replaced to its former pre-operative position the load is reduced by 22.5% as y increases (figure 1.3). This factor must be taken into account when analysing the result of this type of implant load against normal or arthritic hips. The direct print out gait cycle is to be compared with that obtained synchronously by walkpath analysis of this and the contralateral hip with Professor Paul's guidance.

REFERENCES

CARLSON C.E., MANN R.W., and HARRIS W.H. (1974)
    Design of a hip prosthesis containing pressure transducers
    Journal of Biomedical Materials Research, Symposium No. 5, (2),
    pp. 261-269.

ENGLISH T.A. (1975)
    The trochanteric approach to the hip for prosthetic replacement
    Journal of Bone and Joint Surgery, 57A, 8, pp. 1128-1133

PAUL J.P. (1976)
    Force actions transmitted by joints in the human body
    Proceedings of the Royal Society of London, B192, pp. 163-172

RYDELL N.W. (1966)
    Forces acting on the femoral head prosthesis
    Acta Orthopaedica Scandinavica, Supplement No. 8

MEASUREMENT AND ANALYSIS OF MOVEMENT IN THE HIP JOINT

T.A. GORE, B.Sc.[1], M. FLYNN, F.R.C.S.[2], G.R. HIGGINSON, Ph.D.[1],
and R.J. MINNS, Ph.D.[1]

1. Department of Engineering Science, Durham University
2. St. Hilda's Hospital, Hartlepool

INTRODUCTION

The subject of the investigation is the study of all the components of angular motion of the femur relative to the pelvis in normal and abnormal hip joints. The measurements cover walking, climbing and descending stairs, sitting and standing, and global range of one leg while standing on the other. Large numbers are involved, including large numbers of healthy subjects to establish the pattern of 'normal' functioning over a wide age range. For that reason an important feature of the equipment is the near-automatic recording, processing and presentation of the large volume of data.

APPARATUS

The whole system is shown diagrammatically in Figure 1. An electrogoniometer attached to the subject transmits signals of flexion/extension, abduction/adduction and rotation about the axis of the shaft of the femur, together with signals from a footswitch, to a tape recorder and/or an ultra-violet recorder. Signals recorded on tape are subsequently analysed on a digital computer.

The Goniometer

The goniometer consists of three orthogonally mounted capacitive rotary position transducers, arranged to lie as closely as possible to the femur, and adjustable so that the centre of rotation can be aligned with the centre of the femoral head. The goniometer is mounted on a light aluminium alloy 'belt' whose circumference stands clear of the body. The belt is located by adjustable clamps on the bony prominences of the anterior superior illiac spines and the convexity of the sacral region of the spine. The movement of the femur is transmitted to the transducers from a simple knee attachment by a square-section rod sliding in a trunnion. Movement of one limb only is measured at a time. The instrument is symmetrical and can be rotated and inverted for measurement of the other limb.

The goniometer bears a superficial resemblance to that described by Johnston and Smidt (1969). One of the important differences in the new design is that the belt and knee attachment are mounted on the bony prominences of the pelvis and the knee rather than on soft tissue. Johnston and Smidt drew particular attention to that aspect of their design as the main sources of error.

In the analysis of gait and the ascending and descending of stairs, which are cyclic movements, time reference points are required within each cycle. These are provided by pressure-sensitive switches, incorporated in commercially available insoles, which switch a voltage through different discrete levels determined by the contact pattern of the foot on the ground.

Instrumentation

In a study of large numbers of subjects, the acquisition, processing and presentation of data constitute a major part of the investigation. Referring again to Figure 1, the recording system, incorporating a tape recorder and an ultra-violet recorder, is easily portable. Readings from subjects can be taken in any location where there are steps for climbing, space for walking, and a mains electricity supply; the signals can be displayed visually on the ultra-violet recorder and/or stored on tape for subsequent analysis by computer.

The apparatus may also be used in conjunction with a polarised light goniometer which measures absolute rather than relative rotations.

Data Collection and Processing

A standard procedure for collecting data is followed as closely as possible. First the subject is briefed, the belt is fitted firmly but comfortably and a period of acclimatisation is allowed; the subject is asked to walk about during this period to become relaxed in the belt.

The tests start with walking. A datum position is established in an upright stance, feet together, toes forward. Subjects unable to attain this position are examined by standard clinical methods to determine the magnitudes of any fixed rotations. Measurements are then taken from a datum as close as can be achieved to the standard datum, and are subsequently corrected.

The subject is asked to walk along an approximately straight line over a distance of 25 m so that at least ten consecutive steps (20 paces) can be recorded. Of these, five are analysed, taken when the subject is in steady motion, neither accelerating nor slowing down. Active subjects walk at a predetermined frequency of 0.9 Hz (guided by a metronome), giving a period of 1.1 s. between consecutive heelstrikes of the same foot. Infirm patients walk at their own pace, which is noted.

After walking, climbing and descending stairs and sitting and standing are recorded. Finally the subject is asked to describe an arc with the femur passing through the limiting points of movement in the planes of flexion/extension and abduction/adduction, while standing on the other leg; this gives an indication of total or global range of movement.

Individual traces can be recorded for immediate inspection on the ultra-violet recorder, but the more usual practice is to record only on to magnetic tape for computer analysis. For example the analysis of level walking is as follows. The data from all four channels are interfaced to the analogue inputs of the computer. The inputs are scanned at 200 Hz and the data points transferred to computer storage. Eight thousand data points are taken giving a total sampling time of ten seconds. Having loaded the data, the footswitch channel is analysed and the locations of two successive heel strikes are determined. These heelstrikes are taken at least four steps into the run, so that the subject has reached a steady pace.

Locating the heelstrikes also locates the beginning and end of individual steps for the other three channels. The information on all four channels is then normalised to give 200 data points on each channel for each step. After calibrating and scaling these points are plotted: flexion, abduction, rotation being plotted against percentage of walking cycles. Five consecutive steps taken from the middle of the run are analysed and each step plotted on top of the previous one. Repetitive excursions of the plotter give the performance envelope of a specific individual.

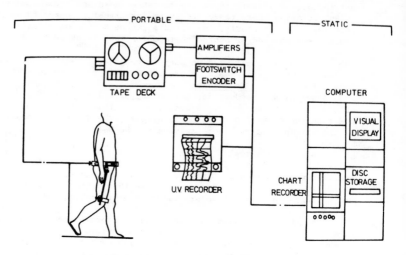

Figure 1.   Layout of Apparatus

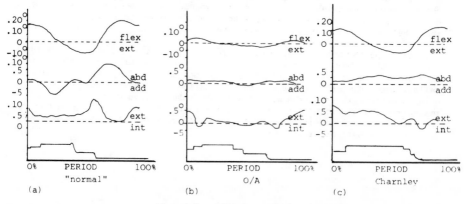

Figure 2.   Average of Five Steps

Because all the traces have been normalised to 200 points, they can be added together and averaged to give an average step, which is plotted as shown in Figure 2. A plot has now been obtained giving simultaneously the angular position of the femur relative to the pelvis in three planes. It is useful to plot this also on a rectangular basis, flexion being plotted against abduction. This allows an easy comparison with the global range.

The other movements are analysed in much the same way. Essentially the only difference is that in the sitting and standing and the global range exercises the footswitch is replaced by a manually operated event marker, which is used to define the limits of the cycle of events.

RESULTS

A lengthy presentation and discussion of results must clearly await a longer publication, as must an analysis of errors. The programme now under way includes ten males and ten females in each of the age decades fifteen to twenty-five years, twenty-five to thirty-five years, and so on up to seventy-five years, all healthy; the healthy set also includes a group of eight males, all nineteen to twenty years old, all between 1.81 and 1.82 m in height and between 65 and 68 kg in weight. The remainder of the present programme will be made up of about sixty pathological cases observed in local hospitals.

Examples are given in Figure 2, which show three records of level walking; one for a healthy female of 32 years, the others for a female of 72 years, with a Charnley prosthesis in one hip and severe osteoarthrosis in the other hip (both are shown). All the records are of the average of five steps. In a paper restricted to this length, Figure 2 must be allowed to speak for itself.

Finally, the system's errors must be briefly described. Errors arise due to the belt slipping because of skin movement over the attachment areas; parallax errors due to the separation of the square section rod and the axis of the femur, and instrumentation errors. A full discussion of these will be presented in a later paper, but briefly they are estimated to be as follows: instrumental, less than 1°; parallax of the order of $\pm 1^\circ$ on flexion and abduction, and calculable; belt slip, most difficult to estimate, and largely dependent upon the subject being tested, of the order of $\pm 2^\circ$ on all components.

ACKNOWLEDGEMENT

The authors acknowledge the financial support and encouragement given to this project by the Research Committee of the Northern Regional Health Authority.

REFERENCE

JOHNSTON, R.C. and SMIDT, G.L. (1969)
Measurement of hip-joint motion during walking, Journal of Bone and Joint Surgery, vol. 51-A, no. 6, pp. 1083-1094

THE USE OF FORCE PLATE ANALYSIS IN THE ASSESSMENT OF TREATMENT FOR TENDON INJURY IN THE RACEHORSE

A.E. GOODSHIP, B.V.Sc., Ph.D., M.R.C.V.S.[1], L.E. LANYON, B.V.Sc., Ph.D., M.R.C.V.S.[1], P.N. BROWN, B.Tech.[1], and C. PYE, B.Sc.[2]

1. Department of Anatomy, School of Veterinary Science, Bristol University
2. Department of Mechanical Engineering, Bristol University

Introduction

Injury of the flexor tendons in the forelimbs of racehorses is a source of great financial loss to the racing industry. Treatments for such injuries are varied, and present evaluation of their success is based largely upon subjective clinical observation. The aim of our investigation is to develop a system for the objective quantitative analysis of both normal and pathological gait in racehorses. Such a system will also be used to evaluate different treatment regimes for tendon injuries. If the system is sufficiently sensitive, it could be of considerable value in the screening of young animals for any functional predisposition to locomotor disorders, before the expensive training programme is commenced.

The problem of estimating soundness and degrees of lameness objectively is a difficult one, only recently being tackled in the human field partly in an effort to quantify the results of prosthetic joint replacement and partly in the growing science of sports medicine. The basic piece of apparatus which has been developed for some of these studies is the "force platform" which, by measuring and analysing the reaction of the foot with the ground, gives some quantitative information related to the animal's or person's performance (Adamson and Whitney 1971, Paul 1972, Paul and Poulson 1974, Payne 1968, Payne 1974). Although some preliminary studies have been made in animals, using this technique to investigate both normal gait and the presence of lameness (Prentice and Wright 1971), there is little evidence of the technique being used to monitor the course of a disease or recovery process and relate this to normal gait patterns.

Method

The system currently being developed utilises a Kistler piezoelectric force platform manufactured specifically for high loads. The stainless steel platform measures 900 x 600mm, contains four transducer pillars each capable of taking 2 metric tonnes vertical force and one metric tonne horizontal forces, and has a minimum natural resonance frequency of 1 kHz. It is mounted on a frame sunk into several tons of concrete in a concrete walkway, both the platform and walkway are covered by a thin non-slip rubber mat. The horses are walked and trotted along the walkway until a sufficient number of "hits" are obtained for each limb. The sequence of right limb and left limb "hits" being random. An attempt is made to keep the velocity constant; it is hoped to use a doppler radar unit to measure the velocity of the animals and the force platform itself to measure the mass of the animals.

The signal from the platform is amplified using Kistler type 5001 charge amplifiers, monitored on a storage oscilloscope and recorded on cassette tape using a Bell and Howell CR3000 FM tape recorder. Force patterns from successful "hits" are then digitised at millisecond intervals using a transient store (Model 512AS, Physical Data), this data is then processed by a Prime 300 computer. The duration of the force is then recorded then the signal is expanded to a constant time base allowing a mean pattern to be obtained from a number of signals. By using this averaging process we hope to reduce inconsistent transients and enhance those related to specific lesions. An indication of likely variation is also given by plotting the mean pattern together with the mean minus one standard deviation (Figures 1 and 2).

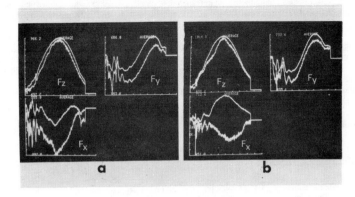

Figure 1   (a) Mean force patterns from five "hits" of the
left forelimb of a horse with a mild strain
of the left superficial digital flexor tendon

        (b) Mean force patterns from five "hits" of the
right forelimb of the same horse. In each
case the upper trace is the mean trace and
the lower is the mean minus one standard
deviation. Relative scales F_z = vertical
force 5 x 10^3 N/V. F_y = backward and forward
horizontal force 1 x 10^3 N/V. F_x = lateral
horizontal force 5 x 10^3 N/V.

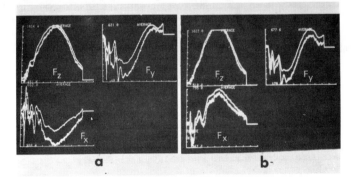

Figure 2   (a) Mean force patterns from five "hits" of the
left forelimb of the same horse as in
Figure 1 four months after treatment of the
tendon lesion

        (b) Mean force patterns from five "hits" of the
right forelimb four months after treatment
of the lesion in the left limb. Scales as
in Figure 1

These mean patterns can then be used for various types of analyses to determine differences in magnitude, duration and frequency content.

Natural variation in force patterns both between limbs and between horses is being ascertained in a representative normal population of horses in training. Once these normal data have been determined they can be used for comparison with force patterns from horses with tendon lesions. The injured horses are being divided into groups, each of which will receive one of the currently used treatments for tendon injury. Force platform data will be recorded from these animals at regular intervals throughout the recovery period to compare their force patterns with those seen in the normal population.

Preliminary Results

Preliminary results from one horse can be shown in Figs. 1 and 2. This horse suffered a mild strain of the superficial digital flexor tendon of the left forelimb.
Fig. 1a shows the mean force patterns from five 'hits' of the left forelimb and Fig. 1b the mean force patterns of the right forelimb both before treatment. In all cases the upper trace represents the mean pattern and the lower trace the mean minus one standard deviation, the relative scales being vertical force $Fz = 5 \times 10^3 N/V$, Backward and forward horizontal force $Fy = 1 \times 10^3 N/V$ and lateral horizontal force $Fx = 5 \times 10^2$ N/V.
Fig. 2a shows similar mean patterns for the left forelimb four months after treatment and Fig. 2b patterns for the right limb at the same time.

Although these are only from one animal differences can be seen before and after treatment. Before treatment the vertical force shows a greater magnitude on the right (uninjured) limb than on the left (injured limb). After treatment the vertical force is still greater on the right limb, but both limbs show greater vertical force than before treatment. The character of the vertical force of the left limb differs following treatment from that seen before treatment.

Discussion

Few if any conclusions can be drawn from the results from one animal at one stage of recovery. However, these preliminary results do show that differences can be detected using this system. It is hoped to monitor these changes throughout the recovery period and, with reference to data from normal horses, ascertain quantitatively the time at which recovery reaches completion.

Although the specific results of this investigation will only be relevant to the racehorse, the procedures adopted are applicable to quantifying locomotor performance in any species.

Acknowledgements

We would like to thank the Horserace Betting Levy Board for providing funds for this investigation and the owners of the horses for their cooperation. Photography was by Mr. D. Telling. The manuscript was kindly typed by Mrs. J. Gillard.

References

Adamson, G.T. and Whitney, R.J. (1971) Critical appraisal of jumping as a measure of human power.
Medicine and Sport, Vol. 6, Biomechanics II. 208-211 Karger Basel.

Paul, J.P. (1972) Design aspects of endoprostheses for the lower limbs.
Perspectives in Biomedical Engineering, editor Kenedi R.M.
Macmillan Press.

Paul, J. and Poulson, J. (1974) The analysis of forces transmitted by joints in the human body.
Proceedings of the Fifth Conference on Experimental Stress Analysis, Udine, Italy. CISM Udine.

Payne, A.H. (1968) The use of force platforms for the study of physical activity. Biomechanics I. 1st International Seminar Zurich 1967, pp. 83-86. Karger 1968.

Payne, A.A. (1974) A force platform system for biomechanics research in sport.
University Park Press 1974.

Prentice, P.E. and Wright, J.T.M. (1971) A platform for measuring the walking forces exerted by the bovine foot.
Journal of Physiology, 219, 2P-4P.

ORTHOTICS DESIGN
AND FABRICATION

ORTHOTICS DESIGN AND FABRICATION

G.K. ROSE, F.R.C.S.

Orthotic Research and Locomotor Assessment Unit,
Robert Jones and Agnes Hunt Orthopaedic Hospital, Oswestry

As a scientific subject, orthotics may not be regarded as an infant but is certainly a late starter from the point of view of research. In dealing with the current status of work in this field one cannot only consider a catalogue of units, workers and products, even if it were within my capacity to cover the world scene, for this would need to be the breadth of our scan. Rather, I have taken it to mean a commentary on the present level of philosophy and experience of *research* with some of the practical difficulties which it presents. I note that the first entry in the Shorter Oxford Dictionary defines status as the "height or acme of a disease" and defines disease as "the absence of ease", so that I think there would be little disagreement if we said that the present status of orthotics is something that we were all very uneasy about.

Of course status has other meanings, in particular standing, and certainly in my own orthotic neck of the woods we are much concerned with that for our patients. Those interested in, and concerned with, the improvement of the orthotic situation often speak about improved status or standing, particularly for orthotists. This should, of course, be primarily an inevitable by-product of increasing professionalism on their part but, alas, one knows that it is not necessarily so. Once again I am dismayed to note, in perhaps the most recent official document that consideration of the struggle for skill is to be substantially divorced from that of financial reward.

In our present stage of development I think we are wise to ask rather simple, fundamental questions such as why centres for orthotic research should be necessary today. After all, orthotics have been available in some form certainly for over four and a half thousand years. In 1490, or thereby, Pieter Breughel showed that life's enjoyment could be expanded by quite simple forms of these and the Industrial Revolution brought its Surgical Mechanists, one of whom, Mr. Gillingham in 1888 said with great insight "a surgical mechanist does not trade in mechanisms as does an iron monger in iron ware. It matters not how beautifully instruments may be made; they are useless, and as so much waste material, without the mechanist's skill in adapting the same to his patients' wants. There are no fixed rules, as in ordinary business, each case has to be made a special study, and is, therefore, an art. Those who devote themselves to this branch of usefulness, alone know the anxious thought and nervous force required in difficult cases".

For those of us who have the temerity to try and inject some science into this art for our varied and manifold motives, these words can touch particularly tender spots; and we know the temptation to advance by applying simply a veneer of science rather than to look at fundamentals.

But to answer the question I raise, history and one's own experience shows that there are currents of thought abroad at a particular time, in larger and smaller events which exert a profound effect on us all whether we recognise them or not and some of these forces in the orthotic world can be identified :-

We live in an age of scepticism. All question authority and
this happy and secure situation for the doctor in which his word was
taken uncritically has gone for ever. Scepticism has its dangers of
course; the tendency to throw out lock, stock and barrel all that has
gone before - the NIMBUS Syndrome - nothing important before us. Such
a process tends to ignore the fact that whatever service we have, with
all its warts, must go on whilst we change it, largely by evolution
with occasionally small mutations.

A second powerful force is the effect of the National Health
Service in this country. The right of every patient is to have the
best tomorrow, if not yesterday, and this can raise powerful political
pressures. In other countries competition of commercially produced
orthoses is important where the purchaser is close to the product.

Again :-

The new Industrial Revolution derives from new materials.
Whilst these bring excitement and promise, this sometimes obscures
the fact that their properties have to be learnt and applied appropriately
and just as importantly, the vexed problems of the interrelationship
between design and material, re-assessed. I live near to what is called
the first Iron bridge in the world but in fact should be more accurately
described as a wooden bridge made in iron, and this is an error which
we must avoid if we are to make the best use of these materials.
As an example I remember an overweight young lady paralysed in both legs
who could not manage orthodox calipers. She has been immensely improved
by the provision of a "tray" of fibreglass, holding her legs in the
appropriate position, into which she can drop these and secure them simply.
An example of the exploitation of a new material.

Last in my incomplete list is the need to use our limited resources, both financialand material, to the best advantage. Ostensibly
this is the motive for much funding and expenditure, but in putting
it forward many of us feel a deep sense of unease. Yet the fundamental
concept, that of producing the most elegant and simple solution is
the very basis of science, as is the design of the simplest, most pertinent
experiment to expose the quickest answer to a burning question. And
what steps do we need to take to choose the question?

In our field there is an absolute, that we must all be involved
in the clinical situation and that in this situation we have to use
all our senses to acquire data; not only just to listen to patients,
parents and our colleagues, but also to go into homes and schools and
see what goes on outside the hospital and workshop environment. The
data so gathered has to be most carefully assessed. The most forthcoming
patients are often those who most readily produce various solutions
which may obscure the value of objective comment. In the world of
swivel walkers it was frequently represented to us that it would be
a great advantage if patients could sit and stand in their orthosis
in addition to ambulate. Having accepted this, it was reasonable to
ask what we knew about the act of sitting and standing and investigation
showed two important points; that whilst doing this :

We normally use hips, knees and ankles in order to keep the
centre of gravity over the support area. The design of apparatus used
at that time would have required us to put in at least nine articulations
with all the problems of locking and unlocking these simultaneously,
maintaining their alignment and mechanical efficiency.

Secondly, that the centre of gravity had to be lowered in a controlled manner and raised by a considerable expenditure of energy and that certainly the problem of the latter was increased if the patient had an exo-skeleton.

The solutions to these problems became ominously complex and we then had of course, to do that which we should have done at the beginning, namely assure ourselves that we were hearing the correct request. What they were asking for was not specifically that they should stand and sit in the orthosis, although that was the solution that occurred to them, but that they could transfer from wheelchair to ambulation independently and rapidly. The problem now had a different dimension and we were able to solve this with all round advantage to our design, producing a simple front opening device into which the patient could transfer in less than a minute and, with relatively little effort, get into the standing position.

Another important lesson this involvement soon brings is the problem of applying the orthodox experimental methodology with its controls to this situation. Patients on the whole are anxious to get on with their daily lives and have neither the time nor inclination to take part in extensive experimental procedures which may in fact reduce their functional capacity, albeit temporarily. Certainly in the world of spina bifida one has to be very careful not to steal educational opportunities from the patient by being pre-occupied with the physical. Equally important, one has to protect them as far as possible against the apprehensions of laboratory investigation which themselves become meaningless if it is impossible to make the patient comfortable and relaxed with their instrumentation, One has to appreciate the enormous psychological distress that any setback consequent upon unsuccessful new designs occasion the patient and the family. Yet either to ignore or to shrink from these problems is to substantially vitiate or even negate one's efforts. Some years ago I saw in a very wealthy establishment in North America a force plate which served a double function by being made transparent and having a camera located beneath it. It was for the investigation of children with cerebral palsy and to ask them to walk on what appeared to be a hole seemed to me unlikely to produce a response characteristic of their usual gait.

Because of the very considerable variations which can occur both physically and psychologically in the subjects we have to investigate, we are often hampered by relatively small numbers in our own clinics so that in this area, as in many others in orthotics, the problem of accurate communication arises. There are two factors concerned here, an accurate and uniform language and the discipline with which it is used. For both these reasons the biomechanical Analysis System of the American Academy of Orthopaedic Surgeons is a welcome and valuable beginning; for, until we can confidently compare like with like, the present problems of sharing our experience will remain.

I make no apology for having dwelt at some length on the patient aspect of research into orthotic design for it is this which makes bioengineers as opposed to engineers. In the earlier days certainly, I often met with the response from an engineer when asking for help, that I simply had to provide him with the specification for what I wanted and he would produce it. But of course, far from being able to do this, all I could do was produce questions in rather vague terms such as :-

How could a patient paralysed in both legs walk?

Or in more limited terms :-

Having regard to past investigations into gait what assessment tools could be applicable to such a patient (one can hardly expect young children or old ladies to have pins driven into their bones, for example) and what new tools of investigation could you suggest. Equally importantly, what tools can we produce with the money and time available so that we would still then have time and funds to actually use them in an investigation? We all know the dangers of a tool becoming an end in itself. I remember early investigation into the wear properties of plastic tiling. It was thought reasonable to produce a device which would simulate human gait on the tiles. The investigator found the data to do this was inadequate and so he moved a step further back and started to investigate the fundamentals of human gait. Not very surprisingly, by the time he had designed and tested his force plate, and then used it on a small number of subjects without advancing the available data, nine-tenths of his time had gone with no answer at all in sight. I suppose it was the inspiring terror of this occasion which led him to sell me his force plate for a nominal sum, put down squares of the material in front of the ticket offices at London railway stations, measure the wear, count the number of tickets sold and thereby produce a useful result in the remaining tenth of his time. A lesson I think for us all. This is not, of course, in any way meant to diminish the value of instrumentation but only a plea that it should be used wisely. This cannot mean that one can always know the potential result of using it. After all we are attempting to explore the most difficult black box situation, a box no-one had a hand in designing and for which we have as yet only the sketchiest blue prints of the early evolving examples. One must not fall however for the charm of the idea that if one can only accumulate enough data something must come out of it, particularly if it can be linked to a computer. Of course it is always possible but it is by no means inevitable. One is encouraged by the on-line analysis of gait producing almost an instant result from the Childrens Hospital Medical Centre in Boston used to solve the problem of whether a below knee orthosis with a fixed ankle can help children with cerebral palsy and if so, how does it do this. And in a different sphere, from Chicago where the biomechanics of the Milwaukee brace treatment of idiopathic scoliotic patients have been analysed through simulation in five computer constructed model spines. The validity of this simultation was then tested by a retrospective analysis of cases, with an 81% agreement between outcome and prediction. Such an investigation is particularly valuable in this situation. As many of you will know the Milwaukee splint was originally designed to correct spinal curvature in three ways all passive :- traction, by three point pressure and by a rotational couple. Of these forces the traction was the first to be critically assessed, simply because it produced unacceptable complications, namely distortion of the growing jaw to which it was applied. The adverse cost of this element of correction, resulted in partial abandonment of it, with the replacement of a passive traction by what was hoped to be an active traction applied by extending the neck over the occipital fixation points. This, in turn, led to a gradual modification of the apparatus to be a much more dynamic corrective device than a passive one. The assessment of such changes in design required two areas of information :-

Firstly :- Knowledge of the natural history of the disease.
This is a feature all too often ignored by those who advocate some
types of orthosis in treatment of conditions which will in any case
recover spontaneously. A sure recipe for success of course.

Secondly :- A careful, comparative follow up and as this may
take at least seven years and perhaps desirably fifteen. One can see
the difficulties of assessing a particular design unless one uses something of the method adopted by Chicago.

There are two other areas on which I must comment :-

The translation of designs from Research and Development into
service.

This is a particularly difficult problem throughout the world,
and one is aware that the majority of devices on which much time and
money is spent in development, will never find their way to the patients
who need them, and in analysing this problem Rancho Los Amigos has
produced a concept, the

      Design   )
      Development   ) D.D.P.
      Production   )

Its complexity is shown in the attached flow diagram. (Fig. 1)

They have said, as I did earlier, that it is virtually impossible
for any one person clearly to state specifications of a device to meet
a patient's needs in engineering terms. An initial attempt can be
made by an effective team - medical, engineering and associated health
professionals who should start with initial performance objectives
and proceed from these to define research and development tasks.

It is not until this device is assessed clinically that many
aspects of the problem not recognised in the beginning may become clear
after which it may be possible to define the specifications in engineering
terms.

The prototype is then redesigned and redeveloped and it is seldom
that only one cycle is required. Rather, the process becomes a continuous
one, with new and improved designs being worked on and evaluated.
The problem of freezing the design for production is an immensely difficult
one for the designer at a time when he is still working on various
improved versions under inevitable pressures from his patients, if
he is, as he should be, closely involved with them. He can be helped
in this difficult decision, if the organisation and instrumentation
for rapid evaluation is available to him. It will in any event require
heart searching and judgement.

Having frozen the design he now has to find someone who will
produce it, again in reasonable time and often in small numbers. This
accomplished, the production side may propose changes in specification
which require further clinical trials.

There is clearly no simple solution, but realisation of its
complexity from the beginning of a project can provide the opportunity
for planning which can minimise the problems.

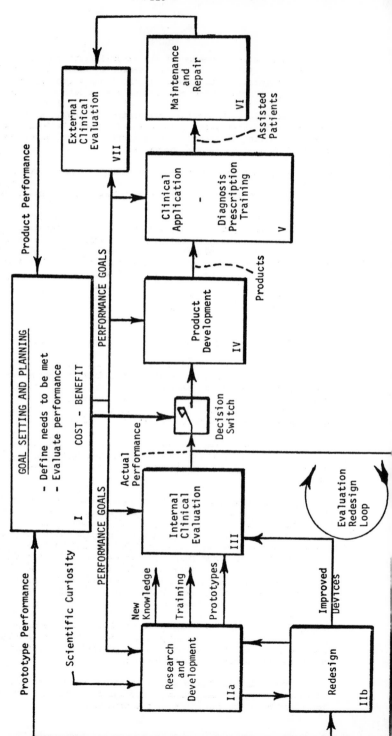

Figure 1   Design - Development - Production Process -
Rehabilitation Engineering Centre -
R.L.A. Hospital

The other point is that of Education in two different aspects :-

The Education of those who are to work in this field and their responsiblity to educate others.

The Education of those coming into the field has been debated at great length. Those, already in it, have often, perforce, largely educated themselves in their new speciality. This has been enormously helped by the team approach. As the situation gets more formal, and we hope more common, the question of special inter-disciplinary courses for Bioengineers has to be considered with all the difficulties that one can envisage. These have often been the subject of late night debate and I cannot hope to summarise results but the greatest difficulty, to my mind, is the danger that people so trained, spend all their working life in this field. I think it of paramount importance that some of their time should have been in industry, particularly having regard to the Design - Development - Production Process. It also has to be faced that to be successful, a special temperament is required to cope with patients and parents, with the inevitable untidiness of medical situations and, not least, the vagaries of surgeons. It is very important, therefore, that those who feel drawn to this speciality have some opportunity to find out whether they would in fact like it and could in fact survive it, before their training starts.

In the other aspect of this matter even the best workers in these units will fail substantially if they cannot pass on their ideas and enthusiasm to the orthotist and the clinician. The best way to do this is to show them that it produces results for their patients.

From the point of view of the orthotist there is, I know, a tremendous enthusiasm and willingness to upgrade their status, at this time, although I think they have not yet quite realised how far they will need to go, and the vast amount of work that is required to do this, coupled with the need somehow for them to set aside time for research and teaching. The Department has taken steps in this direction by allowing the trade to impose a levy to be used for educational processes but there is as yet no similar allowance for research.

Inevitably the most fruitful areas for research are going to be in hospital workshops and yet at this time these are decaying and may yet disappear for want of support, both financial and administrative.

As regards clinicians it must be said that orthotics are vastly undervalued and perhaps over shadowed by biomechanical advances in the world of joint replacement and elsewhere. Yet their correct prescription and production could produce a tremendous benefit for their patients and a diminution in operative treatment. We have somehow to get it over to the clinicians that prescribing an orthosis is a matter of just as great a responsbility as prescribing a drug.

You will have perceived that I have identified five main, inter-related areas of responsibility in Orthotics Design and Fabrication :-

    The Patient
    The Orthosis, and, of course the Interface
    Assessment Service
    Education
    R & D into Service

In our own Unit we have had two large boards prepared, expanding these areas in regard to our own interests. All, therefore, will know what our objectives are and we have found it invaluable to go back from time to time if occasionally, we appear to be in danger of losing ourselves. (Fig. 2)

I have dealt with this matter in a general way, unless we see clearly what we are about, appreciate the tremendous difficulties that lie in our way and yet retain a sense of urgency, the bright vision with which so many of us start, will inevitably become a dull routine. This need not happen, and it has not with those of our colleagues to whose presentations we now look forward so confidently.

REFERENCES

Andriachhi, T. P., Schutz, A. B., Belytschko, T.B. and Dewald, R.L., (1976).
Milwaukee Brace Correction of Idiopathic Scoliosis.
Journal Bone & Joint Surgery 58A/6. p.p. 806-815.

Simon, S.B., Deutsch, S. D., Rosenthal, R. K., Miller, W. and Hall, J. (1977).
The Treatment of Genu Recurvatum in Cerebral Palsy with a Fixed - Ankle Below - Knee Orthosis.   Given at I.S.P.O. World Congress 1977. New York from Children's Hospital Medical Centre, 300 Longwood Ave., Boston, Mass. O2115.

Figure 2

ORTHOTIC RESEARCH AND LOCOMOTOR ASSESSMENT UNIT

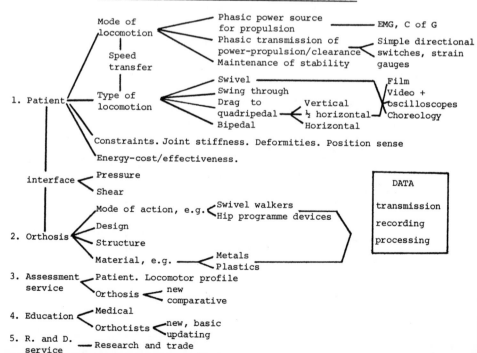

THE INSTRUMENTATION OF HIP-KNEE-ANKLE STABILISING ORTHOSES

G.G. REEVE, B.Sc., M.Sc., A.M.B.E.S.

Rehabilitation Engineering Unit, Chailey Heritage (Craft School and Hospital), North Chailey, Lewes, Sussex; and
Graduate Division of Biomedical Engineering, University of Sussex, Brighton

INTRODUCTION

For upright locomotion the extent of paralysis resulting from the more severe spina bifida lesions frequently dictates the use of full length hip-knee-ankle stabilising orthosis; the design of such calipers is open to question on a materials and structural basis. Any assessment of or improvement to these devices should be supported by quantitative information on their behaviour during normal use, but there is little relevant patient performance data available.

The purpose of this chapter is to present a system developed at Chailey Heritage and the University of Sussex for the investigation of both crutch-assisted locomotion and the corresponding loads resisted by the current joint stabilising orthoses.

The choice of a suitable measurement technique was limited by the nature of the system and in reaching a final decision the following parameters were considered most important:

1. The force system is dynamic but aperiodic and of unknown frequency;

2. the patient/orthosis is subject to gross translation;

3. interference with the patient's normal activity, whether locomotion or play, should be minimal to promote "natural" behaviour;

4. the measurement system should be applied to the patient's own equipment.

The detection of strain manifesting at strategic sites in the caliper was considered the most appropriate method consistent with the above parameters.

INSTRUMENTATION OUTLINE

The strain gauge method combines a good dynamic response with low cost per orthosis and with little inconvenience to the patient. The frequency response demanded of the instrumentation was established by mounting eight linear foil gauges at two sites, hip and knee, on a special full size caliper built to ease the demand for children during the system development. Using a Bruel and Kjaer strain gauge bridge, responses of the form shown in figure 1, the hip site, were obtained.

From this a minimum rise time of 100 ms. may be noted inferring an
equivalent frequency of 5 Hz; this indicated a conservative frequency
response of d.c. to 50 Hz at ± 2000 µs. The substantial negative element
observed between toe off and heel strike is due to isometric contraction
of the abdominal muscles tending to flex both the trunk and orthosis and
is the result of using a normal subject for this experiment.

For the main test programme a suitable gauge configuration was
determined by statically testing typical caliper sections; the site should
comprise two rectangular rosette foil gauges and two linear foil gauges
mounted on the medial and lateral aspects of the dorsal and ventral edges
of the strut respectively. The dynamic nature of these gauge outputs
demands that all signals be sampled simultaneously in order to evaluate the
principal stresses and hence external loading on the orthosis. Thus the
instrumentation system was required to accept eight signals from one site
initially but be sufficiently flexible to permit the addition of
successive eight channel modules as required.

Considering the above factors the following broad specification was
prepared:

1)   an analogue store in the form of a four channel f.m. tape recorder
with audio facilities having a bandwidth of d.c. to 5 kHz;

2)   a portable wheatstone bridge unit to interface the strain gauges;

3)   a portable multiplexer unit to encode the individual signals into
one resultant signal;

4)   a timing or clock unit to drive the multiplexer, the square wave
output from which to be recorded for subsequent decoding of the data
channel;

5)   a calibration system to provide a zero and 1000 µs. offset to the
multiplexed signal at the start and finish of a test;

6)   a wire telemetry system consisting of a miniature multi-core
screened cable sufficiently light and flexible as to be ignored by the
patient;

7)   a differential instrumentation amplifier to drive the above with
variable gain to permit adjustment of strain sensitivity;

8)   a stable d.c. power supply for the bridge, clock and
multiplexer units:

9)   a demultiplexer for monitoring the recorded data during the test.

This specification has been met and Figure 2 shows the final
configuration. The sampling rate of the multiplexer is 1.6 kHz., fast
enough to permit adequate reconstruction of a 50 Hz. triangular waveform.
Both the bridge and the multiplexer/clock units are small enough to be
comfortably mounted on the back band of the orthosis.

With any tape storage system there is a danger of drop out and if this
occurs in the middle of multiplexed data it may scramble the decoded
channels; for this reason a framing or reset pulse is incorporated at the

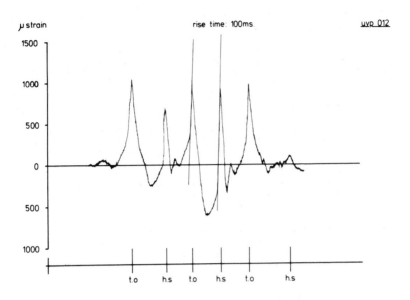

Figure 1   Typical strain-time response curve. Hip site

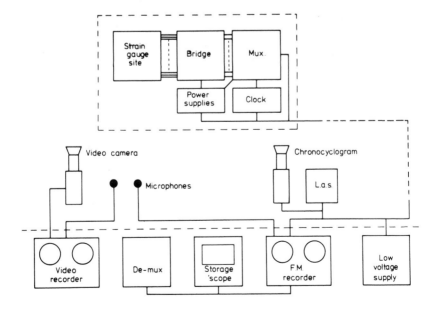

Figure 2   Block diagram of experimental arrangement

end of each set of 8 timing pulses to realign the sequence of decoding should a dropout occur.

The high frequency components in the square wave outputs necessitate recording at a minimum of 15 in/s; this limits continuous monitoring of strain to thirty minutes which has proved quite adequate for the tests to date.

Visual Record Systems

Initial experiments demonstrated the need for some form of correlation between the strain readings and the gait pattern and since some of the children adopt a 'drag to' rather than a 'swing to' or 'swing through' gait with positive foot contact an alternative to the usual gait switches was considered. An easily accessed visual record was desired, preferably of the single plate form, as many of the strain results would be presented in graphical form; the chronocyclograph has proved ideal for these requirements and after considerable difficulties with lighting and exposure acceptable photographs have been produced. Figure 3 shows a typical chronocyclograph obtained in this way; reflective tape is used on the soles of the child's boot to enhance this area which has a tendency to 'ghost'. The chronocyclogram operates at 5, 10 and 20 images per second; this exposure was made at 5 images/second.

Precise correlation between the chronocyclograph and the strain gauge record is achieved by sensing the 'shutter-open' period on the 35 mm. camera and linking this in series with a light activated switch mounted behind the rotating slit shutter. Hence a signal is only output when the camera shutter is open AND an image is present. This signal modifies the clock reset pulse for recognition during processing.

The chronocyclograph is valuable for locomotion visualisation in one plane but correlation is extended using a video camera for general monitoring of the complete experimental session so that turning movements and play activities may be linked with the strain record. Synchronisation between the two recorders is obtained simply by recording an audio channel on both and on playback any shift is easily corrected.

Energy Considerations

Three children were used as subjects during the pilot programme of system development and in 1976 a locomotion study on them was completed by a student at the University of Surrey. The chronocyclographs were used as a tool for this investigation and from the resultant gait analysis much valuable information was obtained. Displacement curves were plotted from the photographs on a Hewlett Packard digitiser from which velocity and acceleration curves of the centre of gravity and shoulder-arm complex were drawn. The energy expenditure is related to those rotational and translational accelerations of the various body segments and it was judged that with sufficient accuracy in plotting the displacements, characteristic acceleration curves would be defined for each child and used to assess the relative energy expenditure for that child under different conditions. At the time of writing plotting inaccuracies have proved an insurmountable obstacle to this approach and an alternative but still non-invasive method of energy assessment is currently under investigation; the mean velocity theory assumes that a subject adopts a walking pace corresponding

to that required for minimum energy expenditure and this information is
readily available from the chronocyclographs and may be supplemented by
monitoring heart rate on one of the spare data channels.

Data Processing

Data processing is performed at the University of Sussex using two
computers linked together, a Modular One and Digital PDP 11 disc oriented
system. The former may be regarded as the interface computer which
communicates with the outside world via the usual peripherals plus an eight
channel ADC, a visual display unit and a digital graph plotter. During
processing a lot of information is handled and stored or rejected; in the
interests of both computer and operator time data is input in real time to
the ADC from the analogue tape recorder. The encoded nature of the
multiplexed signal demands some processing at the time of reading and CORAL
66 was chosen as a programming language for its high speed of execution.
The programme is fully interactive with the operator, resulting in
considerable flexibility in running, an important factor in research studies.

Processing is undertaken in batch form for the locomotion work; a
buffer size of up to 16,000 is available, which, with a clock frequency of
1.6 kHz enables a ten second run to be monitored. The recording of a zero
and 1000 µs offset on the data channels at the start and finish of the test
run minimises effects due to gain changes and drift in the instrumentation
system; further, the use of the clock record to trigger the ADC sampling
of the data channel nullifies any high or low frequency tape transport
fluctuations. Channel sequence perturbations due to drop-outs are automatically eliminated and reset but the number of such resets is displayed
for the operator since they may disturb the continuity of the record.

Demultiplexed signals may be filtered if necessary during display and
if a chronocyclograph has been taken at any point in the sample an image
pulse chain is presented as a modification of the 'Time' scale. If
considered suitable, the demultiplexed, unfiltered data is sent in batch
form across to magnetic disc for storage and subsequent analysis.

At the time of writing full analysis programmes are not running due to
floating point compilation problems but hard copy of the demultiplexed
waveforms is available and a brief discussion of these is presented.

DISCUSSION

Figure 4 shows part of a typical test output drawn on the digital
plotter; each waveform being nominally displayed by 5000 µs. A
chronocyclograph (Fig. 3) was taken during this test and the image chain is
clearly seen along the top of the time axis. The gauge sampling order was
as follows:

    1)   torsion sensitive gauge, medial aspect;
    2)   dorsal linear gauge;
    3)   torsion sensitive gauge, medial aspect;
    4)   medial abduction gauge;
    5)   lateral adduction gauge;
    6)   torsion sensitive gauge, lateral aspect;
    7)   torsion sensitive gauge, lateral aspect;
    8)   ventral linear gauge.

All waveforms are presented with a tension-positive characteristic.

Chronocyclographs are taken either at the start or towards the finish of a test run; physical limitations of the experimental area prevent any extension of the blackout walkway. Figure 3. thus shows one complete gait cycle and part of the second with the subject starting from rest just outside the field of view.

By comparing the images with the corresponding period on the strain gauge output it may be seen immediately that a period of high strain occurred on almost gauges at 'heel strike', the seventh image in the sequence. The subjects body is seen to have been flexed at that moment and evidence for the resultant bending moment is seen in the tensile peak on gauge 1 and the compressive 'peak' on gauge 8. Of interest also at this point, is the considerable positive strain on gauge 4 indicating abduction of the leg; a surprising effect which cannot be fully explained at the time of writing, though poor fit of the caliper may be a contributary factor. Torsional strains were of a low magnitude throughout this test run. Finally, inspection of the image at 'toe off' reveals an extension of the subjects body which manifested in the strain record as a less severe perturbation than that at heel strike.

From the foregoing brief discussion it will be realised that a great deal of additional information is contained in the strain waveforms and the ability to correlate these with the gait in a visual manner has been found most convenient. Without reading too much into these preliminary results the tests carried out to date enhance the importance of 'heel strike' and 'toe off' as events inducing high loading into the caliper and consideration is being given, therefore, to the development of a mathematical model of the patient/orthosis system at these two events. This will seek to predict the dynamic loading on the caliper in response to such variables as patient height, mass and activity level with a view to augmenting the strain gauge information.

In conclusion, a tool has been developed for the investigation of strain in lower limb orthoses and together with the locomotion-visualisation methods will be used for a pilot study at Chailey Heritage. This will be undertaken as soon as analysis programmes are running on the computers.

ACKNOWLEDGEMENTS

The valuable assistance of Mr. A. Brown, Chailey Heritage is gratefully acknowledged and also the generousity of Professor Davis, University of Surrey for the extended loan of the chronocyclogram.

Figure 3   Chronocyclograph.   5 frames/s

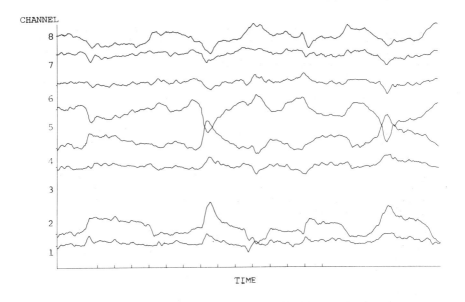

CHANNEL

TIME

Figure 4   Strain gauge waveforms

DHSS BIOMECHANICAL R AND D UNIT FIELD TRIAL OF
CARS-UBC VALGUS/VARUS KNEE BRACE

S.J. COUSINS, B.A.Sc., M.A.Sc., D.L.V. LUSBY, C.Eng., M.I.Mech.E., and J. CHODERA, M.D., Ph.D., O.L.Orth.Prosth.

Biomechanical Research and Development Unit,
Department of Health and Social Security, Roehampton Lane,
Roehampton Lane, London

INTRODUCTION

This brace (Cousins and Foort, 1975; Wassen et al, 1976; Foort et al, 1977) can support a knee that is unstable in the medial or lateral direction. It resulted from a clinic in which a team* isolated and defined the problem from clinical observations, measurements and experimental brace fittings. Out of this came the bracing requirement for force application, in the medial or lateral direction, to occur only at or near full knee extension while leaving other knee motions and other joints unaffected. The resulting brace applies a corrective force that increases as knee flexion decreases while the brace mechanism, that applies this force, leaves other motions free.

From electrogoniometric records of patients (rheumatoid and osteo-arthritis only) with medio-lateral knee instability two key features were confirmed:

　　(a) valgus-varus instability occurs only in stance phase,
　　(b) stance phase flexion is less than ten degrees.

The conclusion, from the bracing point of view, is that an intermittent force application device is needed, stabilising the knee in stance phase only, when flexion is less than about ten degrees. The pivoted circular telescopic tube mechanism is one solution to this problem.

The mechanism shown on the flexed knee of figure 1 can pivot at the thigh and shank cuffs. Between these pivots is a circular tube that telescopes as the knee flexes. A stabilising force is applied to the knee via a triangular knee sling with its apex attached to the telescopic tube and the other two corners connected, anteriorly, to the thigh and shank cuffs respectively. As the knee extends the telescopic tube moves forward pulling the knee sling tight and generating a stabilising force. This force is balanced by forces transmitted via the tube pivots to the thigh and shank cuffs. The tube acts as a beam on the side of the leg and anchors against mediolateral translatory and angular movement. The pivoted telescopic tube, however, allows free flexion-extension and internal-external rotational movements.

Table 1 lists the motions that are free or inhibited and the "Degree of Freedom" (DOF) associated with these motions. The CARS-UBS brace has four DOF blocking only unwanted motions while leaving all others free. This has direct implications for brace prescription. The brace will support a medio-laterally unstable knee even if there is a flexion contracture of hyper-extension of less than about 15°. Internal-external rotational instability, flexion instability and anterio-posterior translational motion are not controlled or restricted.

The brace has been used on patients with rheumatoid and osteo-arthritis
where general or uni-compartmental destruction has occurred leading to
instability and/or pain. The brace has been used to stabilise and protect
after reconstructive ligament surgery. Suitably pinned fractures (fractures
through one side of the tibial plateau for example) near the knee joint
have been protected by the brace until healing was complete. Unstable
implants that cannot be corrected surgically, causing increasing medio-
lateral instability, have also been supported. The brace was applied so
that other rehabilitation processes could continue, e.g. physiotherapy.
Also the brace was used in a protective way by reducing the number of
bleeds a haemophiliac was having into his knee joint from one a month to
one in a year. Many of these example areas of use come from the British
Columbia Field Trial (Truelove et al, 1976; Clark, 1977).

Contra-indications for brace fitting, other than the ones mentioned above
are:

skin sensitivity	lack of balance
circulation problems	obesity
local pain	lack of ability to understand
permanent lack of flexion ability	other untreated problems such
(neurological deficit for example)	as drop foot, short leg, etc.

Most of these could also be seen as general contra-indicators for any
orthotic system.

DESCRIPTION OF BRACE

The brace is prefabricated in one size and its cost is less than 30% of
braces having a similar function. It can support any of four possibilities,
i.e. medial or lateral instability of right or left leg. Because the
brace only performs a medio-lateral stabilising function, as opposed to
weight bearing for example, it has low weight approximately 0.37 Kg which
is 25% of some other braces.

In figure 2 all the components of the dis-assembled brace are laid out.
The waist belt (a) connects to the down strap (b) which in turn is
connected to the thigh strap (c), together forming the basic suspension
system for the brace. The thigh cuff (d) attaches to the telescopic tube
(e) via a pivot (f) as does the shank cuff (g). The knee sling (h)
attaches to the telescopic tube with a back strap (j). The anterior straps
(k) and (m) connect the knee sling to the thigh and shank cuff respectively.

When the brace is fitted the thermoplastic cuffs are adjusted with a heat
gun for customised shaping to the leg(s). Appropriate waist belt, thigh
and shank straps are fitted and a suitable telescopic tube length selected
so that at least ninety degrees flexion is obtained. What remains is the
adjustment of the knee sling straps. The judicious use of straps has had
two results: (1) the brace is lighter, and (2) care must be taken in
arriving at the appropriate strap length to avoid cuff anterior rotation
on the leg. This second point can be explained more clearly with the aid
of a diagram.

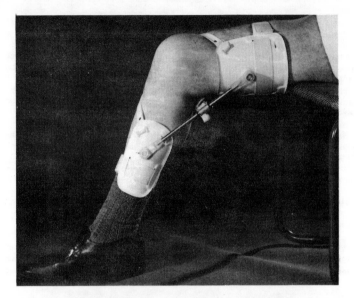

Figure 1   Telescoped and pivoted tube in flexed knee position

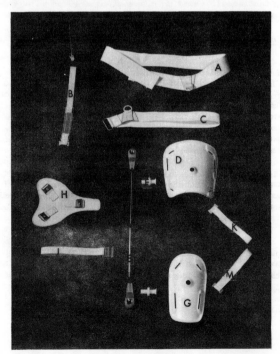

Figure 2   Components of BRADU developed brace

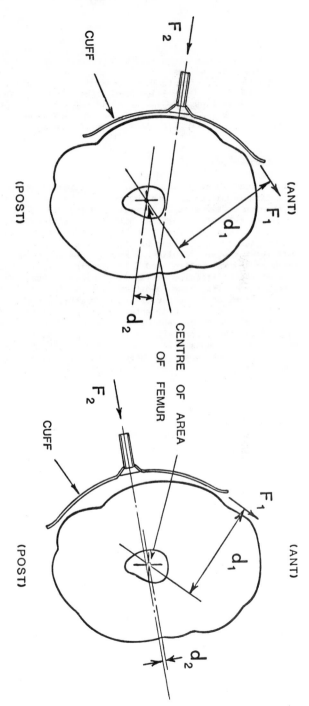

Figure 3   Section through thigh showing forces on cuff

Figure 3 shows a horizontal cross section through the thigh cuff. It is
assumed for this discussion that rotation of the cuff will take place about
the leg surface. Besides the drag force (dependent upon force between cuff
and skin) resisting rotation there is one force from the anterior strap and
another acting through the pivot of the telescopic tube, labelled F_1 and F_2
respectively. A moment balance, given the moment arms d_1 and d_2 in figure 3
shows:

$$F_1 d_1 = F_2 d_2$$

for the cuff to stay stationary. If F_1 approximately equals F_2 then
balancing (equilibrium) must be obtained by varying the position of the cuff
on the leg. If the cuff is positioned anteriorly of the bone, forces may act
to rotate the cuff anteriorly but if re-positioned posteriorly of the bone
then the change of force direction permits balancing of the moments.
This posterior positioning of the cuff is obtained by (1) positioning the
cuff (on the side or) slightly back of the leg before tightening the back
strap of the knee sling, and (2) adjusting the length of the anterior strap
so that the positioning of (1) is possible. Thus, the moment balance is
established. This last condition is satisfied by trial and error adjustment
of the length of the anterior and back straps so that rotation of the cuffs
is not observed. Stopping anterior rotation of the cuffs can be frustrating
unless its underlying cause is understood. Thus it can be seen why obesity
(especially the thigh) will be a contra-indicator for brace fitting because
unfavourable moments will occur as flesh moves uncontrollably relative to
the point of rotation. In these cases rotation of the brace may persist and
other means of controlling it may have to be considered (e.g. modifications
to suspension strapping).

DHSS ASSESSMENT

Already aware of the CARS-UBC Brace and its potential, BRADU began an
engineering assessment of the brace in March this year (1977) with a view
to introducing it officially to the United Kingdom. This assessment took
into account its function, materials used in its construction, method of
assembly and fitting, methods of manufacture, and cost. The various
actions taken are typified by the following examples:

    (i)   The thigh and shank cuffs are now vacuum formed on a
           standard mould in ABS instead of hand forming in PVC,
           and are no longer left and right handed. This reduces
           manufacturing time and eliminates any confusion in
           cuff selection.

    (ii)   It is no longer necessary to rivet buttons to the cuffs
           for strap attachment, e.g. the thigh and shank straps
           simply make a full circle around the leg passing through
           slots in the cuff. This provides cost saving in parts,
           assembly and fitting times, also the danger of setting
           up stress raisers is avoided.

    (iii) The telescopic tube was formerly made in non-stainless
           steel and nickel plated externally; internal corrosion
           was still possible. Stainless steel is now used obviating
           the need for protection at no extra over-all cost.

(iv)   Pre-sized telescopic tubes are now provided in five
       different lengths to eliminate the need of cutting
       to the required length while fitting to the patient.

(v)   Buttons, for strap attachment, are no longer riveted
       to the knee sling but are replaced by fasteners which
       enable the orthotist to make quick, on the spot strap
       adjustments without the need for safety pins and
       subsequent sewing.

A few additional changes have also been introduced subsequent to the fitting
of patients during the trial, e.g:

(i)   The down-strap suspending the brace from the waist
       belt originally passed anteriorly down the thigh but
       during the process of lowering to or arising from the
       sitting position, when the hip joint is near to full
       flexion, the down strap became slack permitting the
       brace to slip down the leg. This has been overcome by
       placing the down strap laterally to the thigh where
       there is less effective shortening and introducing a
       section of elastic into the strap so that tension is
       retained throughout the various positions.

(ii)   Because some patients have RA in their hands it has
       been necessary to introduce small aids to enable them to
       fit the brace. One such aid is associated with the
       strap at the back of the knee. This originally was a
       strap with punched holes which the patient attached to
       a buckle on the telescopic tube. BRADU initially
       changed this to a strap which, fastened permanently to
       the telescopic tube, was attached to the knee sling via
       the adjusting fastener, but this also proved difficult
       for the RA hand because of the need to thread the strap
       through. The end of this strap now terminates in a
       polypropylene, injection moulded clip, which the patient
       is able to slip on and off the telescopic tube quite
       simply; easy adjustment is still maintained.

From time to time it is necessary to make small "tailor made" modificatioms
such as changing the basic curvature of the cuff (reforming is easily done
after warming the material with a hot air gun), lining the cuff where the
shank is bony or tender, and providing a purpose made waist belt where age
has produced an unusual shape around the middle. But essentially we have
a brace which is modular in its construction in which all the parts can be
put together in less than ten minutes; a patient can be examined, assessed
and fitted with a brace in the one visit. It now weidhs 0.37Kg and is
approximately one third the cost of a conventional brace.

BRADU FIELD TRIAL

Before the trial is complete it is hoped that a minimum of fifty patients will be fitted with the brace. Talking to hospital consultants for the provision of patients started at the same time as the engineering assessment. The result has been that these paths progressed together in a relatively short time so that the first patient was fitted in eleven and a half weeks from the commencement of the project.

So far all the patients have come to us via the consultants within the Westminster Group. Approaches are being made and discussions are in hand to widen this field to other areas in the United Kingdom, but in doing so we are anxious to pass on all the information and expertise we can so that patient selection and fitting can be carried out by the indigenous team.

We have now examined seventeen patients all of whom get little or no relief from conventional orthoses and,having made an assessment on the basis of the indications/contra-indications described earlier, eleven have been fitted. None have been straightforward M/L knee instability cases, but each patient is relieved of pain and/or is given increased stability leading to confidence in walking. The success of the brace is being demonstrated by the regular use and comments of the patients. This information is shown in Table 2, together with the reasons for which six patients were considered unsuitable.

Rejections

After wearing the brace for three and a half weeks one patient, an eighty-nine year old female, complained of a low back pain. We have advised that she discontinue using the brace in case the two things are related but because of an accident with her hand in a lawn mower we have been unable to investigate this further.

Mechanical Failure

There has been one very minor mechanical failure which was to the knee sling back strap clip. Initially we hand formed three or four of these in ABS with a hot air gun and it was one of these which failed; there has been no repetition of this with the polypropylene injection moulded clips and none is anticipated.

Patient Follow-Up

We have carried out a check on each patient one week after the initial fitting. In general the second check has been made after a further two weeks and then additional checks carried out at one monthly intervals.

Not only is the patient questioned concerning the benefits gained, and comfort etc but each brace is examined carefully from the mechanical stand point, allowing us to carry out a "LIVE" life test without the enormous expense of special equipment. We are satisfied that even if some part of the brace did fail during the one monthly intervals, nothing disastrous would occur to the patient.

Patients are now being asked to complete a questionnaire when they have
worn the brace for two months which will indicate to us the amount worn,
help given, and a chance to comment generally upon such matters as keeping
it clean etc. Comments made by patients on the questionnaire are typified
by these two quotations:

(i) "It is only possible to go out if wearing the brace ..."
(This lady, at 83, does her own shopping again after not
being able to leave the house for 6 years).

(ii) "Although I still get a lot of pain in the knee after
walking any distance, I welcome the support the brace
offers me, it really is a very great help."

The Future

From the Vancouver field trial and the regular knee clinic a very
conservative estimate of fifty patients per million population will require
the brace. This estimate suggests that, initially, at least 3000 braces
will be required in the UK. Therefore, as soon as we are satisfied with the
standard of development to which the brace has been brought, it is our
intention to hand the complete manufacturing/marketing management over to a
contractor whereby the brace will become available on prescription in the
normal way.

* Rheumatologist, Physio and Occupational Therapists from the Canadian
Arthritis and Rheumatism Society and Medical Engineers from the Medical
Engineering Resource Unit, Division of Orthopaedics, University of
British Columbia, Vancouver, Canada.

REFERENCES

CLARKE B. (1977)
A new approach to bracing the unstable arthritic knee
Allied Health Professions Section of the Arthritis Foundation (USA)
Newsletter 4, vol. 10

COUSINS S.J., and FOORT J. (1975)
An orthosis for medial or lateral stabilisation of arthritic knees
Orthotics and Prosthetics, 4, vol. 29, pp. 21

FOORT J., COUSINS S., HANNAH R., and WASSEN R. (1977)
The CARS-UBC knee orthosis valgus-varus hold
Proceedings of the International Society for Prosthetics and
Orthotics, New York, May 1977

TRUELOVE L.H., FOORT J., McBAIN K.P., CLARK B.M. (1976)
Bracing of the unstable arthritic knee - a new approach
Canadian Association of Physical Medicine and Rehabilitation, January 1976

WASSEN R., HANNAH R., FOORT J., and COUSINS S. (1976)
Fabrication and fitting of the CARS-UBC knee orthosis
Orthotics and Prosthetics, 2, vol. 30

	MOTION	MOTION IS	D.O.F.
ANGULAR	1. Flexion Extension	Free	1
	2. Internal External Rotation	Free	1
	3. Valgus - Varus	Inhibited	0
LINEAR	4. Anterior - Posterior	Free	1
	5. Distraction	Free	1
	6. Medial - Lateral	Inhibited	0

Total D.O.F.	4

Table 1   Motions possible and degrees of freedom

No. of patients	No. of patients Suitable	Age Limit	Sex M	F
17	11	17 - 89	5	6

Sex	Age	Reason for Unsuitability
F	77	Very much overweight. Whole body in too advanced stage of R.A.
F	63	Drop foot and fused hip. Leg length discrepancy for which no correction had been provided.
F	68	Flexion contracture of 17°. Skin and circulatory problems. In great mental distress.
M	70	No instability, but in continual pain.
M	78	Very little V/V instability. Gross A/P instability. (1.5 - 2cm). Flexion contracture of 15°. Ulcers around ankle.
M	80	Weak muscle power and A/P instability. Barely coping with amputation of other leg.

Table 2   Results of BRADU trial to date

THE UNSTABLE ELBOW - THE LIMITATIONS OF ORTHOTIC MANAGEMENT

J.H. MILLER, M.B., Ch.B., F.R.C.S.(Glas. et Ed.)[1]
W.G. DYKES, L.B.I.S.T., and J.V. TAYLOR, F.B.I.S.T.[2]

1 Royal Infirmary, Glasgow
2 National Centre for Training and Education in Prosthetics
   and Orthotics,
   Bioengineering Department, University of Strathclyde, Glasgow

An elbow orthosis may be required in either a protective or a supporting
capacity. Light resting splints of plaster of Paris or plastic provide
adequate protection for painful joints. So far there has been no completely
satisfactory answer to the flail or, in particular, the unstable elbow joint.
The flail elbow is seen as a result of either muscular paralysis, e.g.
poliomyelitis, brachial plexus traction lesions, or, a pseudoarthrosis in
the vicinity of the elbow joint, e.g. an un-united supracondular fracture.
The unstable elbow joint is the result of ligamentous laxity due to either
the destruction of bone, e.g. rheumatoid arthritis, or, the surgical
treatment of an ankylosed joint, e.g. infection, severe rheumatoid arthritis.
Excision arthroplasty restores mobility, unfortunately at the expense of
stability. Such operations have therefore been used sparingly. Recently
there has been renewed awareness of the problems of the unstable elbow
associated with the disappointing results of hinge anthroplasty for both
stiff and unstable joints, particularly in rheumatoid arthritis (Souter, 1973).
Salvage operations have left grossly unstable joints with further reduction in
the patient's independence. Attempts to solve the problem by providing a
stabilising orthosis have met with total failure. This chapter describes the
problems encountered in an attempt to design a functioning orthosis. It does
not pretend to have found the answer. It is hoped however, that the
experience gained will provide a useful background to the future
development of an appropriate orthosis.

BIOMECHANICS

The forces operating at the elbow joint in normal subjects have now been
calculated from equations developed to give their magnitude in either the
static or dynamic states in both the loaded and unloaded modes (Simpson, 1975).
Prediction of how the forearm will move relative to the humerus under such
loads applied via external and internal force systems can be made. There are
no comparable studies of the biomechanics of the unstable elbow joint at
present. Therefore, predictions relevant to normal elbow joint function can
only be used as guides in assessing the effect of similar forces on an
unstable joint. Figure 1 depicts the main muscular forces acting on the
elbow joint during flexion, viz. biceps F1, brachialis F2 and brachioradialis F3. If we assume that F1 = F2 = 2F3 and draw a triangle of forces
the resultant is R. R can then be resolved into its vertical Rv and
horizontal Rh components. This is a stable situation in the intact elbow.
On removal of the lower humeral condyles, however, the horizontal force Rh
produces posterior displacement or telescoping of the forearm bones in
flexion. This is only brought to a halt by the subsequent tension in the
soft tissue, i.e. bunching. Consideration will have to be given as to how
restraining forces might be applied to constrain the ulna/radius and the
humerus to move in the most efficient way in relation to one another. This
analysis must then be related to the development of the orthotic device.

CLINICAL APPLICATION

The most appropriate cases for treatment by such an orthosis would be those in which gross elbow instability is associated with minimal hand and wrist involvement, and perhaps in those severer cases where hand surgery had improved function. Unfortunately many cases of severe rheumatoid elbow disease have at least as marked damage to the joints of the hands and wrist, although the shoulder is perhaps slightly less affected. As in the choice of cases for surgery the great incentive for the use of an orthosis is the bilateral involvement of the disease and its interference with the independence of the patient.

PRESCRIPTION

The detailed prescription of the device must be worked out in discussion amongst the doctor, the physiotherapist, the occupational therapist and the orthotist, taking into consideration the patient's history and medical requirements. The problems encountered even after repeated discussion are best illustrated by the case of Mrs. M.B. This sixty year old lady had severe rheumatoid involvement of her right elbow. Her problem was eventually treated by hinge arthroplasty. When it failed the resultant salvage operative procedure left her with a grossly unstable elbow (figure 2). This functional defect was due to a number of factors:

Problems in the Patient:

    (a) Telescoping of the arm,
    (b) bunching of the soft tissues,
    (c) displacement of the axis of elbow flexion/extension, and
    (d) abnormal forearm rotation.

Telescoping of the unstable joint occurred in active flexion and resulted in posterior subluxation of the forearm bones behind the humerus. Bunching of the soft tissues occurred and produced increased girth at the level of the elbow joint. Also the interference with the axis of elbow rotation restricted flexion and exaggerated extension. The instability resulted in abnormal forearm rotation on abduction and adduction of the shoulder (figure 3).

Because of the severity of her disability, it was decided to try to construct an elbow orthosis which would stabilise her joint. In addition it should allow flexion and extension with the hand in supination during flexion and in pronation during extension.

The Roehampton flail arm splint was used as a prototype. This splint normally consists of a light aluminium alloy structure with cast aluminium alloy joints, except for the shoulder joint which is of stainless steel or chrome alloy. This splint is satisfactory where the elbow joint is intact, e.g. in the flail elbow.

MODIFICATION OF THE ROEHAMPTON SPLINT

In the case under discussion the normal cradle had to be replaced by upper arm and forearm cuffs in order to improve the grip on these parts (figure 4a). The splint, however, proved to be unsatisfactory in the unstable elbow because it did not answer the problems in the patient.

Problems in the Apparatus

Without the orthosis the patient's problem was inability to use the arm due to gross instability in the elbow. With the splint there was marked restriction of all four elbow movements.

SECONDARY PROBLEMS ENCOUNTERED

(a) To prevent telescoping, bunching and displacement of the axis of elbow extension/flexion would have required traction. This would have necessitated counter-traction against the medial wall of the axilla. The resultant pressure there would have produced discomfort unacceptable to the patient. Instead subluxation was opposed by bringing a cuff extension from the upper arm cuff to block the proximal movement of the olecranon. This was only partially successful.

(b) As a result no satisfactory answer could be found to the soft tissue bunching which interfered badly with the fit of the splint and varied in extension and flexion.

(c) The dislocation of the axis of rotation of the natural elbow joint meant that the axis of the orthotic elbow joint could only be aligned approximately. However, it appeared that this was not a great obstacle to reasonable function of the orthosis.

(d) The obstruction to the forearm rotation was due to the difficulty of getting the externally set joints to act in the correct longitudinal axis of the forearm. The forearm cuff would have required to be mobile and rotate round the distal member of the orthosis. This could be achieved by splitting the distal member at the middle third of the forearm and inserting a simple pivot joint. This would allow limited rotation of the distal part along with the wrist cuff. To transmit the rotational forces to the lower member the cuff would require to be closely moulded to the forearm. The difference in the alignments of the two axes of rotation would restrict the actual range of rotation obtained.

The answer may be to accept fixed forearm and wrist cuffs, and where the shoulder is mobile, pronation is certainly well compensated for by abduction, although supination is probably still significantly impaired on adduction. The main problem is in the stiff shoulder where such compensation is obstructed. Even here, however, a certain amount of compensation occurs using torsion of the trunk. This effect was magnified by the resilience of the materials of the support which allowed a little rotation.

(e) Another difficulty is the posterior relationship of the orthotic shoulder joint to the normal joint (figure 4b). There is no problem in the stiff shoulder but in the mobile one abduction results in lateral shift of the

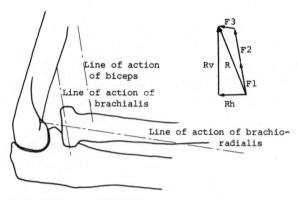

Fl = Force in biceps, F2 = Force in brachialis,
F3 = Force in brachioradialis
R = Resultant force at elbow
Rv and Rh = Vertical and horizontal components of R

Assume Fl=F2=F3

Figure 1   Diagram of muscular forces acting on elbow joint during flexion.
Triangle of forces shows how in the unstable elbow the horizontal
force Rh produces posterior displacement of forearm bones

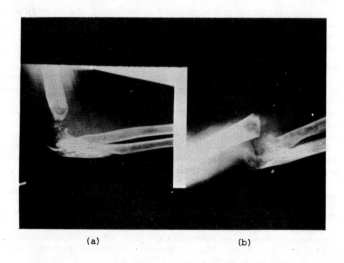

(a)   (b)

Figure 2   X-rays showing in (a) posterior subluxation of the forearm bones
and impingement of the coronoid process against the lower end of
the humerus in flexion; in (b) gross posterior displacement and
telescoping of the forearm bones in active extension

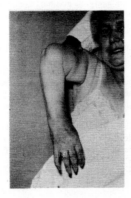

Figure 3 (a)

Figure 3 (b)

(a) shows abnormal forearm internal rotation with the shoulder in abduction
(b) shows abnormal forearm external rotation with the should in adduction

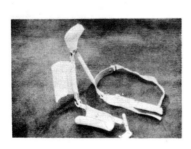

Figure 4 (a)

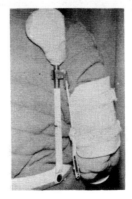

Figure 4 (b)

(a) the modified Roehampton splint

(b) the posterior relationship of the orthotic shoulder joint to the normal shoulder

body strut from the pelvic band and the related orthotic shoulder joint This seriously restricts shoulder movement. In a painless normal joint the resulting pressure could be accepted but in many rheumatoid cases even the slightest pressure produces an unacceptable increase in pain due to the low pain threshold.

Because of these problems it was decided to try to eliminate the shoulder joint and to construct an orthosis consisting of an upper arm and forearm cuff with a light aluminium alloy elbow joint. This also failed. Serious bunching occurred. Even worse was the complete loss of rotational stability, particularly when the arm was used against gravity. Such a splint would be of no use to an active person but could, however, be used as a resting or night splint.

This experience demonstrated that the inclusion of a shoulder joint was imperative. Accordingly, it would have been necessary to modify the upper arm cuff in such a way as to bring it up proximally to enclose the shoulder anteriorly and posteriorly and hold it firmly in position, possibly by a strap encircling the opposite axilla.

WRIST CUFF

Distally, the emphasis is on a comfortable cuff well moulded and padded. This is important because of the frequent involvement of the inferior radio-ulnar and wrist joints in rheumatoid disease.

In rheumatoid arthritis if the elbow disease is severe, the wrist and hand will often be affected to a similar degree. Therefore, we should suggest that to stabilise the wrist the forearm cuff should be extended into a medial or ulnar gutter cradling the hand. Dorsi-flexion and palmar flexion of the wrist would be allowed by a simple flexion/extension joint. The hand would be secured more comfortably by an encircling strap than by a palmar bar which is often uncomfortable.

MATERIALS AND COSMESIS

The materials used must be light and hygienic. Cosmesis requires the use of matt finish, flesh coloured, white materials or covering.

SOLUTION

A useful solution to the problem requires to be simple. Two ideals both for function and comfort would be (a) a universal joint at the shoulder allowing only a limited degree of humeral rotation, and (b) a flexion/extension joint at the elbow allowing some forearm rotation. In practice, however, one would probably have to accept that the simplest answer would be a flexion/extension joint with the forearm held firmly in the mid-prone position.

It is essential that the problems associated with the posterior subluxation of the forearm bones on active use are overcome.

CONCLUSION

The development of a satisfactory elbow orthosis is limited both by
mechanical and pathological considerations. In only a few cases where the
instability is due to disease or is iatrogenic as a result of surgery will
it be possible to ameliorate the disability by the use of such a device.
Attempts to stabilise an elbow joint must be reserved for those few special
cases prescribed on the basis of greater elbow involvement or instability
than hand and wrist laxity.

The design of the elbow endoprosthesis used should allow the preservation
of the ligaments and require minimal bone resection for its insertion.

It would seem imperative to avoid subjecting patients to the implantation
of elbow endoprostheses which require for their insertion resection of a
large amount of bone along with stabilising ligaments and where, if a
salvage operation becomes necessary, they will be left with unacceptable and
untreatable elbow instability. Either the withholding of operative
treatment altogether with the continuance of conservative management or a
stabilising arthrodesis in isolated cases may be better therapy.

ACKNOWLEDGEMENTS

The Authors would like to express their thanks to Professor G. Murdoch,
Professor of Orthopaedic and Accident Surgery, Dundee University, Scotland,
Mr. J. Hughes, Director, and Mr. D. Simpson, Lecturer, both of the
National Centre for Training and Education in Prosthetics and Orthotics,
Department of Bioengineering, University of Strathclyde, The Department of
Medical Illustration and Miss G. Mooney, secretary, both the latter of
Royal Infirmary, Glasgow, for their assistance in compiling this paper.

REFERENCES

ROEHAMPTON FLAIL ARM SPLINT - PROGRESS REPORT
Ministry of Health Research Department, Limb Fitting Centre, Roehampton.
No. 4,5. July - December, 1965. Page 8, no. 4. Page 5, no. 5.

SIMPSON D. (1975)
    An examination of the design of an endoprosthesis for the elbow
    M.Sc. Thesis, Glasgow. University of Strathclyde

SOUTER W.A. (1973)
    Arthroplasty of the elbow
    Orthopaedic Clinics of North America, 4/2, pp. 395-413, April 1973

LUMBAR SCOLIOSIS CORRECTIVE ORTHOSIS

R.G.S. PLATTS, M.A., M.D.

Institute of Orthopaedics, Brockley Hill, Stanmore, Middlesex

The place of brace treatment for idiopathic scoliosis is now relatively
well agreed worldwide. The degree of deformity to be treated by a brace
for a girl with a bone age of four is from 15° to 65° Cobb, whereas the
indications for an adolescent case of say a fourteen year old are much
narrower - say 20° to 40° or 50°. The standard accepted form of brace is
the Milwaukee, which attempts to provide a distractive force between the
head and the pelvis by means of the occipital and mandibular pads. There
is indeed the very clear evidence of an actual upward distractive force on
the chin from the splayed out teeth which some Milwaukee brace wearers
develop. It is none the less a simple mechanical consideration that
distraction is more effective for the larger curves and lateral corrective
forces for the smaller.

A few attempts have been made to quantify the distractive force, provided
by the Milwaukee brace and it can be seen to be between 15N and 45N, which
I would suggest is insignificant mechanically speaking, when one relates it
to the forces in the spine as found for example, by Nachemson, measuring
the intra-discal pressures.

The logical development was the introduction of the so called throat mould
which probably has the same effect of reminding the patient to stand up out
of the brace but has itself virtually no distractive effect. This form is
also now generally accepted.

The super structure of the Milwaukee brace with its metal uprights and neck
ring is clearly undesirable from the cosmetic point of view and it was a
natural progression for attempts to do away with it in view of the
mechanical findings I have mentioned. A number of centres in North America,
Sweden, Italy and France are therefore trying a topless form of brace for
lumbar and thoraco lumbar curves in idiopathic cases.

We have been engaged in this exercise in a small way for two and a half
years now. The brace we have been using has been a moulded plastic girdle
of a medium-high molecular weight polyethylene, moulded to a positive cast
of the patient. The correction of cobb angle which the brace achieves is
obtained in three stages. First, the patient is corrected as much as
possible at the time of casting. She stands in a special frame with elbows
resting on horizontal bars which are adjustable for height and angle and
with knees slightly flexed. The iliac crests are accentuated, if
necessary by straps to the knee bar and if required, slings are passed to
the verticals to press on the rib cage.

The second stage of correction is by modification of the positive cast.
The symmetry is improved and material is cut away where pressure is
required and material added where room is required for tissue to be
displaced.

The final stage of correction is achieved by the addition of appropriate
pads to the inside of the brace. These pads are placed with careful regard
to both the clinical features and the x-ray pictures.

Most of the lumbar curves we have seen are not fully compensated so that the patients display a list of the body to the convexity of the curve. This usually results in more weight being taken on one foot than another. Since the brace is aiming at straightening the whole patient and not just the particular scoliotic segment of the spine, it is very easy to stand the patient with each foot on a weighing scale with the feet equidistant from the centre line and see to what extent the brace is correcting the list and adjust it accordingly.

Another simple method of monitoring the immediate effect of a brace is by accurate measurement of the sitting height. An anthropometer measuring in millimetre increments is used while the patient sits with only underclothes on a hard surface. A standard weight is applied to the measuring arm on the head and this way measurements reproducable within the millimetre scale are obtainable. 5° of Cobb angle correction will give a millimetre or two of extra height. The immediate effect of different placement of corrective pads is therefore discernible and when optimised can be confirmed by radiography.

It is usually possible to gauge how much pressure is being exerted by the lumbar corrective pads by the appearance of the skin but when fitting a new brace or if the brace has not been worn for some hours, it is useful to have an objective measure of the pressure. This is obtained by a simple pressure sensor with an on/off switch indicating separation of the two faces. We find that if in the course of time the pressure threshold falls below 400 Pa. the pad will need building up.

We have so far selected twenty-nine adolescent idiopathic cases with curves whose apex was not above T10 and ranging in severity from 18° to 59° Cobb averaging 33°. The average age of these patients at the start of bracing was 13.4 yrs. and the average Risser sign was 1.3. They were inducted into the brace over three to four days and followed up after three to four weeks and then routinely at four monthly intervals. They were required to wear the brace for twenty-three hours per day, taking it off only for sports and bathing etc. The results of this treatment have been encouraging. One can see (Table 1) as one would expect that the milder curves correct more readily than more severe curves, and this is, of course, an irrefutable argument in favour of catching these cases early by some school screening process.

The published data on the results of Milwaukee braces on lumbar curves is rather scanty (Table 2). The main difficulty being that several authors have not separated thoracic from lumbar curves. From the point of view of the initial correction in the brace - which is only a small part of the whole story - it is evident that our series is not quite as good as Moe and Kettleson's, though it is only fair to point out that theirs included an active exercise programme in the brace; that it is very comparable to Nordwell's and distinctly better than the third author. However, only time will tell the eventual result. I am confident that it will be better than appears here because we are getting better as time goes on. The results of the initial correction now, are distinctly better than our earlier ones. There is also the very important factor of acceptability of the brace. It has been shown by Myers and others and by Clayson and Levine that the Milwaukee brace, unacceptable as it is at the start of bracing, is less and less acceptable as brace wearing continues. We have had no cases of refusal to wear this brace. Therefore, if the clinical results of the lumbar brace are only as good as with the Milwaukee brace, it is still better than the Milwaukee.

The following six cases illustrate the use of the brace:

Case 1: A fifteen year old with 30° thoraco lumbar left sided curve. Initial correction in the brace was to 10° cobb. One year later it was 13° in the brace. Two years later it was 7° in the brace and 12° out of it. She is now being weaned from the brace, wearing it at night only.

Case 2: A 40° right thoraco lumbar curve in a fourteen year old. The initial correction was to 27° in the brace. Sixteen months later 22° in the brace and 31° out of it. She continues to wear it.

Case 3: A thirteen year old with a 27° thoraco lumbar curve which corrected in the brace initially to 14°. One year later it was holding at 15°.

Case 4: A fourteen year old with a 47° thoraco lumbar curve corrected in the brace initially to 28°.

Case 5: A 35° long thoraco lumbar curve corrected to 13° in the brace.

Case 6: A 25° curve in a thirteen year old fully corrected on initial fitting in the brace.

L.S.C.O. results to August 1977

Average curve before bracing - (degrees Cobb) - 33 (n = 29)

Average age at first bracing - (years)   - 13.4 (n = 29)

Average Risser Sign at first bracing   - 1.3 (n = 29)

Average percentage improvement in Cobb angle
on first bracing-

overall	- 37	(n = 29)
for 15°-29° curves	- 47	(n = 14)
for 30°-44° curves	- 30	(n = 10)
for 45° curves	- 23	(n = 5)

Average Cobb angle improvement OUT OF BRACE
after (average) 19.4 months   - 20% (n = 7)

Table 1

Results of Treatment of Lumbar

Adolescent Idiopathic Scoliosis

with the Milwaukee Brace and with the LSCO

Author:	Moe and Kettleson 1970	Nordwell 1973	Keiser and Shufflebarger 1976	LSCO
Number of cases	52	29	37	29
Average curve before bracing	45	32	39	33
Initial correction percent in brace	45	38	20	37
Correction percent at end of brace treatment	23	36	10	?
Loss after one year	5	21	?	?

Table 2

Moe and Kettleson (1970)
Journal of Bone and Joint Surgery, 52A, p. 1509

Nordwell (1973)
Acta Orthopaedica Scandinavia, Supplement 150

Keiser and Shufflebarger (1976)
Clinical Orthopaedics and Related Research, 118, pp. 19 - 24

BODY SUPPORT SYSTEMS

P.J.R. NICHOLS, D.M., F.R.C.P.

Mary Marlborough Lodge Disabled Living Unit, Nuffield Orthopaedic Centre,
Nuffield Orthopaedic Centre, Oxford

INTRODUCTION

Among the patients with severe physical disability there are a small
number who present very severe problems in obtaining comfortable and
functional seating, either in conventional house chairs or in wheelchairs.
These patients present a number of very different problems. Some of them,
particularly those with mental retardation accompanying the severe
disability, require the provision of comfort only. Some require functional
positioning so that in spite of severe deformity or weakness they are
positioned so that they are enabled to use their hands in some functional
capacity. Others require correction of a correctible deformity or
prevention of a progressive deformity, particularly important in those
children who, although having a progressive disability, are likely to
survive into adult life (e.g. spinal muscular atrophy types II and III,
and high cervical lesions of children). In some, the problem of accommodating
severe deformity is accentuated by an associated sensory loss and therefore
a liability to pressure sores when pressure becomes localised.

The types of clinical disabilities which are likely to present for this
form of management are as follows:

> Multiple congenital dysmelia
> Brain damage of all causes, e.g. head injury, encephalitis,
> or severe cerebral palsy.
> Spina Bifida, particularly high lesions and other high lesions
> of the spinal cord (figure 1).
> Osteogenesis Imperfecta.
> Degenerative neuromuscular disorders, e.g. Duchenne muscular (figure 2)
> dystrophy, spinal muscular atrophy, and Freidreich's Ataxia.
> Very rigid patients, e.g. Ankylosing Spondylitis or juvenile
> Rheumatoid Arthritis.

FACTORS CAUSING DIFFICULTY

In tackling these problems the difficulties are largely those of
compromising between various requirements. For example, there is
always likely to be compromise between the provision of maximal total
body support which will tend to reduce any form of voluntary movement
and the achievement of maximum functional activity. Thus, the requirements for support will have to be balanced against the requirement for
active postural movement.

Changes which take place in the shape due to gravity, for example,
collapsing scoliosis from whatever cause, make for difficulties in
positioning the patient in the chair or in the support. If the support
is made to accept the patient in the optimum position, i.e. on stretch,
then it may be difficult for the attendant to fit the child into it
when the child is lifted into the support. Many of the patients who are
referred for body support systems are children and therefore there is
always the complication of growth and the necessary replacement or
reshaping of the support system as the child develops.

When an attempt is made to correct a deformity or to prevent further
deformity taking place, there will almost inevitably be localised areas

of pressure. Any splint which is correcting a deformity will have to act against the deforming sources and thus, in corrective body support systems, there is inevitably going to be some concentration of pressure with attendant discomfort.

Another factor, particularly relevant for children in wheelchairs who attend schools for the physically handicapped or other schools, is the problem of accommodating different types of clothing. There is a considerable difference in size for summer clothing and winter clothing and a closely moulded body support system does not allow for this form of seasonal variation.

CLINICAL CONDITIONS

It may now be helpful to comment on one or two of the commoner problems which we have been battling with over the last few years.

Muscular Dystrophy and Spinal Muscular Atrophy:

In these conditions the problem is one of progressive trunk weakness and the consequent progressive collapsing scoliosis. There is a great need to support the trunk and prevent collapse in order to maintain functional posture for feeding, working, playing and so on, also for preventing loss of respiratory function in the later stages. Furthermore, those children who use mobile arm supports must be supported fully by the trunk; for, if they transfer weight on to the arm supports, they reduce the functional capability of these orthotic devices. (Nichols, 1971) Supporting the collapsing trunk is an extremely difficult orthotic exercise; the trunk weight has to be taken somewhere and it is inevitably uncomfortable. The Milwaukee brace requires some active trunk musculature to obtain its maximal effect and is singularly unhelpful in this group of patients. Usually a total contact brace of the moulded leather type is the conventional answer and many children find these restrictive. They are also time and labour consuming to make, and during the growth spurt are very difficult to keep pace with the child's needs.

There is a difference, however, in our approach to Duchenne muscular dystrophy than to spinal muscular atrophy. If we are sure of the clinical diagnosis of spinal muscular atrophy Type II or Type III, then there is a clear indication that the child may survive into adult life and respiratory restriction is likely to be one of the factors leading to eventual demise. We feel, therefore, that it is extremely important to attempt to prevent the collapsing scoliosis during the early teens and indeed, in some centres, these patients are now being seriously considered for spinal fusion as they approach skeletal maturity.

At Mary Marlborough Lodge we attempt to gain the child's confidence and acceptance of spinal support as soon as there is a clinical indication of scoliosis. Often a conventional Spencer corset is acceptable. We then cast and make a moulded leather jacket, fitting this some six months after starting the lightweight corset. As the scoliosis develops the corset becomes more complex and the child inevitably collapses within the corset and, as the scoliosis becomes more severe, the difficulties of casting and manufacture and the child's distress during the procedure, also increases. In very severe situations with thoracic pelvic contact, polystyrene bead cushions and sheepskin covered cushions may help. In our experience, the best management is a combination of moulded leather jacket and cushioning built into the wheelchair (Nichols & Strange, 1966). However, some children will only accept some form of supportive padding and, if the child refuses to wear a brace, then we have to rely on cushioning to provide the most comfortable and functional compromise we have (figure 3).

Cerebral Palsy:

Cerebral palsy probably provides the largest group of patients referred for moulded body supports and also probably the widest range of problems. Many of the children demonstrate several, if not all, of the features of cerebral palsy, and their requirements for cushioning support or moulded body support systems varies according to the clinical picture. The features which influence the requirements are spasticity, athetosis, joint contractures and deformities, weakness and mental subnormality. Even for those children who are markedly retarded, the modern management approach is to capitalise on all available controlled movements and to encourage every possible intellectual stimulation by movement of voluntary activity. It is probably true to say that the more comprehensive the body support system the more comfortable and quieter the patient remains, but this probably means that less intellectual stimulation can be achieved. Frequently, therefore, there is a conflict of interest between the family, the school and other caring staff and where one group may request a total moulded body support system which makes the child more comfortable, another group will require some system which makes the child more vertical and therefore more available for visual and intellectual stimuli.

Spinal Cord Lesions:

Severe spina bifida lesions may produce a variety of complex problems, particularly of collapsing kyphoscoliosis with anaesthesia of the gluteal and weightbearing lesions. High spinal lesions acquired during childhood (e.g. from trauma) may also result in severe scoliosis and anaesthesia. (McSweeney, 1976). Incontinence often adds a further complication for the orthotists and therapists attempting to manage this type of severe deformity. One particularly interesting attempt to solve these problems is to suspend the patient in a moulded trunk support, the body support being hung from a yoke attached to the wheelchair uprights (Siebens et al, 1972)

Osteogenesis Imperfecta:

Although a very rare disease, osteogenesis imperfecta presents a unique and challenging problem of management, especially in the severe aggressive form. The salient features are bone fragility, long bone deformities, and spinal deformities. In very small children the pain they suffer from fractures and their fear and apprehension at being handled by others than their own parents, adds to the general problems of management. For this group in particular we have been concerned to make a moulded body support system which allows for confident transfer and which can be used for transport, comfort, toileting, bathing and so on. (Williams & Nichols, 1977)(figures 4 & 5)

SUMMARY

Thus, there are a number of complicated problems of severe disability which require some form of body support system. A body support system is required to provide a comfortable sitting position, to overcome weakness and to accept deformity. In some instances it has to attempt to partially to correct the deformity or to prevent the deformity increasing. The system has to improve the functional sitting posture in patients otherwise unable to use their hands, mouths and eyes in order to feed themselves, and to learn and explore their environment (figure 6). The secondary features of the support system are that it shall be available for use in a number of different situations, e.g. as a house chair, a wheelchair, a car seat, and even in the bath and toilet, or it may have to be used as a carrying device.

During the past twelve years we have tried many different techniques at Mary Marlborough Lodge and we are convinced that some form of quick moulded body support system is an invaluable adjunct to our management programme. It is necessary to have the facility for providing a variety of different systems both for the assessment and for the long term management of the severely handicapped and severely deformed patient.

REFERENCES

McSweeney, T.
Deformities of the spine following injuries to the cord.
In 'Handbook of clinical neurology' Volume 26.
Injuries of the Spine and Spinal Cord.
(Ed. R. Braakman)
Elsevier, 1976.

Nichols, P.J.R.
Rehabilitation of the Severely Disabled.
2. Management. (pp 268-9)
Butterworths, 1971.

Nichols P.J.R. & Strange, T.V.
Adjustable wheelchair supports for the paralytic
collapsing spine.
Annals of Physical Medicine, 1966, 8, 266.

Siebens, A et al.
Suspension of certain patients from their ribs.
John Hopkins Medical Journal, 1972, 130, 26.

Williams, E & Nichols, P.J.R.
Management of severe disability consequent upon osteogenesis
imperfecta.
Scottish Medical Journal, 1977, 82, 83.

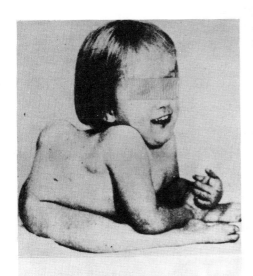

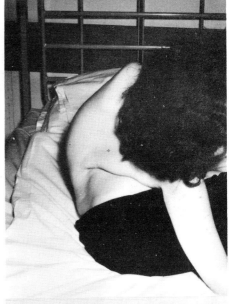

Figure 1   Figure 2

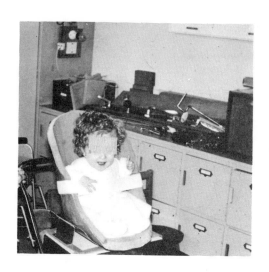

Figure 5

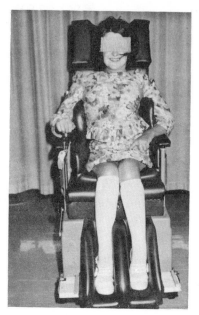

Figure 6

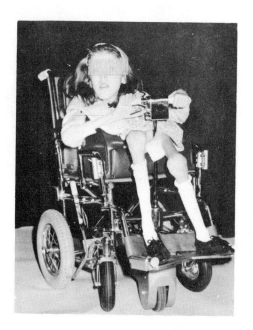

Figure 3

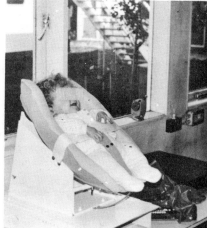

Figure 4

SEATING FOR ASYMMETRIC HIP DEFORMITY IN
NON-AMBULANT MULTIPLY HANDICAPPED CHILDREN

D. SCRUTTON, M.Sc., M.C.S.P.

Newcomen Centre, Guy's Hospital, London

Non-ambulant children can develop asymmetric hip deformity ("windswept" hips) which may lead to hip dislocation and secondary scoliosis. Such deformity usually results from cerebral palsy, but is perhaps more common where (even mild) cerebral palsy is combined with severe mental subnormality. One hip is adducted and internally rotated whilst the other is abducted and externally rotated. The cause of this common deformity is unknown, but is likely to be multifactorial: persisting head turning, gross motor delay, cerebral palsy and severe mental retardation being the most obvious.

In terms of functional restriction, pain and discomfort, debility, stress on nursing staff and the type of residential care required, the Country is faced with a large problem and prevention would save much unnecessary hardship and money. Is total prevention possible? Since we do not fully understand the mechanism of developmental deformity it would be foolish to say "yes", but I am convinced that the majority of these deformities are caused by early inadvertent neglect and that routine physical management (combined with orthopaedic surgery) can prevent some, and alleviate all, of them.

The management of posture is difficult, for one has to find the child early (that is before aged one year) and then convince those looking after him that restrictions of some sort are necessary. By the time the need for restriction is obvious to all, it may be almost too late for solely-conservative management to be effective. Furthermore, for many of these children any activity is seen as good and restriction as counter to their overall developmental needs. No one, let alone a child, can be fixed in one position for long and this means that several positions are needed so that the child can be moved from one to the other regularly and frequently. So we need people experienced in developmental deformity assessing babies, suitable apparatus, a means of acquiring it, and people (frequently the parents) who will apply the regime because they appreciate its significance. This is asking a lot.

Although we do not understand the mechanism of developmental deformity, we can observe its sequence. Mobile deformity precedes fixed deformity, and structural deformity is usually preceded by both. Thus, if we can prevent mobile deformity we may be able to prevent both fixed and structural deformity; "may" because sequence does not necessarily imply consequence.

In an older child it is important to correct the windswept posture in sitting to protect the adducted hip from dislocation and to prevent pelvic asymmetry causing lateral spinal curvature. Left uncorrected (figure 1), sitting becomes increasingly difficult, spinal deformity more likely and the opportunity to learn (or retain) head control is greatly reduced.

It is not easy to control pelvic asymmetry. Attempts to abduct the adducted leg serve only to rotate the whole body, leaving the femoro-pelvic angle

unaltered. The pelvis must be fixed first and only then can the leg
position be corrected. Fortunately the hip joint of the abducted leg is
nearly always very secure, so a horizontal force applied to the femoral
condyles can act longitudinally along the shaft and push that side of the
pelvis posteriorly.

Then, provided the back rest is firm and the seat not too long, the pelvis
is located and the other leg may be abducted effectively (figures 2, 3 and
4); the foot being kept in towards the mid line to rotate the hip
externally.

This is but one example of the type of consistent postural correction
needed in early childhood for many of these children. Correction is not
always easy and simple homely apparatus is required. It may not seem a
grand challenge to the engineer, but it could reap profound rewards for the
children.

ACKNOWLEDGEMENT

The author is grateful for permission to reproduce the figures and some of
the text which is based on a chapter in "The Care of the Handicapped Child",
editor J. Apley, Clinics in Developmental Medicine, Spastics International
Medical Publications, Heinemann, London 1978.

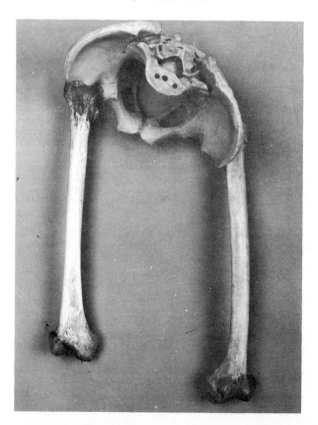

Figure 1   Superior view of the typical pelvic and femoral positions
            of a "windswept" child when sitting on a chair

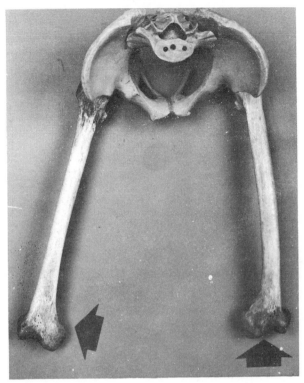

Figure 2   The position corrected by a posteriorly directed force applied to the femoral condyles of the previously <u>abducted</u> leg to fix the pelvis and allow another force to abduct the opposite (right) leg

Figure 3   A child in such a chair

Figure 4   Detail of the straps on the chair. The crutch block is there only to mount the strap, not to hold the child in position

ONE APPLICATION OF CARBON FIBRE REINFORCED PLASTIC
FOR ORTHOTICS FABRICATION

R.L. NELHAM, B.Eng., C.Eng., M.I.Mech.E.

Rehabilitation Engineering Unit, Chailey Heritage Hospital, Chailey, Sussex

INTRODUCTION

A physically handicapped person often requires an appliance, the size
and weight of which, whilst essentially factors of the design, usually
increase with degree of disability. Hence, the most severely handicapped
tend to be further handicapped by the additional weight of their appliances;
assuming, of course, that the method of handicapping racehorses also applies
to human beings!

At Chailey Heritage the orthoses worn by the children born with spina
bifida have been the subject of investigation. These hip-knee-ankle
orthoses (HKAO) can weigh from about 7% to 15% of the child's body weight,
the lightest and, hence, smallest of the children carrying the largest percentage weights. The orthosis weight tends to level out at about 7% of body
weight for a child weighing 60Kg (Fig. 1) and, therefore, an adult wearing an
orthosis of this type could be carrying 5% to 7% of his body weight as
additional equipment.

Improvements in these ratios, and in cosmesis, are being achieved in
various countries by forming sheet plastics to produce close-fitting shell
orthoses. However, this technique is not widely used in Britain for Spina-
Bifida patients.

LIGHT WEIGHT MATERIALS

Weight saving is a function of the specific properties of materials
rather than their absolute properties except in the case of cosmetic or
shell orthoses where shape makes a contribution. Without considering the
specific gravity of materials it is difficult to justify an alternative to
steel (Fig. 2a) but when these absolute properties are divided by the
specific gravity of the materials, the resulting specific properties present
a completely different picture (Fig. 2b). High specific strength and stiffness materials other than carbon fibre reinforced plastic (C.F.R.P.) such as
boron fibres, silicon whiskers, etc., can be included in these figures but
within the limits of practicability and economy, C.F.R.P. possesses the
highest specific strength and stiffness of all common materials and therefore offers the largest potential gains in weight saving.

DESIGN AIM

C.F.R.P. has been used for the manufacture of the Chailey Harness for
upper limb externally powered prostheses for over seven years and its use
for orthoses has been investigated during this time. Current investigations
are being supported by the Department of Health and Social Security. The
aim has been to produce a composite that would replace existing steel or
alloy struts and which could be introduced into the present orthotics
service with the minimum reorganisation or upheaval. It is considered that
the orthotist or orthotic contractor should not have the task of laying up

the pre-impregnated carbon fibre using wet lay up techniques because not only is this an unpleasant and tedious task but it introduces such problems as quality control of the strut and duplication of some manufacturing equipment. Therefore, the design aim is to produce a composite strut that has a reasonable shelf life and can be formed to shape using similar techniques to those used for steel or aluminium alloy.

CONSTRUCTION OF C.F.R.P. STRUT

C.F.R.P. requires a consolidating pressure during the cure cycle to remove excess resin, reduce voiding and produce the shape required. This is usually achieved during press moulding of the shape which is not practical with the bespoke nature of the construction of orthoses. A thermoplastic matrix system appears to be attractive for this application since it is feasible that moulded or pultruded, profiled sections could be produced in suitable lengths. These could be heated by the orthotist to form the shape required but the high moulding pressures and temperatures, typically $12MN/m^2$ and $300^\circ C$ respectively, associated with thermoplastic matrices have to be maintained during forming and this would require complex and hence expensive tools. For this reason investigations into thermoplastic matrices have been temporarily abandoned.

Thermosetting epoxy resins require a relatively low pressure of approximately $700KN/m^2$ and can be readily moulded or shaped by hand at room temperature in the pre-preg or uncured condition using suitably designed simple tools to prevent fibre damage. Some method of retaining this shape during a cure stage or transportation in its uncured condition is required since in this state and during the early stages of the cure cycle its structural properties closely resemble those of sticky string!

Two methods of retaining the formed shape have been investigated. In one, the resin impregnated carbon fibre or pre-preg is pulled into an aluminium alloy tube which is then rolled to an oval section (Fig. 3) to consolidate the composite. In the other, the pre-preg is laid into the channels of a small aluminium alloy I-beam and consolidated by tape winding with a heat shrink tape (Fig. 3). Each of these methods has advantages and disadvantages associated with uniformity of section shape, cosmesis, economic use of carbon fibre and handleability.

It has been decided to adopt the section that includes the I-beam in order to maximise the efficiency of use of the relatively expensive carbon fibre which, in this section, lies furthest from the neutral axis. In the absence of patient performance specifications, the bending moment to yield the strongest of the common orthotic steel sections, namely 60N-m, has been taken as a guide to the requirements of the composite. This results in a section size that produces a composite with a specific gravity of less than 1.8 compared with that of aluminium alloy of about 2.8 and that of steel of about 7.5. It is envisaged that this composite can be laid up and heat shrink tape wound on at some centralised manufacturing unit before being supplied in suitable lengths to the orthotist for him to cut and form to the shape required.

MANUFACTURE OF ORTHOSES

Storage The resin system used in the composite must have a long shelf life and most thermosetting epoxy resins can be stored in a domestic type freezer for considerable periods of time. Laid up composite struts have been stored in the pre-preg condition at $-20^\circ C$ for at least a year with no apparent loss of flexibility at room temperature or deterioration of the strength and modulus of the cured composite and a storage period of say four years would appear to be feasible.

Forming Since the strut contains continuous fibres, bending it can buckle or break these fibres thus considerably reducing the strength and modulus of the composite. Most bends in orthotic structures are made in the mediolateral plane to accommodate anatomical profiles and are basically offsets. It is therefore possible to induce two bends simultaneously, i.e. induce an S-bend (Fig. 4) such that the fibres tending to buckle on the concave or compressive side of one bend are taken up by the required slip on the convex or tensile side of the next bend. In this way fibre slip is not required over the whole length of the composite, only in the region of the S-bend, and buckling of the fibres can be minimised or eliminated. Tests to date have established that this approach is feasible and suitable designs of bending tools are currently being investigated. Most incidences of a single bend occur towards the end of a strut at a hinge joint or an interface with other components and it is easier to induce fibre slip over the short length at the end of a strut.

Where a bend needs to be applied in the anteroposterior plane to accommodate, say, a fixed flexion deformity, it is not considered practical to form the strut since the I-beam buckles and causes buckling of the fibres. Suitably designed angle connector plates could probably be used in this instance, but to date this aspect has not been investigated.

Fitting Once the struts have been formed and the orthosis assembled, a trial fitting has to be carried out. In the uncured or pre-preg condition the composite has no structural strength and the aluminium alloy I-beam is not sufficiently strong to support the patient's weight. In the fully cured condition, maximum structural properties are achieved but the shape of the composite cannot be altered. A partial cure is required such that a percentage of the ultimate strength and modulus can be realised but modification of the shape is possible, if required. The resin system currently used is a modified epoxy and heating it to approximately $120^{\circ}C$ for one hour produces a partial cure giving approximately 50% of its ultimate properties, sufficient in most cases to carry out a trial fitting. Modification of the shape can be carried out by reheating the composite locally with, for instance, a hot air gun and resetting the bend with the bending tools. One of the current investigations is directed towards the establishment of a limit, if any, on the number of times a bend can be reset. When a satisfactory fit has been achieved the orthosis is replaced in the oven at $150^{\circ}C$ for 3 hours to cure the composite fully. Once cured it can be covered in the normal way.

INTERFACE CONNECTIONS

Since it is impossible to change significantly the shape of the cured C.F.R.P. strut it must be replacable, otherwise the orthosis would have to be scrapped in the event of a breakage or discrepancies in the shape or alignment. It is not advisable to drill holes in a C.F.R.P. composite since the continuity of the fibres is destroyed and the strength of the composite reduced. Failure is usually interlaminar shear as the drilled fibres pull away. Bolting (or screwing) and gluing is more successful but produces a joint which is not easily demounted. Interface connectors are being investigated, the current design of which clamps onto the C.F.R.P. strut and bolts to the mating structure. The clamp becomes bonded to the C.F.R.P. during the cure cycle, remaining demountable from the mating structure.

FAILURE BY DELAMINATION

One major problem being investigated is the delamination of the C.F.R.P. from the I-beam during use of an orthosis or during bend testing of the strut. Since the linear coefficient of thermal expansion of the C.F.R.P. is very small and negative and that of the aluminium alloy I-beam large and positive, thermal stresses are induced in the composite during the cure cycle. If a glue line of suitable thickness between the C.F.R.P. and the I-beam can be maintained, this should, in theory, overcome the problem. Etching solutions for the I-beam and film adhesives at the interface between the I-beam and C.F.R.P. are being used to produce such a glue line and results to date look promising.

COSTS

If carbon fibre were to be introduced into orthotic practice there would obviously be an increase in the cost of materials. Some savings have to be made, therefore, in the manufacturing process in order that the cost of orthoses does not escalate alarmingly. Without describing current practice in Great Britain or detailed modifications to it, it may be possible to carry out more manufacturing in the clinic situation to the extent of achieving the fitting stage at the first clinic visit. Fewer patients could be seen but quicker delivery of orthoses would ensure more satisfactory results. These are as yet untried suggestions which may help to prevent the cost of C.F.R.P. being a prohibitive factor in its use.

CONCLUSIONS

Benefits to the patient are difficult to cost but it is believed weight saving is high on the list of patient requirements. An experimental orthosis constructed at Chailey using the C.F.R.P. in the aluminium alloy tube as side members achieved a weight saving of 38% over the weight of the child's previous orthosis, which he had outgrown. Further improvements could have been achieved by replacing the steel in the corset and bands with lighter materials, but a great deal of work remains to be performed first on the struts. C.F.R.P. offers a great potential for reducing the weight of conventional orthoses and investigations are continuing into its orthotic applications.

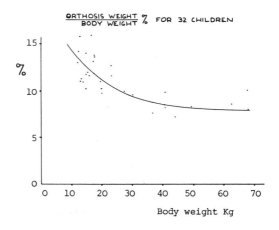

Figure 1

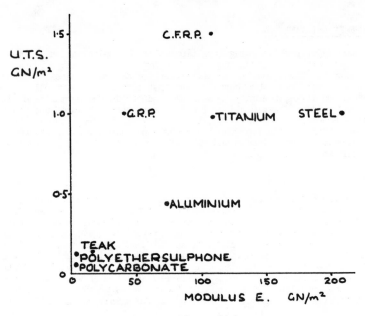

Figure 2(a)

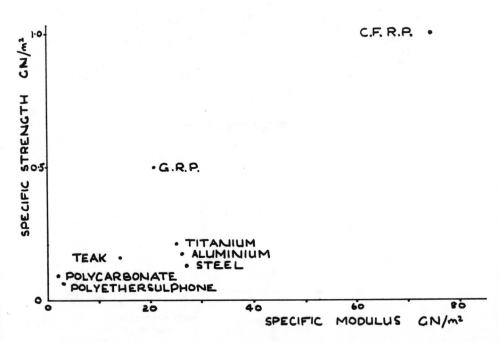

Figure 2(b)

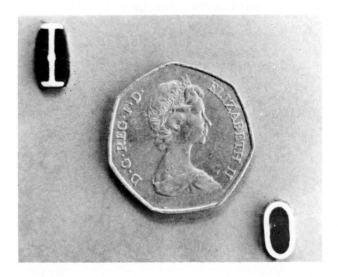

Figure 3   CFRP in the aluminium alloy tube and laid
            either side of the I-beam compared in size
            with a 50 pence piece

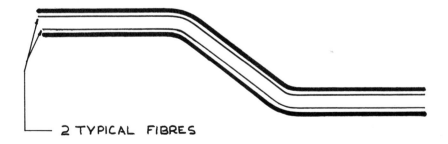

2 TYPICAL FIBRES

Figure 4   Diagram showing how the lengths of paths for all fibres throughout
            the section remain constant when an S-bend is introduced

THE USE OF CARBON/GLASS FIBRE HYBRID LAMINATES
FOR THE CONSTRUCTION OF ORTHOSES

G.R. JOHNSON, B.Sc., Ph.D.

Department of Rheumatology and Rehabilitation,
Derbyshire Royal Infirmary, Derby

1. INTRODUCTION

A large proportion of the disabled population require some form of external support, either for fractures or weakened muscles or to improve the stability of mechanically impaired joints. The requirements of these devices (orthoses) are that they should be lightweight, strong and cosmetically acceptable. The bulk of existing orthoses are manufactured from metal and other conventional materials and their design has evolved little in the past 50 years.

Although the existing designs are largely based on metals, some advances have been made using thermoplastics - particularly high density polythene and polypropylene. A typical example of one of these designs is shown in Figure 1 illustrating the Stanmore caliper using a vacuum formed shell of high density polythene. This orthosis has the advantages of improved cosmesis and lighter weight over the conventional design (Tuck, 1974) but suffers from some difficulties which result from the design limitations imposed by the requirement for a fixed geometry. These limitations will always exist when isotropic materials are used but can be avoided by changing to materials having directionally dependent mechanical properties. The possibility of using fibre reinforced materials has been investigated with a view to solving this problem and achieving further reductions in weight.

2. CHOICE OF MATERIAL

It was stated in the introduction that high stiffness and strength to weight ratios are desirable to produce improved designs of orthoses. There is, however, the further requirement that there should be no possibility of catastrophic mechanical failure which could injure the wearer. Therefore, while carbon fibre might appear to be the ideal material from the point of view of stiffness and strength, its brittle nature makes it unsuitable unless combined with some other material to absorb energy at fracture. It was this requirement that led to the investigation of glass/carbon hybrid materials which have been shown to have an improved capacity for energy absorption, exhibiting what can only be described as yield properties (Hancox and Wells, 1973). The remainder of this chapter will be concerned with the design of one particular component in carbon/glass hybrid materials.

3. CHOICE OF COMPONENT FOR DESIGN STUDY

It was decided, for the initial design study, to attempt to produce a component which was already in service in another material and which might benefit from improved mechanical properties. One orthosis, which has already been referred to, is the Stanmore caliper which uses a moulded high density polythene shell fitting behind the lower leg and inside the shoe. The plastic component is attached to steel side members with hinges at the knee and a moulded cuff at the thigh. The advantages of this orthosis are a considerable reduction in weight over a conventional long leg caliper together with improved cosmesis. This orthosis has been well received by both patients and clinicians. However, it was believed that further benefits might accrue from the use of carbon fibre reinforced materials for producing the moulded shell. This component was, therefore, chosen for the design study.

4. DESIGN PARAMETERS

The prime requirements of the shell are that it should be sufficiently strong to carry the imposed loads and that it should be thin enough to fit inside the patient's shoe without causing discomfort. It must possess not only adequate rigidity to render it stable but also flexibility in the heel to allow, or even assist, ankle movement. The design parameters which have been examined are, therefore, as follows:

(a) bending stiffness of the heel section:
(b) flexural strength of the heel section:
(c) torsional stiffness along the major axis:
(c) suitability for attachment of associated hardware.

4.1. BENDING AND TORSIONAL STIFFNESS

In order that realistic comparisons should be possible between the fibre reinforced and conventional shells, it was decided that the new component should have the same bending and torsional stiffnesses as the original high density polythene item. These characteristics of the heel section of a Stanmore cosmetic shell have been measured statically in the laboratory and were established to be approximately:

$$EI = 1.7 \text{ N.m}^2$$
$$GJ = 1.1 \text{ N.m}^2$$

Tests have been carried out to measure the flexural and shear moduli of laminates with different fibre configurations. The principal study has been of combinations of 1:1 carbon / glass unidirectional hybrid cloth laid either side of a woven glass core (see Figure 2). The variations of the moduli E and G with the fibre angle θ for this type of laminate are shown in Figure 3.

In order to calculate the bending and torsional stiffnesses of the proposed cosmetic shell, it was assumed that it took the form of an open cylinder. It was then possible to calculate the moments of inertia and, therefore, the stiffnesses of components of different radii and shell angle ϕ. Examples of this can be seen in Figure 4.

4.2. FLEXURAL STRENGTH

The most highly stressed area of the shell is likely to be the section around the heel which is subjected to a cyclically varying bending moment resulting from the ground reaction force at the foot. Furthermore, in order that a shoe may be worn comfortably with the orthosis, it is essential that the material around this area should be as thin as possible. It has been estimated that this section of the orthosis should be able to withstand, under fatigue conditions, a cyclical bending moment of amplitude 20 Newton-metres approximately if it is assumed that the appliance is relieving the limb of 50% of the ground reaction force.

It was decided that the heel sections should be cyclically tested in the laboratory and a rig has now been constructed to fatigue test these components in flexion at a loading frequency of 1 Hertz. This apparatus applies a fixed amplitude deflection to the specimen and has a facility to measure the load applied. Tests carried out so far indicate that these sections should have a fatigue life in excess of 3,000,000 cycles.

4.3. FASTENING OF SIDE MEMBERS

The attachment of metallic components to laminates can present problems arising from the difference in the elastic moduli of the parts to be fastened.

Furthermore, in this particular application it is essential that catastrophic failure should not occur. It is also essential that the orthotist should be able to assemble the orthosis using conventional techniques and that adjustment should be possible at this final stage - a requirement which precludes the use of moulded-in fastenings.

A study has been carried out, therefore, of the strength and failure characteristics of fastenings using combinations of rivets, screws and adhesives. Initially the tests were carried out by loading single lap type fastenings in pure shear at an extension rate of 1 cm. per minute. The load-deflection traces were recorded and it was possible to detect. from these, the load at which failure commenced as well as the maximum loading achieved. It was concluded from these tests that, in the case of a joint using adhesive or rivets alone, catastrophic failure can occur without prior warning, whereas if combinations of screws or rivets with adhesives are used then the mode of failure is progressive.

On an orthosis it is unlikely that a joint would be loaded in pure shear because of the bending of side members required to accommodate deformities. Further testing is now being carried out of fastenings offset from the line of application of the load to produce a peeling action at the joint. It has been established from these tests that, under static loading conditions, a fastening constructed from self-tapping screws and adhesive is capable of carrying a load of twice body weight. A programme of fatigue testing of these fastenings is now in progress.

5. PRODUCTION OF CUSTOM ITEMS

While hand lay-up is an ideal process for the production of prototypes, it is not considered suitable for use by the existing orthopaedic appliance industry which is based on traditional engineering skills. It is likely, therefore, that an application utilising shaped laminates can only be adopted if there is some simple method of modifying a range of stock items to fit individual patients. There appear to be two possible methods of achieving this: (a) Modification by vacuum forming methods of shells with a thermoplastic matrix: (b) Vacuum forming of a thermoplastic lining on a range of stock components. At present, method (a) seems unlikely to be acceptable owing to the high cost of high performance thermoplastic resins and the difficulties of imposing large strains on a matrix reinforced by essentially inextensible fibres. It does, however, seem likely that it will be possible to fit a standard shell with, say, a foamed polythene liner which could be suitably modified by a vacuum forming technique.

These problems have yet to be examined in detail.

6. COSMETIC APPEARANCE

It is essential that the orthosis should be flesh coloured to produce minimal visual impact on the leg and; in the case of a laminate, this must be achieved by the pigmentation of the matrix resin and/or by the application of a coloured outer skin.

It has been established that the basic colouring can be achieved by pigmentation of the matrix although this does not mask the black colour of carbon fibre sufficiently. However, it has been found that a good overall appearance can be obtained by applying a gelcoat pigmented to flesh colour. It is important that this coat should be flexible to prevent cracking occurring around areas which are cyclically deformed. It must also be borne in mind that a large range of tones may be required to suit the whole population.

7. CONCLUSIONS

The above study has shown that it is possible, on a laboratory scale, to produce carbon/glass hybrid laminate shells as components for a cosmetic caliper. Whether such components can be adopted for regular use depends upon a proof of reliable service and advantage to the patient. It is also important that the problems of producing custom items are resolved.

The economics of using these materials are not yet clear. However, at a time in which the costs of thermoplastics and alloy steels are rising sharply, the cost of carbon fibre has been steadily falling. It is believed, therefore, that provided an economic method of production is available, carbon and glass fibre components will come into use in future designs of orthoses.

8. ACKNOWLEDGEMENTS.

The author would like to thank Mr. L.N. Phillips, RAE, Farnborough, and Mr. J. Johnson, Rolls-Royce Ltd., Derby, for the help with this project, and Dr. G.M. Cochrane, Department of Rheumatology and Rehabilitation, Derbyshire Royal Infirmary, for his clinical advice and encouragement.

References

1. Hancox, N.L. and Wells, H. (1973). Izod inspect properties of carbon fibre/glass fibre sandwich structures. Composites 4, 26.

2. Tuck, W.H. (1974). The Stanmore cosmetic caliper. J. Bone, Jt. Surg., 56B, 115.

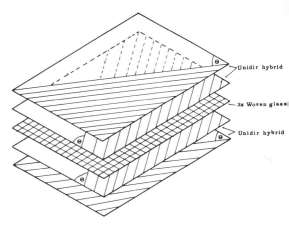

Figure 1   Stanmore Cosmetic Caliper

Figure 2   Lay-up of hybrid laminate

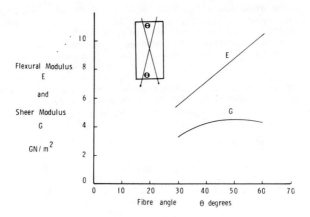

Figure 3   Variation of moduli with fibre angle

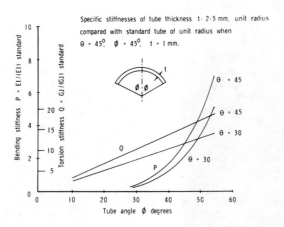

Figure 4   Mechanical properties of hybrid shells

RESEARCH AND SERVICE APPLICATIONS OF VACUUM CONSOLIDATION

J.D. HARRIS, M.A., C.Eng., M.I.Mech.E.

Oxford Orthopaedic Engineering Centre,
Nuffield Orthopaedic Centre, Oxford

For the development and manufacture of orthoses and prostheses, particularly where the requirement concerns the individual shape of the patient or of a limb, the technique of vacuum consolidation is very appropriate.

It depends on the characteristics of particles of matter to lock together when contained in an impervious bag and evacuated. The bags so constructed become highly adaptable moulds. When thin and elastic material is used for the bag and it contains fine free flowing granular powder, its capability to conform to the shape it is placed against is extremely good. Slightly evacuated the bag can be manipulated and shaped. Using more than one vacuum bag a complete mould system can be built up to encase the limb. Subsequently these moulds can be replaced without the limb in position, and a cast made of the limb, or body shape.

As used by the Mary Marlborough Lodge in the Nuffield Orthopaedic Centre in Oxford, a primary application of vacuum consolidation is to obtain the shape of patients with serious neurological or spinal disorders who require more seating support than can be provided by wheelchairs or cushioning. Conditions giving rise to this requirement are reported elsewhere by Dr. P.J.R. Nichols.

First, the patient seating shape is obtained for function and comfort by seating him in a large vacuum consolidation bag (figure 1). This is made to conform by manipulation, and the shape is then retained for assessment (figure 2).

This system is also used at Chailey Heritage (Craft School and Hospital) for disabled children.

In Oxford we go on to reverse the shape by transferring it to a second bag; placing this into the cavity formed by the patient. This second bag then becomes the mould onto which the Plastazote seating shell is formed (figure 3). It is also used to shape both the reinforcing plastic outer liner and the upholstery material, to complete the seat unit (figure 4).

Another application is to obtain an accurate replica of the foot of the patient under load bearing conditions, for the analysis and design of shoes and insoles (figure 5). For this, one vacuum consolidation bag is used. This is first evacuated, and subsequently allowed to deform under the weight of the patient (figure 6). From this a plaster of Paris cast is taken and the shaped insole made to conform to this cast.

This foot shape is also the basis of a full leg cast. Onto this lower bag two further bags are moulded in a partially evacuated condition and shaped to the patient's leg by using elastic bandaging or an elastic gaiter. Using this method the bag is then allowed to flow freely and adapt to the limb shape under atmospheric pressure, before being locked up (figures 7 and 8). By this means the parting lines between the moulds are also closed.

At any convenient stage in the process, modifications to the shape of the mould and thus the casting,can be made, to relieve pressure or decrease the support of the orthosis.

Vacuum consolidation moulds, from the point of view of the patient, are clean and conform to the body very readily. There is no change of shape when they are evacuated. Since they can be separated easily, this stage of the process causes minimum distress even when painful or fragile limbs need to be replicated. The system is being used successfully for the contouring of supports for osteogenesis imperfecta patients and for the preparation of splints on extremely painful limbs where the use of a plaster of paris bandage would be impracticable.

The technique is still at a development stage, and lends itself to considerable adaptation to suit the individual requirements of the physio-therapist or technician who needs to obtain a representation of individual limb or body contours.

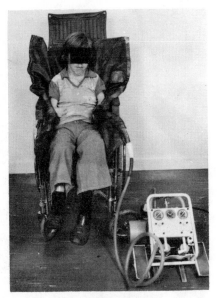

Figure 1   The patient seated in the
vacuum consolidation bag

Figure 2   The patient shape retained

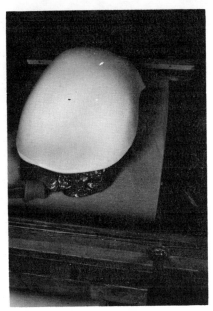

Figure 3   The seating shell on the
mould

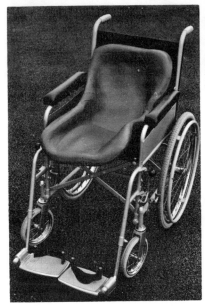

Figure 4   The individual seating
unit

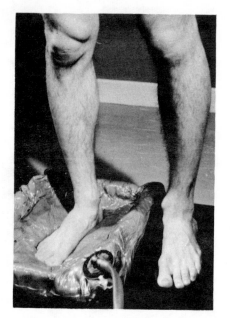
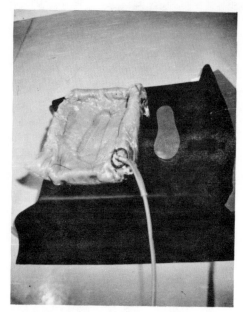

Figures 5 and 6   Foot contours obtained under load bearing conditions

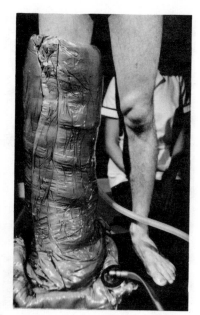
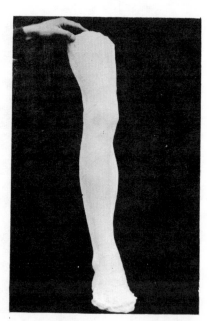

Figure 7   A leg mould by vacuum
                consolidation

Figure 8   A cast taken from a
                full leg mould

VACUUM CONSOLIDATION TECHNIQUES FOR LIMB REPLICATION - SOME PRACTICAL EXPERIENCE

G.R. JOHNSON, B.Sc., Ph.D., and G.R.H. CROOKS, S.R.O.T.

Department of Rheumatology and Rehabilitation,
Derbyshire Royal Infirmary, Derby

INTRODUCTION

Replication of the shape of limbs is essential prior to the production of splints made from materials which cannot be moulded directly to the patient. It is essential that any process used for this should be fast, accurate and cause the minimum of inconvenience to the patient. A further requirement, if it were available, would be the facility to modify a cast during the replication process in order to ensure that the limb was in the best possible position.

Probably the commonest method consists of applying plaster of Paris bandage to the limb in order to produce a negative cast. This must then be cut off the patient and prepared for the casting of a positive replica. However, this process is slow and messy, and so is not usually well received by the patient. Furthermore, it is not possible to modify the shape of the plaster bandage shell once the plaster has set.

PRINCIPLES OF VACUUM CONSOLIDATION

The vacuum consolidation process, in which a bag containing a particle filler becomes rigid when evacuated, has been in existence for a long time. It has been used successfully with bags containing polystyrene beads, for the replication of body contours prior to the production of moulded body supports in several centres. However, the process, in this form, has not been sufficiently accurate for the reproduction of limb shapes for the manufacture of orthoses. The accuracy of the process is dependent upon the size of the filler particles and the wall thickness of the bag. Recently, the use of small particle fillers and bags constructed of 25 - 50 micron polyurethane film, which has been pioneered by the Oxford Orthopaedic Engineering Centre, has made this procedure sufficiently accurate for orthotic manufacture. The bags containing the filler are reusable and, in any case, their capital cost is low.

EQUIPMENT REQUIRED

The equipment required to carry out this type of moulding is simple and inexpensive. The moulding bags are constructed from low cost materials and can be easily made using conventional plastic welding equipment. A vacuum source is, of course, essential but this will be a standard supply in many hospitals. Filtration of the system is important to prevent the ingress of filler particles into the vacuum pump. Originally open cell polyurethane foam was used for this, but more recently commercially available glass fibre filter elements have been found to be entirely reliable and satisfactory.

The facility of modification of a mould can be achieved by bleeding a small amount of air into the vacuum supply so lowering the vacuum in the bag. This can be achieved simply by fitting a valve, which can be vented to atmosphere, into the vacuum supply. It may be advantageous to arrange for this valve to be foot operated although in the present example a hand operated valve has been used without difficulty.

METHOD OF MOULDING

The exact method of use is best illustrated by a description of the process used to replicate the shape of a lower leg prior to the production of an ankle foot orthosis. For this type of moulding the bag is laid in a canvas harness and the patient seated alongside with his lower leg resting on the bag in a horizontal position (see figure 1). The bag is then formed around the limb by hand pressure from beneath the harness and then evacuated. The patient is stood up with his leg weight-bearing in the resulting mould. It is now necessary to modify the mould to the leg in a weight-bearing position and the ankle at a right angle (see figure 2). When a small amount of air is admitted to the bag, the mould can be deformed by hand to fit the limb. The bag is then, once again, evacuated and the resulting moulded cavity can then be filled with plaster of paris to cast a replica of the limb. The plaster cast produced by this process is illustrated in figure 3 where it can be seen that there is only the minimum surface dressing to be carried out.

The above method is clearly usable for the replication of any body shapes and it has been found, by the authors, to be particularly useful during the manufacture of orthoses for both the upper and lower limbs as well as for the production of custom moulded body supports.

CONCLUSIONS

Vacuum consolidation provides a quick accurate method of reproducing limb and body contours. The process causes the minimum of inconvenience to the patient; a further advantage of the process is that modification is possible during moulding - something which was hitherto impossible when using conventional plaster of Paris techniques. It is believed that vacuum consolidation moulding will provide a low cost, convenient replacement for plaster of paris bandage in many applications, and open the way to the use of new materials and moulding processes for the construction of orthoses. The process is now being used routinely by the authors for replication of both the upper and lower limbs.

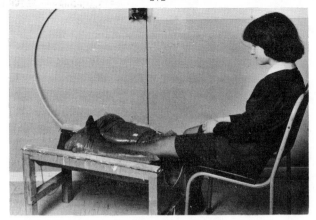

Figure 1   Vacuum moulding bag and harness

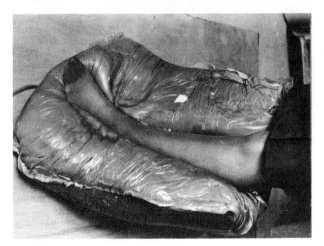

Figure 2   Cast of lower limb while weight-bearing

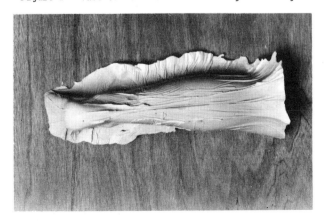

Figure 3   Final plaster cast